# Working in Sport and Recreation

## A Practical Approach

**Rob Saipe**

MA

Stanley Thornes (Publishers) Ltd

First published in 1999 by:
Stanley Thornes (Publishers) Ltd
Ellenborough House
Wellington Street
CHELTENHAM
GL50 1YW
United Kingdom

99  00  01  02  03  /  10  9  8  7  6  5  4  3  2  1

A catalogue record for this book is available from the British Library.

ISBN 0–7487–3899–1

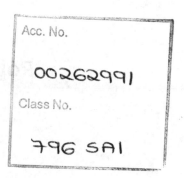

Cartoons by Jean de Lemos

Typeset by the Florence Group, Stoodleigh, Devon
Printed and bound in Great Britain
by Redwood Books, Trowbridge, Wiltshire

# Contents

# Dedication

To DABS

# How to use this book

This book is an essential text for people studying, teaching and working in sport and recreation. It can also be used as a reference and resource book as all sections are clearly identified.

The book is appropriate for a range of courses. It develops underpinning knowledge for

- NVQ2: Operational Services (mandatory and optional units)
- NVQ2: Coaching, Teaching and Instructing (mandatory and optional units)

and may be of use to Level 3 students and teachers.

The book is indispensable for the existing GNVQ in Leisure and Tourism and addresses the new proposed units. Students taking several other courses (British Sports Trust Leaders and Hanson Awards) should also find it useful and the text supports many Governing Body Leaders Awards and Professional Body Awards such as ILAM.

The text is divided into 10 chapters, each covering key themes in the courses listed above. Within each chapter is a range of features designed to aid learning and act as reminders of important facts:

**'This chapter covers'**   Lists all the main headings in each chapter, so that readers can see at a glance the topics that are relevant to their particular area of study.

**Case studies**   A number of case studies in each chapter, each describing a realistic situation and asking the reader to think deeply to solve further problems.

**Remember points**   Essential, quick reminders of important issues.

**Good practice boxes**   Practical tips that will help to improve the ways you do things.

**Activities**   Small tasks that are to be performed individually or in groups.

**Key terms**   A list at the end of each chapter identifies technical terms and words that the reader should have learned from the text of that chapter.

Operational Services – Level 2 – Mandatory units

| Chapter | Unit C35 | | Unit C32 | | | | Unit C33 | | Unit A52 | | | Unit C22 | |
|---|---|---|---|---|---|---|---|---|---|---|---|---|---|
| | C35.1 | C35.2 | C32.1 | C32.2 | C32.3 | C32.4 | C33.1 | C33.2 | A52.1 | A52.2 | A52.3 | C22.1 | C22.2 |
| 1 | | | | | | | | | | | | | |
| 2 | | | ● | ● | ● | ● | ● | ● | | | | | |
| 3 | ● | ● | | | | | | | | | | ● | ● |
| 4 | | | | | | | | | ● | ● | ● | | |
| 5 | | | ● | | | | ● | ● | | | | | |
| 6 | | | | | | | | | ● | | | | |
| 7 | | | | | | | | | | | | | |
| 8 | | | | | | | | | | | | | |
| 9 | ● | ● | | | | | | | | | | ● | ● |
| 10 | | | | | | ● | | | | | | | |

Unit C35: Deal with accidents and emergencies; Unit C32: Develop and maintain positive working relationships with customers; Unit C33: Make information and advice available to customers; Unit A52: Support the work of a team; Unit C22: Contribute to maintaining a safe and secure environment

Operational Services – Level 2 – Optional units

| Chapter | Unit C13 | | Unit C12 | | | Unit C34 | | | Unit C31 | | | Unit A53 | | Unit C23 | | Unit C27 | |
|---|---|---|---|---|---|---|---|---|---|---|---|---|---|---|---|---|---|
| | C13.1 | C13.2 | C12.1 | C12.2 | C12.3 | C34.1 | C34.2 | C34.3 | C31.1 | C31.2 | C31.3 | A53.1 | A53.2 | C23.1 | C23.2 | C27.1 | C27.2 |
| 1 | | | | | | | | | | | | | | | | | |
| 2 | | | | | | ● | ● | ● | ● | | | | | | | | |
| 3 | ● | | | | | | | | | | | | | ● | ● | ● | ● |
| 4 | | | | | | | | | | | | ● | ● | | | | |
| 5 | | | | | | ● | | | | | | ● | | | | | |
| 6 | ● | ● | ● | ● | ● | | | | | | | | | ● | ● | | |
| 7 | | | | | | | | | ● | ● | | | | | | | |
| 8 | | | | | | | | | | | | ● | | | | | |
| 9 | | | | ● | | | | | ● | | | ● | | | | | |
| 10 | | | | | | | | | ● | | | ● | | | | | |

Unit C13: *Maintain sport and recreation equipment and facilities*; Unit C12: *Provide equipment for activities*; Unit C34: *Solve problems for customers*; Unit C31: *Receive customers and visitors*; Unit A53: *Improve own and organisational practice*; Unit C23: *Clean and tidy sport and recreation areas*; Unit C27: *Deal with substances hazardous to health*

| Chapter | Mandatory units | | | | | | | | | | Optional units | | | | | | | | | | | |
|---|---|---|---|---|---|---|---|---|---|---|---|---|---|---|---|---|---|---|---|---|---|---|
| | Unit D43 | | | Unit D44 | | | | | Unit C35 | | Unit B11 | | Unit D13 | | | Unit C32 | | | | Unit B12 | | |
| | D43.1 | D43.2 | D43.3 | D44.1 | D44.2 | D44.3 | D44.4 | D44.5 | C35.1 | C35.2 | B11.1 | B11.2 | D13.1 | D13.2 | D13.3 | C32.1 | C32.2 | C32.3 | C32.4 | B12.1 | B12.2 | B12.3 |
| 1 | | | | | | | | | | | | | | | | | | | | | | |
| 2 | | | | | | | | | | | | | | | | ● | ● | ● | ● | | | |
| 3 | | | | | | | | | ● | ● | | | | | | | | | | | | |
| 4 | | | | | | | | | | | | | | | | | | | | | | |
| 5 | | | | | | | | | | | ● | | | ● | | | | | | ● | | |
| 6 | | | | | | | | | | | | | | | | | | | | | | |
| 7 | | | | | | | | | | | | | | | | | | | | | | |
| 8 | | | | | | | | | | | | | | | | | | | | | | |
| 9 | ● | ● | ● | ● | ● | | | | | | ● | ● | ● | | ● | | | | ● | ● | | |
| 10 | ● | ● | ● | ● | ● | ● | ● | ● | | | ● | ● | ● | | | | | | ● | ● | ● | ● |

Unit D43: Prepare for coaching sessions; Unit D44: Conduct coaching sessions; Unit C35: Deal with accidents and emergencies; Unit B11: Support the development of the sport/activity; Unit D13: Maintain sport and recreation equipment and facilities; Unit B12: Provide equipment for activities Unit C32: Develop and maintain positive working relationships with customers; Unit B12: Provide equipment for activities

GNVQ *Leisure and Tourism Advanced*

| Chapter | Unit 1 | Unit 2 | Unit 3 | Unit 4 | Unit 5 | Unit 6 | Unit 7 | Unit 8 | Unit 9 | Unit 10 | Unit 13 | Unit 14 |
|---|---|---|---|---|---|---|---|---|---|---|---|---|
| 1 | ● | | | | | | | | ● | | | |
| 2 | | | | | ● | ● | | | | | | |
| 3 | | | | | | | ● | | | ● | | |
| 4 | | ● | | | | | | | | | | |
| 5 | | | ● | | | ● | ● | ● | | | | |
| 6 | | | | | | | | | | ● | | |
| 7 | | | | | | | | | | ● | | |
| 8 | | ● | | ● | ● | | | | | | | |
| 9 | | | | | | | ● | | | | ● | ● |
| 10 | | | | | | | ● | | | | ● | ● |

Unit 1: *Investigating the Leisure and Tourism Industries*; Unit 2: *Human Resources in the Leisure and Tourism Industries*; Unit 3: *Marketing in Leisure and Tourism*; Unit 4: *Finance in the Leisure and Tourism Industries*; Unit 5: *Business Systems in the Leisure and Tourism Industries*; Unit 6: *Developing Customer Service in Leisure and Tourism*; Unit 7: *Health, Safety and Security in Leisure and Tourism*; Unit 8: *Event Management*; Unit 9: *Sport and Physical Recreation*; Unit 10: *Leisure Centre Operations*; Unit 13: *Planning for Sports Coaching*; Unit 14: *Techniques for Sports Coaching*

# Acknowledgements

I would like to thank Ruth Hease for her word processing skills, the Academy and STAR for permission to take photographs, Rodney Wells for his assistance with the 'Good practice' ideas and illustrations, Ronnie Miller for his proofreading and Jo and my family for their love and support.

# 1 Introduction to sport and recreation

This chapter covers:
➤ The structure of sport and recreation
➤ Working in sport and recreation

Sport is played and watched by thousands of people every day in the UK.

It plays a very important role in the national economy in terms of consumer expenditure and provides full-time, part-time and voluntary work for many.

People participate in sport and recreation for many reasons: to improve their health, for enjoyment, to have challenges, to be part of a team, to earn money. The continual growth in sports provision has extended for many the opportunity to participate in and to observe sport. Likewise, the opportunity to work in sport and recreation continues to expand.

## The structure of sport and recreation

The structure of sport and recreation in the UK is complex, with many facility providers and administrators, each having their own aims and objectives. Different facility providers very often have similar objectives and the administration of the industry is controlled by many bodies and agencies who also have their own influences on the structure and organisation of sport. It is important to note that other factors influence this structure, including the media, politics, sports agents and fashion.

### Facility providers

Facilities can include:
- sports and leisure centres
- exercise and fitness clubs
- swimming pools
- outdoor adventure centres
- sports stadiums
- community centres
- sports and social clubs.

These are provided by the public, commercial or voluntary sectors. The type of facility will depend upon the people for whom it is being provided, the goals of the provider and the resources available.

1

It is important to note that public, commercial and volunteer organisations interrelate and often work together to achieve set goals. For example, a commercial provider might sponsor an event run by a volunteer organisation.

### Public sector
The co-ordination of sport in central government is found in the Department of Culture, Media and Sport and the Minister for Sport is responsible for overseeing government policy. Regionally it is the local authorities who are large providers of sports and recreation facilities. Their objectives have traditionally centred around 'providing for the community' and increasing participation.

Compulsory competitive tendering was introduced to improve the efficiency of local authority-run facilities. Commercial organisations have an opportunity to 'tender' to manage the facilities. Even though this is to be phased out and replaced with 'best value', it is fair to say that managers of local authority facilities are more accountable for their services, pricing and quality than commercial providers.

Also included within local authority sports provision are some school sports facilities. Some school sports centres are open to the public after school; these are called 'dual use facilities' and are run by the local authority. Other schools manage their own facilities.

### Commercial sector
Some facilities are run by private organisations in order to make a profit. They tend to be more sports specific (e.g. professional sports clubs, ski centres or adventure sports) or exercise clubs in hotels. In most cases facilities and equipment are modern, and strong competition often means that the quality of service is high.

It is common for privately owned organisations to provide sport and recreation facilities for their staff. These are often heavily subsidised by the organisation and are used to help keep staff motivated whilst providing them with an opportunity to keep fit.

### Voluntary sector
Much of the organisation of sport and recreation in a community falls within the voluntary sector and includes:
- community centres
- youth clubs
- local sports clubs (e.g. outdoor bowling).

Each of these clubs is administered by a committee and aims to cater for the needs of its members. Facilities tend to be more basic than those provided by the commercial sector: for example, a scout hut, or a squash court attached to a rugby club.

Within these clubs many volunteers are working to enable others to participate in sport. These volunteers are responsible for managing and coaching teams and help to run the facility. Some positions within these organisations (such as bar staff) may be salaried. This sector relies very heavily on donations and fund-raising activities in order to survive.

## *Administration of sport and recreation*

There are several organisations and agencies that have responsibilities for the administration and co-ordination of sport in the UK. These bodies are not centrally co-ordinated, but each has its own aims and responsibilities. Examples include the various governing bodies of sports and the National Coaching Foundation.

### The UK Sports Council

This is an autonomous body within the Department of Culture, Media and Sport. It is divided into four national councils – for England, Wales, Scotland and Northern Ireland – which are then further split into regions.

Each council focuses on main policy areas. For example, those of the English Sports Councils are:

- *Development of excellence*: supporting governing bodies, the six national sports centres and the British Sports Academy.
- *Young people*: supporting schemes aimed at encouraging young people to participate in sport.
- *National Lottery*: distribution of grants from the Lottery Sports Fund and advice on applications.

The sports councils also receive funding from central government, to pay for their staff and buildings and to provide an information service to the public. Some of their grants are spent on governing bodies of sport and sports clubs.

### Sports agencies

Each sports agency is an independent body, with its own responsibility within the complexities of the co-ordinating sport. They rely on public sector funding or donations and generally provide information, advice and support.

- The British Olympic Association is responsible for the UK's Olympic matters. This includes raising funds, and putting together bids to host the games.
- The Sports Aid Foundation is a fund-raising body which issues grants to performers who show potential for excellence but are not yet eligible for Lottery funding. Their slogan is 'Giving Britons a Better Sporting Choice'.
- The Central Council for Physical Recreation represents the sports governing bodies. It receives funding from the UK Sports Council and uses this to relay the views of its members to the government. The British Sports Trust is its charitable arm, which develops and administrates courses in sports and outdoor leadership.
- The National Coaching Foundation also receives funding from the Sports Council and has regional offices throughout the UK. Its aim is to develop coaches and coaching through courses, providing coaching aids and information.

### The governing bodies of sport

These bodies have traditionally been responsible for organising competitions and enforcing the rules of their sport. They often have regional associations and local sports clubs affiliated to them.

The governing bodies have salaried staff, including chief executives to administer their sport and control their finances. They aim to:

- raise funding, including sponsorship
- develop coaching and leadership awards
- select a national team.

In some of the more popular team sports, such as football, rugby league, rugby union and basketball, the larger clubs have formed their own premier leagues and have organisations to represent them. However, individual teams and players still belong to the national governing bodies and are thus eligible to represent their country, if selected.

Disability Sport England is principally a fund-raising organisation which runs local and national events for disabled sportspeople. There are many organisations that represent individuals with specific disabilities.

**Professional associations**

Several key organisations have a significant impact on the sport and recreation industry:

- The National Training Organisation for Sport, Recreation and Allied Occupations (known as SPRITO) has a unique role, linking industry and government. It aims to set and implement training and education standards, to represent, consult and lead industry and to promote government initiatives.
- The Institute of Leisure and Amenities Management (ILAM) represents its members by providing training, information and professional support. ILAM also acts as a voice of the industry.
- The Institute of Sport and Recreation Management (ISRM) provides standards for training and education of sports facility operators.

# Working in sport and recreation

There has been a significant increase in the number, breadth and variety of jobs and opportunities for working in sport and recreation. This is a result of increases in provision of facilities, as generally more people are:

- taking more holidays
- retiring younger
- wanting to enjoy participating in and watching sport
- becoming more aware of health and fitness.

Participation figures are increasing, as are the numbers of courses aimed at maturing skills for those working in sport and recreation. It is difficult to obtain a job, but keeping up with trends and developments can help you to secure work in the industry.

## A developing industry

The advancement of facilities and promotion of sport and recreation has created many new and varied careers. Educational establishments provide qualifications to prepare people for working in the industry and innovations are numerous.

## Trends and developments

Approximately two in every three people take part in some kind of sporting activity. Men tend to participate more than women and older people less than younger. These statistics are obviously broad figures: in some activities, such as aerobics or outdoor bowls, these generalisations do not apply. However, it is important to monitor the trends and developments that are occurring in the industry so that you are prepared for finding work and diversifying.

The growth in exercise and fitness clubs over the last decade is clearly evident. Here are some practical methods for identifying trends and developments:

- read a daily newspaper and relevant magazines and journals
- visit conferences and exhibitions
- use the national agencies and governing bodies to be aware of policy changes and new initiatives
- watch the media for news of developments in other countries.

## Courses and qualifications

Many courses and qualifications are provided by colleges, agencies and governing bodies.

- Vocational courses are more specifically related to the skills and experience required for working in the industry. These include NVQs and coaching courses, both of which also provide underpinning knowledge of their subjects.
- Non-vocational courses, such as sports management degrees, tend to provide more theoretical knowledge but often contain practical elements.
- Individual qualifications are provided by the industry representatives such as the ILAM and ISRM. These are aimed at those already working in the industry.

The qualifications and course to take depends upon the nature of the work you want to do, the requirements of the industry and the organisation you wish to work for.

## Careers in sport and recreation

Despite the growth of variety and opportunities in the industry, there remains great competition for jobs. In each career you are likely to need a combination of training, education and experience before progressing to a managerial position.

Here are some of the areas for careers in sport and recreation:

- *Coaching and leading activities*. You might work with individuals, groups or teams. There are organisations who run activities for children in the school holidays, and opportunities to work on summer camps abroad. It is very difficult to become a full-time coach and job security depends often on the results of your athletes. However, there are opportunities to assist or coach on a part-time basis.
- *Sports and recreation facilities*. You might initially work as a lifeguard, outdoor recreation assistant or sports assistant, progressing to duty officer and facility manager. Work can include preparing and cleaning facilities, leading activities and coaching.

- *Exercise and fitness*. You could work as an instructor, helping users to meet their exercise and fitness needs by setting up fitness programmes, demonstrating and supporting participants during workouts.

- *Sports medicine*. For those who have the necessary qualifications, opportunities are expanding for specialists in treatment of sports injuries – doctors, physiotherapists, osteopaths etc. There are also introductory courses on treating injuries, giving nutritional advice and improving fitness. This work could be in a part-time capacity at a local sports club or team.

- *Sports journalism*. Few openings occur in television, radio, or the national newspapers but starting in local radio stations or newspapers is a good way to gain experience.

- *Sports development*. Governing bodies and local authorities appoint officers to develop target groups such as young, retired or disabled people or to develop specific sports such as tennis or volleyball.

- *Sports retailing*. Sports clothing is fashionable as well as functional and many new retail outlets employ staff to sell to and advise customers.

- *Sports performer*. The more popular sports offer great financial rewards to successful full-time professionals. Some sports, such as football and cricket, pay players on a part-time basis.

---

**ACTIVITY**

Look in newspapers and journals for job adverts. What skills are required for the job? What pay is offered?

---

## Working in the industry

Working in sport and recreation can be very rewarding, depending upon the type of job, the organisation and people you work with and the responsibility you have. Whatever particular job you want to obtain, the industry requires certain characteristics and skills of all staff within it; these you must identify. Obtaining work can be difficult but by being prepared and thoughtful in your approach you can greatly increase your chances of securing work.

┌─ REMEMBER ─┐

*Enthusiasm is infectious.
Enjoy what you do.*

└────────────┘

### The nature of the industry

Many people choose to participate in sport and recreation in their leisure time – primarily evenings, weekends and during holiday periods. Working unsociable hours is commonplace and many people work shifts.

Providing a service means that an assistant's role is likely to include cleaning and preparing facilities for use. You will often work in groups and teams, depending on the size of the facility.

The industry also requires people to work full-time, part-time or on a casual basis so that facilities can meet the differing needs in busy and slow periods. This also enables those working in the industry to combine coaching, leading activities, working part-time in facilities, teaching swimming and playing sport.

## The work

Some managers seek people with 'personality', as it is essential to be able to communicate positively with customers and create a positive and happy environment to work in. As a sports and recreation outdoor assistant in a centre you may be asked to:

- provide customers with information
- provide a healthy and safe environment
- deal with accidents and emergencies
- put up and take down equipment
- deal with substances hazardous to health
- operate and maintain equipment
- clean and tidy facilities, both indoors and outdoors
- lead activities and assist more qualified staff
- plan and deliver exercise and fitness sessions
- follow standard operating procedures.

Working as a coach or leader you are also likely to be involved in:

- marketing activities
- organising events
- programming activities
- purchasing equipment.

Perhaps above all else you are likely to deal with children, and as such you can be a role model, emphasising good behaviour, equality and safety.

## Obtaining work

This can be a very competitive industry and the more experience, qualifications and training you have the more likely you are to succeed. The conventional approach is to apply for vacancies and follow the recruitment and selection process. You will need to develop your skills and techniques, such as writing an application letter, creating your curriculum vitae (CV), completing application forms and interviewing.

Further practical steps to help secure work:

- Approach organisations and facilities you want to work in. This is best done by making an appointment to see the manager.
- Sell yourself. Show potential employers that you are enthusiastic, able and flexible.
- Get a foot in the door. If no full-time opportunities are available, are part-time or casual jobs available? Depending on your circumstances, offering yourself on a voluntary basis shows commitment and can quickly lead to paid work.
- Develop your performance. Follow instructions and procedures, be positive and do not be afraid to suggest ideas that you have thought out carefully.

---

REMEMBER

*You will probably need public liability insurance and undergo a police check if coaching young children.*

# 2 Caring for customers

This chapter covers:
➤ Who are the customers?
➤ Meeting customer expectations
➤ Developing positive working relationships with customers
➤ Providing information and advice to customers
➤ Receiving customers and visitors
➤ Customer feedback

Participants select facilities and services on their quality, cost, accessibility, time and mobility. Whatever the reason, as customers we would all like to feel cared for. How your customers perceive the organisation you work for will be a major factor in whether or not they choose to use your services.

Many organisations realise the importance of caring for their customers and have policies (and in many cases, specialist departments) focusing on customer care. All members of the organisation must work together to ensure that their customers needs and demands are met.

## Who are the customers?

Within the sport and recreation sector, customers are referred to in many different ways depending on the amount they pay, the activity they are participating in, and the people with whom they are participating.

### Defining the customer

A customer may be defined by different organisations according to different criteria, such as whether or not they are booking facilities, using facilities or are simply visiting. Many organisations consider their staff as internal customers and therefore include them in their policies for customer care.

**Customers, consumers and clients**

If you wanted to reserve an Astroturf pitch at a leisure centre you would invariably be offered a range of prices (based, for example, on whether you made a regular long-term booking, or simply a one-off booking). As the person making the reservation you would be the *customer* and the person with whom staff will initially come into direct contact. If the booking is done on behalf of a team, the team is *also* the customer and very often referred to as the *client*. The players within the team are those using the facilities and are known as the *consumers*. They participate in the activity and therefore use the facilities.

### Members and visitors

The terminology and structures in place in a club are similar to those in a leisure centre. By joining a club (usually by paying) a person becomes a *member*, which entitles them to certain privileges and services of the club. A member may bring a *guest* with them, who is a non-member but would like to use the facilities. This guest would have to sign in and pay for a specific activity or for a range of activities for the whole day.

There are many opportunities in popular sports for organisations to entertain clients in corporate hospitality suites. These provide the client (whoever is paying for the suite) with a means of entertaining prospective customers. All of these *visitors* will be spectators. Very often these prospective clients come as a group and may enjoy a tour of the facilities before the event. Visitors who are not coming to participate include:

- sales representatives
- technicians
- health and safety inspectors.

Many people enjoy spending their time watching sport and recreation. Spectators may be part of a supporters' club or of a special members' club, or may simply be observing a game of bowls in the park. However, they are all still classified as visitors to your organisation. This is an important factor when we come to discuss legal responsibilities.

## ACTIVITY

Here is a list of the several different types of people to whom you may have to offer customer service. Working in pairs, write no more than one line to describe each.

- Members
- Users
- Clients
- Participants
- Consumers
- Players
- Clubs
- Non-members
- Visitors/group visitors
- Spectators

## Types of customer

Having identified who the customers are we must now examine the types of customers. This becomes essential in recognising the specific demands that each type may have.

### Special needs

Just about everyone has special needs, from arm bands for those who cannot swim to left-handed golf clubs, and it is your job to meet them if at all possible. However, the term 'special needs' refers specifically to people with disabilities and requiring, for example, wheelchair access or Braille facilities. There are approximately six million adults with one or more disabilities in Britain and around 350 000 children under 16 with a disability. There are many different categories of special needs but the current trends are to focus on the sport and activity and not the disability.

The Disability Discrimination Act 1994 makes it unlawful for people who provide goods, facilities or services to the public to discriminate against disabled people. Put simply, you have to treat disabled people with the same priority as you would treat able-bodied people.

### Customers with learning difficulties

People with learning difficulties are often outwardly normal looking but may have difficulty in presenting and retaining information. This may mean that traditional ways of providing information do not initially work and it is possible that your normal methods of communication and information are not being understood. Carefully select shorter, simpler words and speak slowly and clearly. Demonstrating will certainly be better than long-winded explanation.

### Customers with physical difficulties

It is easier to identify the special needs of people with physical difficulties. Those with wheelchairs, crutches or an arm in a sling need information on access, how to avoid using stairs, directions to lifts, special needs toilets, hand rails – and must be given this information without being patronised. When offering help to a blind person do not grab, pull or push his or her arm. Do offer your arm so he or she can follow your movements.

### Language barriers

You might come into contact with individuals who have speech impediments, or who cannot speak English at all. If they need directions, using visual aids will be a great help. Always have to hand a map of the facility in which you are working, or a diagram marking out key areas. Where appropriate, ask individuals to write things down. Repeating the information is a method to confirm understanding. These methods also very often work with people who are hard of hearing.

### Men and women

Except for a few sporting and recreational facilities which are restricted to either men or women, most facilities and activities have equal access. Apart from the obvious provision of separate shower and toilet facilities, most equipment and activities are accessible to and provide for both sexes. Regardless of whether the organisation provides communal changing/locker areas or mixed activities (e.g. fitness sessions in the gym), some men and women are more comfortable perhaps swimming or using the gym with people of their own sex. It has become an approved practice to programme these activities earlier in the evening for women as they often have the greater safety concerns.

> **REMEMBER**
>
> *People with learning difficulties require above anything else your patience and understanding – and often more of your time.*

It is easy to make sweeping generalisations about the needs and wants of men and women – that men are more competitive, aggressive and physical and women are subservient and feminine and thus avoid physically pushing themselves to the maximum. Such generalisations are patently absurd. We can, however, predict that five-a-side football pitches are usually used by men. It is important, therefore, not to confuse traditional usage of facilities with the behaviour of those using them.

### Young people

This is a difficult age group to specify, but people of 16–30 years old have drawn much attention from organisations such as the Sports Council. It is an age group where many stop participating in sport and physical recreation. Those continuing to participate are often targeted by advertisers because they tend to be more aware of the stimuli given by advertisements and organisations in general: value for money, cleanliness, quality, choice, modern equipment or the latest technology.

Being aware of the youth culture is a good step to understanding its behaviour and meeting its needs. This age group tends to be people who are, or appear to be, busy and need information quickly.

### Children

Organisations that encourage families to use their facilities are often aware that children have their own special requirements: for example, shower start buttons that are lower down, shorter tennis racquets, soft balls or purpose-built play areas. It is also accepted that children generally need greater supervision and patience.

Children are difficult to generalise as a homogeneous group. Many different social and psychological factors affect how they behave and how they learn:

- family
- peers
- environment
- age
- gender
- intelligence
- innate abilities.

Trying to acquire as much information as possible concerning these factors will aid in your planning, preparation and delivery of activities.

Safety is a major concern for all parents, guardians and those working with children. The Childrens Act 1989 places clear responsibilities on all staff who manage, provide and supervise activities for children. These include providing and maintaining services for children with disabilities and providing information on services. It is also the responsibility of all those working with children to be aware of child protection issues and to know where to seek help and advice.

### Ethnic groups

In communities where a particular ethnic group is in the majority one often finds purpose-built facilities with staff who are highly aware of their customers' needs – e.g. Sikh centres which have women-only days and

**REMEMBER**

*When dealing with all customers keep good time and be succinct when giving information.*

are closed on religious holidays. Non-purpose-built facilities and organisations have a responsibility to be sensitive to their customers' requirements. Making yourself aware of the beliefs of the major religions will provide greater understanding in determining behaviour. Jewish people, for example, who celebrate New Year around October, may cancel a long-term booking for that week but would expect to recommence the activity the following week.

As well as religious differences there are cultural differences of which to be aware. These are historically found in religion but also include inherited ideas, beliefs, values and knowledge that combine to determine social behaviour. It is unreasonable to expect people working in the industry to be fully aware of the religious and cultural needs of all ethnic groups but it is their responsibility to have an open mind to develop knowledge, and to respect the values and beliefs of others.

### Elderly people

Senior citizens are often stereotyped as resistant to change, unfit and unhealthy. This is a completely inappropriate view: very many older members of society are regular participants in activities offered by sports and leisure centres and respond well to new developments. Elderly people should not be patronised, although it should be recognised that some individuals have special needs.

### Customers from overseas

With the increased opportunities of access, some facilities and events are more likely to attract foreign visitors. The regularity of these events will determine whether staff are given specific training, and you should use supporting visual methods with a range of languages and accepted diagrams. Be aware of events going on in your area that might attract visitors from overseas – you may be called upon to help. Do *not* shout to try to make yourself understood.

---

REMEMBER

*Use simple language, gestures and diagrams to aid explanation and be patient and encouraging at all times.*

---

PROGRESS CHECK

1   What is the difference between a customer's wants and their needs?

2   List three actions you can take to assist people with learning or physical difficulties.

3   Why do you need to know the cultural differences of your customers?

4   In what ways can you help to ensure you meet the needs and demands of children?

5   What items would you want with you to help meet the needs and wants of any customer?

## Meeting customer expectations

Organisations realise the importance of having and maintaining a positive image, which is often measured by how it meets the expectations of its customers. Creating a positive first impression and maintaining the standards set are the keys to success.

## First impressions

First impressions are incredibly important. They give perceptions of the individual and the organisation that are lasting and difficult to change. Caring for customers begins as soon as they enter the premises, which includes the car park, public areas and the reception area.

### Preparing for the customer

This should starts at the end of the previous day's work or shift. You must ensure that your work environment is left neat and tidy and that all equipment and information is stored correctly and safely. Before each working day or at the beginning of your shift you should prepare for the customer by:

- dressing appropriately and looking smart every day
- checking your appearance throughout the day
- ensuring your work environment is tidy and well prepared
- having all relevant information at hand.

### Welcoming the customer

The following tips will help create a positive image of yourself and the organisation. They will help to make that first impression a good one when welcoming the customer.

- Establish eye contact.
- Greet customers as they enter your facilities.
- Treat colleagues with respect.
- Smile – with sincerity.
- Do not talk negatively about the organisation in front of customers.
- Be attentive! For example, always remember the customer's name.
- Introduce yourself and wear a name tag.

---

GOOD PRACTICE ▷    *Make yourself a checklist of the above points and ensure they are always achieved. They should become second nature.*

---

**REMEMBER**

*There is no second chance to make a first impression.*

Having made a good first impression, this needs to be sustained by knowing what your customers expect from you. The key points above will set the standards for efficiency and a positive image of the company. This is a major contributor in providing a feeling of satisfaction for the customer and the likelihood of 'repeat business'.

## Maintaining standards

Having made a good first impression you have to maintain the standards set by being aware of the role you play and the environment you are in.

### Appearance

Dressing appropriately for the environment in which you are working is a means of maintaining a smart appearance. The state of your uniform

**Figure 2.1** *Greeting your customers like this could easily put them off!*

sends a clear and visible message about your standards: replace it as soon as it begins to look substandard. Keep your name and department badge clearly visible at all times. This gives the uniform an individual identity and makes you appear more approachable.

### Attitude

A positive mental attitude is maintained by many sports men and women to reinforce their successful performance. However, it is probable that your customers have been at work all day and are pursuing a leisure activity and the last thing they wish to see is the person providing their activity showing signs of having had a long and difficult day. Always smile with sincerity and perform all your routine and non-routine duties with a professional approach. We all can have 'off' days but these should be the exception rather than the rule.

### Knowledge

Learn the customer's name! Try several methods to improve your memory: word association activities, read their membership card, the name on the booking sheet, on the computer screen or a class list. Learning names is a major step towards winning friends.

You need to know the facilities, activities and services you offer. If you are unable to answer a question reply positively by saying that, although you can't help them, you know someone who *can*.

### Cleanliness

Irrespective of the systems in operation and the numbers of customers and visitors, it is the responsibility of all employees to maintain the highest possible standards of cleanliness, not only in their immediate area but in the whole facility. Maintenance of the facility is often carried out by specialists and contractors but you still have the responsibility to record and report any substandard equipment.

**Surroundings**

The environmental conditions of the facility (temperature and lighting) can often be varied to suit an activity or a specific area. They need regular checking. It is difficult to meet everyone's individual demands but you must record and report any malfunctions or trends in complaints.

## ACTIVITY

Working in small groups, select a sports facility you have recently visited or worked for and, using the following list, comment on whether you feel there was an acceptable level of service.

- Was there a waiting time for use of facility?
- Were there flexible opening hours?
- Were all staff wearing uniform?
- How flexible was the range of prices and admissions?
- Were there any hidden extra costs?
- Was the environment clean, tidy, comfortable?
- Were all facilities in working order?
- Were complaints dealt with within an appropriate time?

## PROGRESS CHECK

1 List five methods to help ensure you make a good first impression when meeting a customer.

2 In trying to maintain standards, why is it important to be wearing a uniform and name badge?

3 Why is it important to remember a customer's name, and how can you ensure you do this?

4 What would you do if it was brought to your attention by a customer that the entrance area was untidy?

5 If there was a problem with the temperature in the gym area what should you do?

# Developing positive working relationships with customers

In a highly competitive industry, attracting customers is difficult enough; retaining them through repeat business can be even harder. Identifying the customers and offering a service which meets their needs can be a major step towards attracting and retaining customers.

## Making the customer the priority

The organisation will have a target of customers it wishes to attract – such as businessmen – but the target group will not all necessarily have the same needs and wants. By developing an understanding of customer requirements you will be best able to meet their expectations, secure their business and retain their services in the future.

15

### Needs and wants

We can clearly identify the basic needs that an organisation has to meet. These include emergency evacuation procedures, security and hygiene facilities. However, it can be harder to satisfy people's wants. These differ from needs as they are individual desires and are not essential as needs clearly are. Because people's wants are applicable only to them it can be difficult for an organisation to satisfy everyone. Nevertheless, it must remain a goal to discover people's wants and, wherever possible, to satisfy them.

### Prospective customers

Very often, attention to detail may well attract the prospective customer – individuals or groups who are not yet customers but who may become so in the future. For example, marketing specialists in the major banks realise the importance of attracting young people, who might not hold operating accounts now but are sure to do so in the future.

Recognising prospective customers is an essential part of an organisation's success. Having identified who your customers are and having worked to meet their expectations, it is likely they will visit and use your facilities or services again. A key factor to their continuing as your customer is to develop your working relationship with them. This depends on your communication skills, especially in dealing with customer complaints. Word of mouth information on how good your organisation is quickly spreads – but word of mouth on how bad your organisation is spreads even more quickly.

## CASE STUDY

The Funbury Leisure Centre has a swimming pool which is predominantly used by schools and a local college during the day. In the evenings it tries to cater for other groups by holding women-only sessions, giving swimming lessons and 'swim and gym' sessions. On Saturday mornings an inflatable is placed in the pool for families and children.

One Saturday a woman brings her 10-year-old son for the inflatable session. She is the customer and the boy is the consumer. They have different needs and wants that are recognised by the person taking the booking and the staff working at the poolside. The mother and the centre need the child to be safe during his swim and to have fun, and this is reaffirmed by the staff as they explain the supervision practices. The child just wants to have a good time and is encouraged by the poolside staff to enjoy himself.

1   What other needs and wants might the mother have?
2   Who might be prospective customers?

## *Communication*

Basically, we communicate to impart information, and hence pass on knowledge, to others. A working relationship can be developed only if the person you are communicating with understands the message you are sending.

16

### The communication process

When communicating we start with an idea, which we must pass on to the recipient. The recipient interprets the message and will invariably respond to it. There are many factors (often referred to as 'noise') that can affect how well the recipient understands the message. These include not being able to speak the same language, a lost letter, being unable to read someone's handwriting, being in a noisy room or being unable to hear someone on the telephone.

### Communicating effectively

To avoid such undesirable consequences you should pay close attention to all the forms of communication you use with your customer and try to reduce the noise in all of them. Effective communication avoids misunderstandings, helps decision-making, enhances the organisation's reputation and makes the running of your operations more efficient. Above all, you will be better able to understand the needs and wants of your customers and improve your working relationship.

## Dealing with customer complaints

There will be times when a customer approaches you with a complaint. Whether or not you are directly responsible for the problem you must accept responsibility on behalf of the organisation.

REMEMBER

*Poor communication can result in:*

- *lack of information*
- *time wasting*
- *misunderstanding*
- *confusion.*

**Figure 2.2**   *Try to deal with complaints promptly and efficiently*

GOOD PRACTICE ▷   *When dealing with a complaint you should remain calm and attentive and establish the nature of the complaint. Reassure the person that your organisation takes all complaints seriously and that you will ensure that something is done about the complaint.*

### Taking action

If the problem is straightforward you should attempt to deal with it as soon as possible. Delays will only increase the complainant's annoyance. In all circumstances you should record the information, inform your line manager and tell the customer what you are doing and what will happen next. This provides the customer with a feeling that something positive is happening. However, do not make promises you cannot keep! Whatever the outcome, thank the customer for pointing out the problem.

**Figure 2.3**   *Give the impression that you care about the customer's needs*

GOOD PRACTICE ▷ *Try to ensure that a complainant leaves the premises feeling that this was a one-off incident and that you are a caring organisation striving to make improvements and satisfy their needs.*

ACTIVITY

Working on your own, state which of the following you believe to be true and which you believe to be false:

- If customers do not complain it means we are performing well.
- We can afford to lose one customer.
- Even if we resolve the complaints, they will still talk badly of us, so we have lost them anyway.
- Customers enjoy complaining.
- We should make it difficult to complain so that only genuine complaints get through.

Some of the do's and don'ts in dealing with complaints and challenging customers:

- *Do* keep calm at all times.
- *Do* speak softly; it often defuses the situation.
- *Do* be attentive.
- *Do* take action.
- *Do* deal with emotions first.
- *Do* let the customers voice their views.
- *Don't* make promises you know you can't keep.
- *Don't* blame or contradict the customer.
- *Don't* pass the buck.
- *Don't* blame your colleagues.

## ACTIVITY

In small groups devise and discuss a list of five benefits to your organisation of receiving complaints.

## PROGRESS CHECK

1 What can be the results of poor communication?
2 Why is it important to record a customer's complaint?
3 Why is it best to try to deal with a customer's complaint as soon as you are aware of it?
4 If you are unable to help a person with an enquiry what should you do?
5 List three do's when dealing with customers who are making complaints.

## Providing information and advice to customers

We have already identified the need for effective communication, which lies at the root of establishing the information and advice that is needed and providing the answers. We provide information and advice to customers and visitors in a number of ways.

Spoken communication on the telephone and face-to-face contact are essential factors in the impression created on the customer. The voice needs to be loud enough to be heard. Accents are not generally disapproved of unless they are so strong as to be incomprehensible. For obvious reasons, slang and bad language are discouraged. Much of the advice given about how to talk to customers implies that common sense should be used.

## Contact by telephone

Initial problems can be created because it is difficult to establish a positive relationship without seeing someone in person. In these circumstances information must be gleaned from verbal cues without the benefits of body language etc. However, you can provide a positive image by preparing for telephone calls. Have a note pad and pen with you, keep information close at hand, and keep your booking diary in easy reach.

### Receiving a call

- Use a pro forma to record details of calls.
- Greet the caller and give the organisation's name.
- Make notes of important details.
- Confirm these details with the caller: 'Can I check that I have all the relevant details?'
- Do not waffle. Answer questions concisely whenever you can. If you are unable to do so, assure the caller that you will be back shortly with all the details.
- Give the customer a closing line that leaves a good impression, such as 'I am pleased to have been able to help you. If there is anything else please do not hesitate to phone back.'
- Putting people 'on hold' means we are getting more accustomed to *Greensleeves*, *The Entertainer*, *She'll be Coming Round the Mountains* (etc.), or a disembodied voice saying 'your call is placed in a queue'! Be aware of your system and how long people may have had to wait. Phone in yourself and see what happens.

### Making a call

- Check that you have all the information you need before making the call.
- State who you are, the name of your company and the purpose of your call.
- Check whether you have called at a convenient time.
- Make a note of any details that have been agreed or actions that must be taken as a follow-up to the call.
- Give the customer an opportunity to respond to what you have to say.
- Again, make sure that the customer is clear about details and is satisfied with what has been agreed.

Many people believe that smiling whilst speaking on the telephone automatically makes the speaker sound more pleasant.

## Face-to-face contact

Face-to-face contact is the most important form of contact in many leisure businesses. The attitude and professionalism of the staff are crucial factors in determining whether customers are enjoying themselves and will return.

---

REMEMBER

*Aim to create a pleasant, reasonable, informal style which puts people at their ease whilst giving a favourable impression of the company providing the product or service.*

---

REMEMBER

*Customers want to hear a bright, friendly voice on the other end of the line.*

---

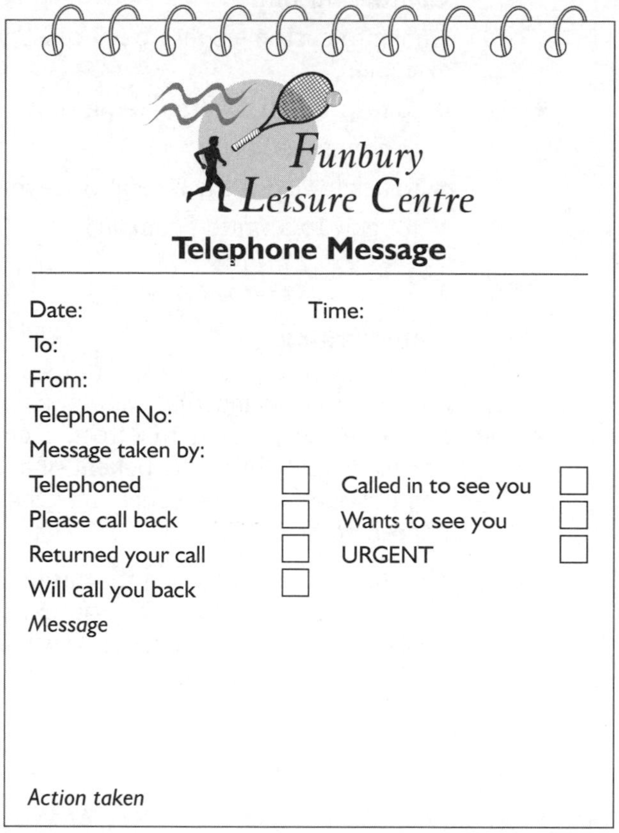

Funbury Leisure Centre

**Telephone Message**

Date: Time:

To:

From:

Telephone No:

Message taken by:

| | | | |
|---|---|---|---|
| Telephoned | ☐ | Called in to see you | ☐ |
| Please call back | ☐ | Wants to see you | ☐ |
| Returned your call | ☐ | URGENT | ☐ |
| Will call you back | ☐ | | |

*Message*

*Action taken*

***Figure* 2.4** *Always use a standard form to record telephone messages*

## The welcome

Successful contact often begins with a warm welcome. Customers will probably make their minds up quickly whether they like someone or not and so most companies strive to ensure that their employees make a good first impression. Appearance often governs first impressions of people. As well as being generally smart in appearance, leisure staff should wear a uniform. This has the dual benefit of making a statement about the company image and enabling the customer to identify staff easily.

However, you are not providing a good service simply by looking presentable. You must respond to your customers' needs, and the first skill required to do this is an ability to listen. Frequently the customer will be seeking information and it is important that this information is accurate, unbiased and helpful. Explanations should not be too technical or hurried. Employees should be given sufficient training about the product or service they are providing.

## Contact by mail

Writing to customers may be necessary for a number of reasons. For example:

- to respond to a written request for information
- to confirm bookings
- to acknowledge the receipt of payment
- to reply to a written complaint.

### Letter writing

Whatever its purpose, every letter should be clear and accurate. Spelling and punctuation must be correct, paragraphing logical and the layout neat. The use of standard letters, such as in response to a customer complaint, may bring the benefit of accuracy but will certainly give the impression of an impersonal organisation which is not particularly concerned about the individual customer.

The standard of care given to written forms of communication should be the same as that given to any other aspect of customer service. The quality of written communication will affect the customer's image of both you and the organisation.

| ACTIVITY | In groups of three, examine three different methods of written communication and identify any mistakes in them using the guidelines described above. |
|---|---|

## Displaying information

Where information is located and how it is presented are essential factors in avoiding repetition of this information. Many signs, such as those for men and women, have generic pictograms. Some signs must conform to European legislative requirements – for example, exit signs must be in pictures, not in writing. The following is a list of popular items of information that will be on display.

- Location of facilities.
- Products and services on offer.
- Times of services.
- Costs of products and services.
- Terms and conditions of taking part in the activities available.
- Instructions – e.g. on how to operate equipment, lockers.
- Health and safety information, including 'no go' areas, exit and emergency areas, how to prevent accidents and injuries.

**Notice boards**

Much of this information is often found on notice boards. Thought must be given to location, size, layout, colour, design and possibility of vandalism.

● Check to see that the displayed information is up to date and in the relevant location.

● Suggest a person be responsible for the notice board as part of his or her daily duties.

● Remove unauthorised information promptly and report it.

● Regularly check the quantities of information sheets/leaflets etc. and have a restocking system.

## PROGRESS CHECK

1 Why is it a good idea to have a note pad next to the phone?

2 What should you do if you cannot provide an answer to a customer who has phoned with an enquiry?

3 In what circumstances would you need to write to a customer?

4 What can you do to ensure that most customers will see the information you have displayed?

5 How can you ensure that notice boards are regularly updated?

## Receiving customers and visitors

Once all efforts have been made to create a positive first impression the processes of controlling entry and enrolment must be performed competently and efficiently. Keeping accurate registers of customers and numbers of visitors is essential for health and safety. The point of entry must be monitored to ensure there is no unauthorised access.

Taking bookings and payments are key financial procedures that demand complete accuracy, and booking procedures are discussed in Chapter 7.

### Controlling entry

This is an essential part of receiving customers and visitors. For health, safety and security reasons, an organisation has a legal responsibility to know who and how many people are on the premises. It is also necessary to complete all the enrolling and financial procedures your organisation may have, such as taking registers and processing payments.

**Preparing for customers and visitors**

Market traders refer to this as 'setting your stall out'. This commences with the physical availability and proximity of all documentation so that it can be accessed easily. Registers and booking systems, whether manual or computerised, should be checked to see who is booked in for the day and what activities they are doing. Having knowledge of your working environment by knowing exactly where information and facilities are can help you receive your customers and visitors more efficiently.

**Figure 2.5**   *Make sure the map you give your customer is one they can carry around!*

*It is now common for large hotels to give maps of their facility to their customers. Depending upon the size of the organisation, one or more copies of the layout of the facility should be at hand, to aid customers.*

Understanding the organisation's procedures and policies usually comes with training and experience. Confirm the policies and procedures that are most likely to be used that day (these may be as straightforward as recording payments or dealing with a suspected stolen credit card).

Before commencing your work shift or session:

- try to identify your general duties and anticipate the day's happenings
- take time to check the day's bookings and activities and ensure that the equipment and personnel are in place to deliver the services requested
- identify where special needs are to be met. You may need to deal with people with disabilities, VIPs, larger than average groups of visitors or customers who have requested special conditions. For example, a martial arts group might have invited an overseas VIP guest to demonstrate new techniques and he or she will require an appropriate welcome.

In an industry that relies heavily on flexible part-time, casual and voluntary workers it is advisable to confirm who is in work throughout your shift and what their roles and responsibilities are so that prompt action can be taken if assistance is required. Check the organisation's diaries and communicate with key personnel. It is a good idea to inform the appropriate members of staff about any customers who have special needs or medical conditions. This information can be obtained from the customer when he or she completes the membership/enrolment forms – relevant medical information is usually required – from a child who has recently suffered a dislocation to a swimmer who has a verruca.

**Admission procedures**

Each organisation will have its own procedures for admitting customers and visitors. The following items of good practice will underpin any of these systems.

- Acknowledge customers promptly. If you are dealing with a telephone call or are presently engaged with a customer, make every effort to acknowledge new arrivals and inform them you will deal with them shortly.

- Greet customers politely and with a smile. Your organisation may have a corporate style and phrase to use but try to be genuinely interested in welcoming the customer so as not to sound 'programmed'.

- Record personal details by confirming the booking, scanning in the membership card or getting new customers to complete the registration form. Whichever system is used it should confirm who the customer is and what facility or activity they are involved with.

- Maintain the activity registers accurately and clearly. At any given time you should be able to give the exact number of customers in the facility and what they are registered to do. This is essential for fire safety and evacuation procedures and as a method of ensuring that the safe numbers of people undertaking each activity are not exceeded.

- Take care with payment! Each organisation should have a system for recording and receiving payment. Whether this is done through a cash register or manually, ensure that customers have paid for the facilities to be used. Secure the payments in the till and give the correct change and a receipt. If there are any doubts always follow security procedures or inform your line manager.

- Direct customers and visitors, once they have registered and paid, to the appropriate facility using the signs and perhaps a map as visual aids. Modern leisure complexes can be extremely large, and directing the customer/visitor straight to the facility will help to maintain a positive first impression. Wherever possible, taking the person to the facility is the best situation – many supermarkets employ this method to help customers find products.

## Enrolling customers/clients

Most leisure facilities offer a range of programmes, including courses, activities and events. It is essential you have good 'product knowledge' of what your facility has to offer. Receiving customers and enrolling them correctly depends on knowledge of the facility's programmes, and is required by health and safety legislation.

**Providing information**

Leaflets are the most popular method of providing information about the facility and the courses or programmes in which a customer can enrol. You should offer the relevant leaflets to your customers, supporting the information on them with an explanation of the products and services of the organisation. You must clarify:

- terms and conditions of membership
- prices and concessionary rates

- facility hire, including times and availability
- cancellation policy
- health, safety and security issues
- course information.

Much of this information is constantly changing – keep your knowledge up to date and have all reference material close at hand.

## Funbury Leisure Centre

**Membership**
There are a range of memberships to choose from, including Standard, Extra and Off Peak. New members receive a special introductory pack including discount vouchers.

**How to Pay**
You pay a joining fee (which can be spread over six months) and a monthly fee, which can be paid by direct debit. For more information ask at reception.

**Cancellation Policy**
You may cancel your membership at any time. If you cancel within one month of joining, you will receive a refund of 50% of the joining fee.

**Facilities**
The centre offers the following facilities and sports:
- Swimming pool
- Squash
- Badminton
- Indoor tennis
- Aerobics
- Fitness studio
- Sauna

**Health and Fitness Consultation**
Before using the fitness studio you must attend a health and fitness consultation with one of our trained instructors.

**Courses**
We run coaching courses at regular intervals. For information on these courses, ask at reception

**Funbury Leisure Centre, Funbury Road, Anytown**
Opening Hours: 8AM–10PM daily

**Figure 2.6**  *The information a leaflet should provide*

## Confirming information

People wishing to enrol on programmes or courses are often unsure of what they really want. Learn more about their needs and wants by asking questions that are open ended.

This is all part of the sales process. You have a responsibility to make a genuine effort to enrol the customer on the right programme or activity for them. If you cannot meet their exact requirements, is an alternative programme available? In all cases the information you give must be correctly described and accurate. Failure to do so may not only give your customer an unpleasant experience but could also lead to prosecution under the Trade Descriptions Act.

Once you have provided the information requested it is essential that you check the details the customer is giving. All enrolment forms must be completed fully and legibly. Politely clarify any item that is not legible and amend where necessary.

The process of enrolment usually concludes with the exchange of money. Ensure that the correct change and a receipt are given. All monies and forms should be processed in accordance with the systems and financial procedures of the organisation.

## PROGRESS CHECK

1   Why is it important to know the environment you work in?

2   What is the process for admitting customers?

3   When enrolling children for an activity what information should be kept on the register?

4   When working on reception what procedures and policies are you likely to need to know about?

5   How can you ensure you have enrolled a person on the correct programme?

## Customer feedback

A customer, having purchased a product or a service from you or your organisation, will have perceptions and opinions on their 'purchase experience'. Discovering and monitoring what these views are can improve the service you offer. A customer may approach you unexpectedly with a complaint (this is known as unsolicited feedback) or you may have asked for the information through a customer comments system – this is solicited feedback. In all cases you can learn a lot from this feedback.

### Customer comments

Customers not only need an avenue to express their points but also need to feel confident that something will be done about them. This is where feedback needs to be processed and evaluated effectively. Where customers are unsatisfied, services should be improved wherever possible and the information relayed to the customer.

**Receiving customer comments**

These may be of a positive or negative nature. Both can aid learning and must be taken seriously. Be sure to:

- listen to the feedback rather than rejecting it
- be clear about the points being made
- make appropriate efforts to confirm the issues rather than taking just one view
- ensure you record accurately the type, time of the feedback and from whom it was received
- process the feedback through the system as soon as possible
- wherever possible, offer solutions

- thank the person for their comments and ensure that their views will be listened to.

### Customer comment system

A customer comment system is a method by which a customer can record their opinions on a pre-designed comment form. He or she could be asked to give a series of graded opinions on specific issues or may have the opportunity to write detailed comments leading from more open-ended questions.

Many organisations offer incentives, such as vouchers, for customers who use their formal customer comments system. This not only acts as a method to encourage return visitors but also provides feedback on which to measure the customer's perception of the quality of the products and services of the organisation.

**Figure 2.7** *Customer comment card*

Some important points about a customer comment system:

- It should be located in a position which is easily accessible for customers.

- The form should be simple to complete, using questions that are unambiguous and not misleading.

- The time taken to complete the comments should be as short as possible. Using diagrams (as in Figure 2.7) could help to attain this target.

- A formal written comment system should exist alongside other methods, such as face to face and (where appropriate) surveys. This variety encourages customers to raise any concerns during their visit, and allows you the opportunity to put things right immediately.

- The completed comments should be processed in a reasonable time. This includes recording the data, analysis, monitoring and response.

> REMEMBER
>
> *Always thank customers for completing and returning their comment sheets.*

## Surveying customers

By undertaking customer surveys an organisation is proactively seeking the opinions of its customers and potential customers. Surveys usually involve taking a sample of customers and directly asking their opinions on a number of issues, by mail, phone or face to face. A survey allows the organisation to target specific groups at specific times, to target opinions on specific activities and courses or to discover what programmes customers would like to see. These methods are more direct than acting simply on feedback but are often more costly and depend upon the skills of the interviewer.

### Customer survey system

- A survey should not be done in isolation. It should form part of a feedback system or be carried out on a regular basis.

- The people surveyed should be allowed to remain anonymous.

- Leading questions should not be asked. Leading questions are questions where an expected answer is sought – for example, 'The coach was really good, wasn't he?'

- A representative sample of interviewees should be taken.

- Clearly identify your aims and objectives before issuing the survey. This helps to ensure that the questions asked are valid and that useful information is gathered.

- Wherever possible, impartial employees or non-employees should administer the questions.

- Interviews should be conducted only with interviewees who have agreed and have the time available, and interviewers should not take time out of their working day to do the interview unless authorised to do so.

- Analysis of the information received from customers can be quite difficult and is often undertaken by senior management.

## Solving problems for customers

Most people accept that problems occur but cannot accept them not being corrected promptly, so solving a customer's problem will enhance their opinion of you and your organisation. Gathering information, offering solutions and taking immediate action are the essentials of solving problems for customers.

### Gathering information

Through administering a customer comment and survey system the organisation should be able to identify their customers' perceptions of problems. Many organisations keep a complaints book to record

- who made the complaint
- the nature of the complaint
- the date and time of any incident
- the action that was (or needs to be) taken.

These points must be summarised to identify complaints that need urgent attention or which are recurring problems. Any that can be dealt with simply and cost-effectively should be corrected immediately; those that require further attention must be processed as quickly as possible. It may be necessary to pass comments to the appropriate people or departments or your line managers.

Keeping a complaints book enables you to obtain key information. Using a variety of sources and consulting the appropriate personnel will give a balanced perspective of the problem. You should also be aware if any problems are related to legislative or legal issues. Any complaints where a visitor's safety is a concern must be investigated immediately!

### Proposing and delivering solutions

Offering to solve a customer's problems shows initiative and willingness to meet their needs. The ability to find solutions that fulfil your customer's needs will leave him or her with a much more positive opinion of the organisation than when the problem arose. They are certainly more likely to tell other people of this experience – for example, the Marks and Spencer's policy on exchanging garments without problems is nationally recognised.

When trying to propose solutions for customers it is a good idea to try the following.

- Discuss the problem with your colleagues and seek their advice. This not only shares a problem (offering more ideas for a solution) but also makes colleagues aware of a problem that may arise again.
- Examine the organisation's policies. There may be precedents for refunds, exchanging goods, goodwill offers. Policies may list situations where you are to refer to line managers.
- Suggest alternative products and services the organisation has to offer. This may help to keep the customer and introduce them to another part of the organisation. For example, offer use of an outdoor Astroturf facility if the sports hall is not available.

- Try to offer more than one choice, with the last resort being a full refund.

- Explain the reasons behind each option you offer. Most negative feelings about a problem experienced by a customer can continue to manifest but telling the complainant why the problem has occurred and what you propose to do about it is evidence of an organisation which is listening to its customers and is hence more likely to retain their custom.

**Taking action to deliver solutions**

It is important, when taking action to solve a problem, to show that you are using initiative at all times and communicating in a polite and friendly manner. However, standard procedures, which have often been designed from experience and with the objectives of the organisation in mind, must be followed. Standard procedures may include the following:

- Checking the problem, recording it and then ensuring the correct level of authority is dealing with it.

- Alerting colleagues and management to recurrent problems and informing them of the range of solutions you offered and those that have been most successful.

- Informing the customer of the outcome of the complaints procedure.

## CASE STUDY

A couple arrive to play badminton but see that the court has not been set up on time. This has happened three weeks in a row and they decide to approach a sports assistant and complain. The assistant puts up the net and, having resolved the immediate complaint, assures the couple that the incident will be reported. The management assess why the changeover had not been completed on time and implement changes to the staffing rota to ensure that there will be no repetition of the incident.

The assistant, after having reported the incident and recorded the necessary details, informs her line manager of the problem; she visits the couple at the end of their session and explains the procedure for complaints. She thanks them for bringing it to the attention of the centre and assures them that their complaint is being taken seriously and that the problem will not happen again.

1   What is the advantage to the centre of the efficient handling and processing of a complaint?

2   What is the role of the sports assistant and why are her actions so important?

## PROGRESS CHECK

1 Why is it a good idea to have a customer comment system in your organisation?

2 What are the key ingredients of a customer comment system?

3 Why is it important to record the comments of customers?

4 Why is it important to quickly find solutions for customers?

5 How would you deal with a customer who has booked to play badminton at the same time as someone else?

---

### KEY TERMS

*You need to know the meaning of the following words and phrases. Go back through the chapter to make sure you understand.*

Activity register
Customer comment system
Ethnic groups
Prospective customers

Communication process
Customer survey
Product knowledge
Special needs

# 3 Providing a healthy, safe and secure environment

This chapter covers:

➤ Examining your responsibilities
➤ General law on health, safety and security
➤ Maintaining a healthy and safe environment
➤ Maintaining a secure environment
➤ Dealing with accidents, injuries and emergencies

Providing a healthy, safe and secure environment should be the utmost priority of any organisation and individual. Within sport and recreation there are many statutes and guidelines covering health, safety and security, but it is not the aim of this chapter to describe all of them. Often, many sporting and recreational organisations, especially those in the voluntary sector, are not bound by legislation. In most instances, however, individuals working in the industry can be found negligent for wrongful actions.

Whether you are simply coaching outdoor hockey to 12-year-old students after school or are working in a multifaceted leisure centre, you need to be committed to providing a healthy, safe and secure environment by identifying your responsibilities and following approved practices and guidelines. Many organisations are trying to raise awareness of the significance of health and safety and security of those working, participating in or watching sport and physical recreation.

## Examining your responsibilities

You have responsibilities for the health and safety of yourself, your colleagues and visitors to your facility. Understanding your legal duties and maintaining and raising awareness of health, safety and security issues can help to ensure that safe procedures are followed.

### Sources of law

Laws on health, safety and security derive from a number of sources and cover a wide area for those working in sport and physical recreation.

**Common law and civil liability**

This is an area of law that has been created by previous civil cases, in which precedents have been established. Courts base their judgments on earlier decisions from accumulated case law. These cases are normally heard in County and High Courts. Individuals (the plaintiffs), bring action

33

against another party (the defendant), to claim damages for losses incurred. The penalties that can be imposed by the courts are known as civil liability.

**Statute law and criminal liability**

Criminal liability refers to the penalties that can be imposed by the criminal courts. These courts (Magistrates and Crown Courts) have the power to issue fines, impose imprisonment and remedial orders. This law is enforced by representatives of the government such as the police and the Health and Safety Executive.

Statutes – Acts of Parliament, such as the Health and Safety at Work Act – are designed to regulate the behaviour of organisations and individuals. They also encompass regulations such as the Control of Substances Hazardous to Health (COSHH), which have been created in consultation with industry and local authorities. Guidelines and codes of conduct, often produced by specialists, also play a major role in providing a healthy, safe and secure environment by determining – amongst other things – standards and approved practice.

## ACTIVITY

In groups of three or four find examples of codes of conduct and guidelines for different sports and organisations. Discuss their similarities and differences.

## GOOD PRACTICE ▷

*Familiarise yourself with relevant legislation, including basic hygiene, food safety, contract law, discrimination and legislation involving the environment.*

**Figure 3.1** *Keep up to date on current legislation*

### Raising awareness

There can be no doubt that health and safety issues have risen in importance for all those involved in sport and physical recreation. Awareness has been heightened by recent 'disasters', mainly at soccer stadiums, where many spectators lost their lives – Bradford, Heisel and Hillsborough are just three such venues. New guidelines and legislation have brought structural changes to major sports facilities and altered many operating procedures. Individuals are more aware of their right to pursue compensation if they feel they have suffered damages as a result of someone else's negligence.

Insurance companies now have specific policies offering protection against negligence claims by those participating, organising and coaching sports activities. Membership of a governing body now usually includes similar insurance. It is the responsibility of all those working in sport and physical recreation not only to protect themselves against legal action but also to actively seek and employ measures to ensure the health, safety and security of customers, visitors and participants. One of the most effective methods of achieving this is to be involved in a safety programme.

**Safety programmes**

A safety programme typically has three main elements:

- *implementation*, which includes setting objectives, seeking advice and implementing safe systems of work
- *monitoring*, which is concerned with ensuring that policies and practice achieve the objectives
- *evaluation*, which examines what has taken place, evaluates and reviews and, where appropriate, recommends improvements.

As a member of the work force you can have a major role to play in the safety programme.

- Take time to read your organisation's policies regarding health and safety.
- Correct colleagues who are breaching policy.
- Promote safe practice by encouraging discussion with participants.
- Use visual means (e.g. posters) to promote safe practice.
- Report unsafe practices to your safety officer or line manager.

---

## ACTIVITY

In pairs, design a poster that would highlight the importance of health and safety for all those visiting a leisure centre or health club.

---

## PROGRESS CHECK

1   What are the main differences between civil and criminal liability?
2   What are the three main elements of a safety programme?
3   Why is it a good idea to raise awareness of health and safety for all those involved in sport and physical recreation?
4   How can this be done?
5   If you saw an unsafe incident at work what would you do?

---

# General law on health, safety and security

It is the overall responsibility of the owners of facilities to provide and maintain safe conditions for those working in or visiting their premises. However, it is the responsibility of all those involved in sport and physical recreation to act in a manner which does not endanger themselves or others who may be affected by their actions.

It is important to understand the main health, safety and security legislation as well as the common duty of care and occupier's liability. The Children's Act will be covered later in the book.

## The Health and Safety at Work Act 1974

This is the main piece of legislation. It has been somewhat expanded in European legislation – the Management of Health and Safety at Work (Regulations) 1992, known as the 'six pack' – but its overall aims remain.

- Secure the health, safety and welfare of people at work.
- Protect people other than those at work (e.g. participants) against risks to health and safety arising from the activities of people at work.
- Control handling and storage of dangerous substances.
- Control the emission into the atmosphere of noxious or offensive substances from premises.

The main aim of the act is to involve everyone – management, owners and employees – to make them aware of the importance of health and safety.

## Employers' responsibilities

It is the duty of the employer, as far as is reasonably practicable, to safeguard the health and safety and welfare of the people who work for them – and that of non-employees (customers, visitors, members of the general public) on the premises. These duties are:

- to provide and maintain plant, equipment and systems of work which are safe and which are not a risk to health
- to provide safe storage, handling and use of substances that could cause risk to health
- to provide appropriate information, instruction and training for employees in regard to health and safety
- to make certain the workplace is monitored and maintained in a safe condition.

## Duties of employees

Under the Health and Safety at Work Act the employee also has responsibilities. This is an attempt to reduce the risk of accident or injury to everyone in the workplace and to promote responsible behaviour. Employees must:

- take reasonable care of their own health and safety
- take reasonable care of the health and safety of others who may be affected by their actions
- co-operate with the employer and other relevant organisations to ensure that the requirements of the act are met (this includes notifying supervisors of unsafe equipment or practices)
- not misuse equipment provided to maintain health and safety.

## Health and safety inspectors

Inspectors can be appointed by the Health and Safety Executive, from the local authority or the fire service. These people may visit your place of work and can legally:

- enter the premises at any reasonable time
- measure, test, inspect and photograph as they wish
- take samples, equipment or substances from the premises.

If the Inspectors see the Act is not being enforced they can:

- serve a prohibition notice, stopping an activity likely to cause serious injury

---

REMEMBER

*If you are ever unclear about your duties, ask your line manager.*

- serve an improvement notice, requiring action to be taken to remedy faults within a period of not more than 21 days
- prosecute any person contravening a statutory provision.

GOOD PRACTICE ▷ *Within your systems of customer care you and your colleagues should obtain identification from visiting health and safety officers. If you are asked to, assist the inspectors on their visit, ensuring that cover of your duties has been arranged.*

**Figure 3.2** *Don't leave groups unattended*

**The organisation's policy**

The Health and Safety at Work Act also requires that any organisation has a safety committee, safety representatives and devises a policy statement containing the following information.

- The organisation's commitment to health, safety and welfare at work.
- The hierarchy within the organisation, identifying those responsible for health and safety.
- All relevant codes of practice and advice covering the particular functions carried out at the premises. These include emergency first aid, pool and ice activities.

*European directives*

A further set of directives on health and safety has come from the European Union. They cover:

- Health and safety management, encouraging a systematic approach to health and safety, including risk assessment.
- Safety of work equipment. Employers should ensure that employees use the correct equipment, that it is well maintained, and that employees are trained in its use.

# Funbury Leisure Centre
## Skating Safely

**1** Choose the correct boot size. Normally you should use at least a half size bigger than your regular shoe size.
Skates must fit tightly. If your skates are loose they will not support your ankles. If they are too large you will develop blisters and discomfort.

**2** Tie the laces using the correct method (see illustration). Loosen all laces, fully insert your foot and pull up your socks – making sure there are no wrinkles.
Push your foot back to ensure correct location of heel.
Tie the laces, leaving the first laces relatively loose to ease your toes, then tie firmly around your ankles. Reduce the tightness until the top of the boot is loose enough for you to be able to insert a finger between the boot and your sock.

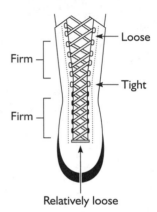

**Figure 3.3** *Safety advice on using skates*

- Manual handling of loads. Many back injuries are caused by incorrect handling and lifting. Manual handling of loads should be avoided, those that cannot be avoided assessed and steps introduced to avoid injury (these might include diagrams of how to lift loads, such as that in Figure 3.4).
- Workplace conditions. These general requirements focus on the environment, safety, facilities and housekeeping. The workplace conditions directive covers a multitude of issues from lighting and ventilation to cleanliness.
- Use of personal protective equipment. Appropriate and well maintained equipment should be used by trained personnel.
- Display screen equipment. Problems with the use of such screens (usually attached to a computer) range from headaches to repetitive strain injuries. Employers have a duty to ensure work design (how work is done), that users take adequate breaks and are well trained to reduce health-related risks for people using display screen equipment.

## Control of Substances Hazardous to Health

It is highly probable that even in the smallest of sport and physical recreation premises there will be substances that can be hazardous to health. These can include chemicals for cleaning and disinfecting, treating water or marking out grass pitches. Employers are required

---

**REMEMBER**

*Be familiar with the operations and systems used in your workplace which affect workplace conditions.*

---

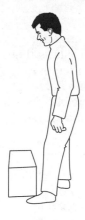

**Stop and think.** Plan the lift. Where is the load going to be placed? Use appropriate handling aids if possible. Do you need help with the load? Remove obstructions such as discarded wrapping materials. For a long lift – such as floor to shoulder height – consider resting the load mid-way on a table or bench in order to change grip.

**Don't jerk.** Carry out the lifting movement smoothly, keeping control of the load.

**Place the feet.** Feet apart, giving a balanced and stable base for lifting (tight skirts and unsuitable footwear make this difficult). Leading leg as far forward as is comfortable.

**Adopt a good posture.** Bend your knees so that your hands, when grasping the load, are as nearly level with your waist as possible – but do not kneel or overflex your knees. Keep your back straight (tucking in your chin helps). Lean forward a little over the load if necessary to get a good grip. Keep shoulders level and facing in the same direction as your hips.

**Move your feet.** Don't twist your trunk when turning to the side.

**Keep close to the load.** Keep the load close to your body for as long as possible. Keep the heaviest side of the load next to your body. If a close approach to the load is not possible try sliding it towards you before attempting to lift it.

**Get a firm grip.** Try to keep your arms within the boundary formed by your legs. The optimum position and nature of the grip depends on the circumstances and individual preference, but it must be secure. A hook grip is less fatiguing than keeping the fingers straight. If you need to vary your grip as the lift proceeds, do this as smoothly as possible.

**Put the load down, *then* adust.** If precise positioning of the load is necessary, put it down first, then slide it into the desired position.

**Figure 3.4** *Lifting heavy objects safely*

to identify, assess, monitor and control all substances hazardous to health under the 1988 Regulations. Failure to comply constitutes an offence under the Health and Safety at Work Act 1974.

Substances have many different properties and potential to cause harm. The human body may be at risk through inhalation via the nose, ingestion via the mouth and absorption via the skin. All potentially dangerous substances must be handled and stored correctly.

## Occupiers' Liability Acts 1957 and 1984

Organisations who own land and premises have a duty of care to ensure the safety of visitors to their premises. Greater care is required where children are involved, as what might be considered safe for adults is not necessarily so for children. Examples might be broken glass in play areas, trees which could easily be climbed, or ladders left alongside buildings.

### The Public Health Act 1936

The main focus of the Act provides local authorities with extensive powers to specify means of escape from buildings. Under local laws there are sections on 'undesirable people'. Action may be taken to remove 'undesirable' people who are likely to influence the Health and Safety of people in the facility. This normally applies in situations where visitors fail to comply with instructions from staff or whose conduct is unsociable.

### The Trade Descriptions Act 1968

Consumers and visitors have legal rights. The Trade Descriptions Act protects customers against providers falsely describing their products and services. Descriptions of products and services, usually found in sales and promotional literature, must be true at the time of going to print. This act also applies to verbal descriptions.

### Activity Centres Act 1995

This act is aimed at improving the health and safety at outdoor activity centres. Centres that are run commercially or by a local authority need a licence to operate adventure activities for children under 18. Strict criteria regarding emergency and operating procedures, staff and ratio of staff to children are enforced.

### Other relevant laws and regulations

- Employer's Liability Act 1969
- Safety at Sports Grounds Act 1975
- Fire Precautions Act 1971
- Sale of Goods Act 1979
- Food Safety Act 1990
- Children's Act 1989
- Electricity at Work Regulations 1989
- Health and Safety (First Aid) Regulations 1981
- Data Protection Act 1984

### Civil law

In civil law an individual can bring an action against a defendant in order to seek compensation for damages caused by an alleged breach of duty.

### Negligence and a duty of care

In order to be awarded damages it must be established that negligence occurred and that:

- a duty of care was owed
- this duty of care was breached
- actual harm occurred to the plaintiff.

This duty of care is said to be owed to our 'neighbour'; in legal terms anyone who can be affected by our actions. It extends to users, spectators and colleagues and (in the case of sport and physical

40

recreation) participants. In the case of participants there are obvious and inherent risks in many sports, especially those involving physical contact. Whether adults or children are involved you can follow local authority and governing body procedures to help ensure you have fulfilled your duty of care.

## Security and the law

It has been argued that the level of criminal activity escalated in the 1980s and early 1990s. Fitting car and house alarms, carrying personal security devices, carrying less money and not going out alone at night are all evidence of the continuing concern for security of possessions and people. A sports and recreation facility and its owners are concerned with the security of:

- property and buildings
- visitors and participants
- staff
- information
- money.

Legislation and responsibility for security can be found in many different sources, although much of it can be found in Health and Safety at Work Act 1974.

### The Data Protection Act 1984

Many organisations have computer systems, which may be networked internally and externally. The Data Protection Act covers all organisations that store personal information about staff and members on their computers. Such an organisation must register with the Data Protection Register. The Act attempts to safeguard the general public from inaccuracy and misuse of information. Under the Act customers are entitled to see any information held about them on computer. They have a right to compensation for inaccuracies and to have the inaccuracies rectified.

### Exclusion clauses

People expect a certain degree of security for themselves and their possessions when they are participating in sporting activities. Many centres offer lockers, supervised storage areas or locked rooms to help ensure personal belongings are protected from thieves. However, most systems are not foolproof and providers have clauses excluding their liability from theft of personal belongings.

---

### REMEMBER

*The public should be made aware of any exclusion clauses before they purchase an entrance ticket.*

---

PROGRESS CHECK

1  What are the main elements of the 'six pack' regulations?

2  Identify two responsibilities of employers and two duties of employees regarding health and safety.

3  What does COSHH stand for?

4  What is the main purpose of the Data Protection Act?

5  What is an exclusion clause and where might it be used?

# Maintaining a healthy and safe environment

Health and safety are an ongoing concern for all people, especially those on duty. Potential problems can be avoided by staff being alert and attentive to problems arising at the facility. More formal procedures, including safety checklists and risk assessment, should be taken in line with European legislation.

## Identifying the hazards in the working environment

A hazard is something with the potential to cause harm. Hazards can include machinery, property and methods of work. Having a basic understanding of the areas where potential hazards exist will help to prevent incidents and increase safety awareness.

### Ventilation

The workplace needs to be adequately ventilated. Fresh, clean air should be drawn from outside to replace humid air and provide movement, giving freshness without causing draughts. Many centres use heating equipment, which can cause fumes and vapours, and fresh air is required to provide adequate ventilation.

### Temperature

A customer's comfort can depend on air temperature, humidity and air movement. Personal preference (whether spectating or participating) makes it difficult to have a temperature that satisfies everyone. In offices and areas where people are more sedentary, a good guideline temperature is 16°C. In areas where more physical effort is involved this can be reduced by 3°C or appropriate ventilation provided.

### Lighting

Inadequate illumination does not enable people to work and move about safely. Light bulbs that have worn out must be replaced. Domestic bulbs can be easily changed but any that need to be fitted by trained/industrial personnel must be reported to the line manager and recorded in the incident book. Automatic emergency lighting must be powered by an independent source and should be regularly checked.

### Electrical hazards

These include power sources and power-operated equipment. Plugs and sockets should be complete with no parts missing. Evidence of burn marks could indicate faults. Extension leads are a potential hazard and should be used only as a last resort. People should not be unnecessarily put at risk by such hazards. Any defects must be immediately reported.

### Noise

Excessive noise is usually associated with special events and where certain sound systems are in operation. Noise and vibration should be monitored to ensure that regulations are being met.

### Dry sport and recreation areas

- Floors can be slippery if not kept clean and free from obstruction. They are potentially hazardous when wet, especially immediately after cleaning.
- Damaged equipment must be reported and removed from use. Maintenance systems and regular checks will help to avoid problems.

- Light fittings should be covered and guarded, preventing damage from broken glass. This should include scoreboards and other similar fittings.
- Fitness equipment should be used only following instructions. Notices and diagrams of instruction on usage will provide good 'memory joggers'. Space for use, instructions, facilities for wiping down after use and protective fittings all require attention.

### Wet sport and recreation areas

- Surfaces need to be regularly cleaned and non-slip steps and diving boards must be safe to use.
- Signs can be useless if they are not clear and identify hazards, such as 'cleaning in progress'. Clear signs are needed on depths of water.
- Water should be safe to swim in. You should be able to see the bottom of the pool at its deepest part. There should be no adverse effect on eyes or skin, nor should there be any objectionable odours. Regular water tests identify problems early.

**Figure 3.5**  *Always be alert to the needs of your customers*

GOOD PRACTICE ▷     *A good tip is to ask regular swimmers for their views on the conditions of the water.*

### General areas

- Changing rooms, toilets and showers should be regularly cleaned. Floor tiles should be complete and not coming loose. Seats and doors should be safe and securely fitted. Cleanliness is the key to avoiding unhygienic conditions. Blocked drains and moulding limescale should be cleared. No cleaning equipment should be left out and COSHH regulations should be followed. Toilets not functioning properly should be clearly marked 'out of action/order' and the time when they will be functioning again given. Water temperature should be monitored, especially in the showers.

- The entrance should be well illuminated with restricted access and exits. Barriers and exit routes must be clear from obstruction and have clear signs directing visitors. The requirements of people with special needs should be met.
- Spectator areas, especially seats, should be safe and checked regularly. Steps and handrails must be in good condition and not slippery. Emergency exits must be free from obstruction and well marked.
- Working long shifts can be tiring and staff can become complacent with routine matters and checks. Where health and safety is involved no situation should be compromised to save time and money.

Despite all the efforts made by the organisation to provide information to the customer, instructions are not always followed. People running in the swimming pool areas, dropping litter, or not showering before swimming are commonplace.

---

REMEMBER

*Take your breaks, and concentrate on key situations and on key tasks.*

---

GOOD PRACTICE ▷  *Approach such people and politely but firmly remind them of their responsibilities.*

---

**Figure 3.6**  *Be firm but polite when reminding people of their responsibilities*

## Risk assessment for health and safety

A hazard is something with the potential to cause harm. A risk identifies the likelihood of harm from a particular hazard. It can also indicate the consequences of the risk – e.g. potential number of people involved.

Under EU regulations risk assessment is required by every employer to identify the risks to the health and safety of their employees whilst at work and those visiting and using the facilities.

44

The self-employed person still needs to carry out risk assessment and take corrective measures where risks have been identified.

EU regulations require that 'regular' systematic general examination of the work activity is undertaken and recorded, usually once a day. A more thorough and detailed assessment should be performed once a month.

GOOD PRACTICE ▷

*Get into the habit, when entering a sports hall or walking onto a pitch, of undertaking and continuing to carry out risk assessment. Is the floor becoming dirtier and therefore too slippery? Is it getting too dark? Is someone playing too aggressively?*

**Carrying out risk assessment**

- Ensure relevant risks are addressed by:
  - identifying hazards
  - assessing if there are relevant acts or regulations to be complied with
  - assessing the risk – no hazard, no risk
  - including all machinery as well as work activity.
- Examine actual systems of work:
  - where work practice differs from the manual
  - non-routine operations.
- Identify those who may be affected: employees, visitors, participants, night security, cleaners, neighbours, people with special needs, inexperienced members of staff.

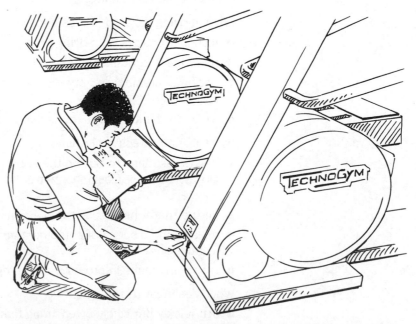

**Figure 3.7** *Risk assessment should include machinery as well as activities*

- Monitor existing preventative and precautionary measures. These may need adapting or changing where they are not working effectively.
- Record the findings. This is normally done in writing but can be done by other means (e.g. electronically).

A copy of a risk assessment form is shown in Figure 3.8.

## ACTIVITY

In pairs, design an appropriate form for identifying hazards at your college/place of work and undertake a risk assessment.

### Taking preventative and corrective action

Having correctly identified problems through risk assessment or following up on information received, take action promptly and effectively.

**Handling substances hazardous to health**

The following steps examine how to prevent harm when handling substances hazardous to health and offers procedures for dealing with spillages.

When identifying the substance and the risk involved:

- read the labels clearly
- refer to guidelines on the type of risk – e.g. inhalation of dust
- identify who, apart from yourself, may be at risk
- take steps to inform people of the risks and take action to prevent harm – for example, erect warning signs
- where there is no label or clear indication of contents do not open. Inform the line manager.

When moving hazardous substances:

- read instructions on moving them
- never leave containers unattended
- once a container is empty, dispose of it as per instructions – never re-use
- focus on the job: distractions may cause poor handling.

When using protective clothing:

- always take time to put on the appropriate clothing (overalls, goggles, gloves, boots or mask), no matter how silly it may look, or how long it may take
- ensure that it has been stored and maintained correctly
- replace and dispose of equipment and clothing to the manufacturer's instructions
- report any faults in protective clothing to your supervisor.

When dealing with spillages:

- act quickly but safely by ensuring that no harm can be caused to yourself or anyone else – use barriers, warning signs etc.

# SAFETY SECTION –
# MAIN RISK ASSESSMENT

*Funbury Leisure Centre*

Date ............................ Last assessment ............................

Directorate ............................

Activity situation ............................

Site or client location ............................

| Task or activity | Hazards identified | Degree of risk — Seriousness | | | | | Degree of risk — Likelihood | | | | | Risk rating | | Persons at risk | | | | |
|---|---|---|---|---|---|---|---|---|---|---|---|---|---|---|---|---|---|---|
| | | No injury 1 | Minor injury 2 | Three day 3 | Major injury 4 | Fatal 5 | Certain 5 | Probable 4 | Possible 3 | Remote 2 | Unlikely 1 | Initial risk rating | Final risk rating | Employee | Young person | Contractor | Public | Visitor |
| | | | | | | | | | | | | | | | | | | |

Risk scores: 0–8 = Low risk
9–15 = Medium risk
16–25 = High risk

IRR = Initial Risk Rating
FRR = Final Risk Rating

SAFETY OFFICER – MS P. WINGROVE
THE COUNCIL HOUSE, COLLEGE ROAD,
DONCASTER Ref/MRA 11/9/93

**Figure 3.8** *Sample risk assessment form*

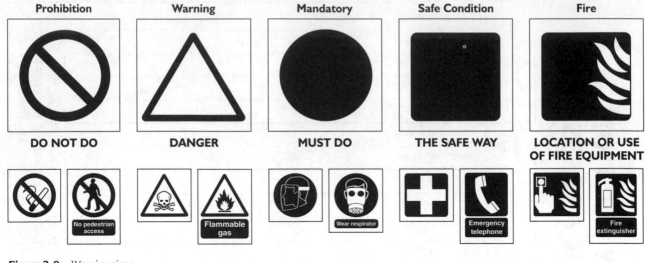

**Figure 3.9** *Warning signs*

- follow manufacturers' and organisational guidelines for spillages. There is great danger in mixing certain chemicals or adding water to chemicals
- where necessary, get help from a colleague
- report the incident clearly. Identify the chemical involved, where the spillage occurred and the action that was taken. This report may initially be given verbally but it is good practice to write the incident down at the first available moment.

**Storing substances hazardous to health**

Time should be spent in selection of a suitable storage area. This will normally be an area that

- is used for the sole purpose for chemical storage
- is fireproof, dry and well ventilated
- has appropriate fire extinguishers with instructions
- has appropriate warning signs and instructions for use
- is locked and secure
- has first aid and emergency instructions.

Once you have used the substances you should follow the system at work related to storage. It will no doubt include the following points.

- Return substances to storage immediately after use. Ensure that the container is capped and returned to its position in storage.
- Avoid placing incompatible substances together. Read the labels and follow the manufacturer's instructions.
- Check for hazards. This may include identifying out-of-date substances, defective containers or simply an untidy storage area. Follow the guidelines for disposing of substances and report any inconsistencies that cannot be dealt with simply.
- Neatly update the records for storage and record any other action you have taken – e.g. disposing of defective containers.
- Leave the storage area as you would like to find it. Lock the room and return the key to the appropriate area.

**Taking action**

All actions should be taken promptly and in line with organisational procedures. Actions are likely to include

- removing and reporting hazards, such as a blocked exit or poorly stored chemicals

- using correct procedures, as indicated on the container, to deal with spillages of hazardous substances

- cleaning up spillages as soon as you are able and using signs to warn others (e.g. 'Caution: wet floor')

- reporting damaged equipment, where the risk of injury has increased, immediately and leaving instructions warning people against using the equipment

- being aware of the manuals and guidance documentation for health and safety

- keeping a health and safety booklet, perhaps used at induction, at your place of work. It should contain concise, relevant details on legal duties and responsibilities, examples of the job, accident and emergency procedures, documentation process and sources of reference

- undergoing training, which should be of high priority and ongoing (new standards and methods are being introduced all the time)

- taking care when handling heavy loads. Do not attempt to lift anything too heavy or to a height that causes you to be unbalanced. Always wear protective gloves and footwear where appropriate. When attempting to lift try to secure a good grip and bend your knees before lifting. Always ensure that you can see where you are going and move heavy loads in stages, especially when moving them to different heights. Use step ladders rather than creating 'ladders' from boxes

- following your responsibility under health and safety legislation. All employees have responsibilities, but the action you take should only be in line with the level of responsibility you have. Evacuation decisions are usually made by management, but any employee could be responsible for removing obstacles from exit routes immediately

- reporting problems promptly. A spoken report may be the quickest and most effective way of initially reporting a problem but this needs to be quickly followed up by a written report in the incident book or a relevant form. Ensure all colleagues are aware of the incident, especially those not working at the particular time of the incident.

PROGRESS CHECK

1  What is the difference between a hazard and a risk?

2  Name five hazards you might expect to see in your local sports centre.

3  Why are regular tests carried out on the water in swimming pools?

4  What is the first thing to do when you have spilt a chemical substance?

5  Give three good tips for handling heavy loads.

# Maintaining a secure environment

Effective security is the responsibility of everyone working in the organisation. Some staff may have specific responsibilities for security, including protecting people and properties, but general staff have responsibility for security by being aware of hazards and by taking positive action to avoid potential breaches of security.

Providing a secure environment is good for the organisation because it

- encourages people to visit the facility
- reduces fraud and theft
- reduces damage to the property.

## Identifying the security hazards

Hazards regarding security generally arise from four main areas:

- people
- property
- money
- information.

### People

'People' include colleagues and visitors to the facility, whether they be participants, spectators or contractors. All employers have a legal duty under the Health and Safety at Work Act 1974 to ensure the health and safety of their staff and avoid hazards in the workplace. Providing a safe working environment that is free from violence is also important. In a service industry there is much contact between staff and customers, and people working in sport and physical recreation can expect sometimes to encounter uncomfortable (and perhaps violent) incidents during their course of work.

The design of the entry point to the facility is essential for security. It must allow

- space for queuing
- a secondary entrance for disabled people
- control of customers through the reception area.

If you are working on reception do not let yourself get distracted and allow people to enter the facility without being accounted for and without paying. Apart from the loss of income, the record of numbers of people in the facility for safety and evacuation situations will be inaccurate.

Sport and leisure facilities often attract large groups of people and sometimes having a good time is at the expense of other individuals. Excessive consumption of alcohol increases the likelihood of unacceptable behaviour and must be dealt with severely.

### Property

This includes the fixtures and fittings of the building as well as personal belongings. Criminal damage to property and equipment can be a regular occurrence, depending on the location of the facility. Many modern design features are aimed at deterring this type of crime, yet robbery and vandalism remain part of modern-day behaviour and security provision is taking on more importance.

Damage to property and fittings, graffiti on walls, broken windows and stolen cars are perennial problems for those working in sport and physical recreation. The growing number of private security firms is testament to the increase in such damages.

### Money

The industry often revolves around financial – and more specifically cash – transactions. It is usual to pay for sport and physical recreation, whether spectating or participating, with cash rather than credit card. Inefficient systems for handling cash can put staff at risk of attack or produce opportunities for dishonesty.

Receiving money, storing it and transferring it to the bank create opportunities for those wishing to steal cash. Fraud is also a concern. It is likely to come in the form of forged currency or stolen cheque books and cards.

Theft of goods, cash or information by customers or staff is a potential problem. Equipment may be taken, such as free weights from a gym, or stock stolen by staff or customers. Client and staff personal belongings are always potentially at risk.

### Information

The leisure industry is growing, as is the technology used by organisations looking for an 'edge' over their competitors. Through compulsory competitive tendering, use of technology has extended into the public and voluntary sectors. The development of customer profiles and direct mail marketing have led to organisations storing vast information on

## CASE STUDY

Two members of staff are changing over the equipment in the sports hall for five-a-side football and notice a group of three men who were in the bar drinking alcohol earlier. One of the men has smashed a glass on the floor and another, insistent that he wants to go for a swim, is threatening a colleague.

The first considerations are to the safety of staff, other visitors and to the men causing the problem. One member of staff goes to inform the line manager, the other goes to assist the colleague being threatened. The men are firmly asked to stop what they are doing and are informed that the incident is being reported. When the duty manager and two other members of staff return the men are seen off the premises.

The area where the glass has been smashed is cordoned off and the glass is removed and disposed of safely. Special materials are used to clean the spilt drink and COSHH practices, indicated on the cleaning store cupboard, are followed.

1   On what grounds could you refuse entry to the person wanting to use the pool?
2   What further action should be taken by the staff?

people and their habits. It is essential to have a secure means of storing information about customers, employees and financial position of the organisation.

## Risk assessment for security

As in the health and safety checks, it is the responsibility of the employer to identify risks in security and to impose systems to reduce the likelihood of criminal activity. As part of daily health and safety checks it is possible to include security checks and assessments. Other security checks may be carried out before special events or extensive changes to the facility or the programme.

### Undergoing a security risk assessment

- Ensure risks are addressed by identifying hazards and knowing the relevant acts or regulations to be complied with. Assess risk – if there is no hazard, there is no risk. Cover all internal and external areas as well as the activities.
- Examine the systems of security and find out where actual practice differs from the manual and what the non-routine operations are.
- Identify the people involved. Do employees have sufficient training, alertness? Are staffing levels appropriate? Who are the potential and likely visitors? Do we need specialists?
- Monitor existing preventative and precautionary measures. These may need to be adapted or changed. Are signs and access areas giving enough clear instructions? Are records of cash accurate? If not, what is the system for handling and storage? How is it recorded, transported and deposited? Is lighting sufficient?
- Record the findings by writing a report of the security check, which could include an action section that can be given to the appropriate manager. For example, if a window lock is coming loose, maintenance needs to be informed so that they can repair it immediately.

## Taking preventative and corrective action

Problems and issues will arise. It is important never to panic and to respond positively by taking the recommended course of action. However, prevention is better than cure and you can take many steps to avoid problems arising.

- Be alert and aware of anyone who looks suspicious or anything which may threaten security – ladders left unattended, fire exits left open, etc.
- All keys should be clearly labelled and the people who have access to them strictly monitored. Always know who has the master keys. Never leave keys around and report loss of keys immediately.
- Access areas need to be adaptable to control people moving into and out of the facility. This may be dependent upon a sudden number of visitors or an emergency situation. Using a simple rope system with clear signs can alleviate potential problems.
- Regular patrols are essential. Wherever the opportunity arises, patrol key areas – changing rooms, car parks, exit doors.

- Cash should always be handled away from the customers and other unauthorised persons. Never count the float where you can be seen. Follow company procedures, neatly record transactions and file receipts.
- When dealing with people, especially visitors, you should always ask what they are participating in or what they are spectators of and give them clear directions as to how to get there. Monitor suspicious people regularly. Disruptive people should be challenged politely. Never put yourself at risk.
- When handling cheques and credit cards, use a standard and approved system making usual checks. Report any 'problems' immediately to the duty officer.
- When handling computerised information back-up disks are essential.
- Deal with people asking general questions regarding programme costs etc. straightforwardly. More unusual questions regarding individuals or the business should be monitored with suspicion.

Security hazards identified through assessment must be followed up. When reporting problems always use the incident report form to support any spoken information you may have passed on. Inform colleagues of any relevant information that may affect them in the course of their work.

GOOD PRACTICE ▷

- *Check price boards to ensure that price changes have been adjusted accordingly.*
- *Remove all outdated brochures and other promotional materials.*
- *Check wording of literature to ensure there is nothing misleading – for example, don't label something as the latest training and fitness equipment when it clearly is not.*

**Figure 3.10** *Keeping the notice boards up to date indicates a well managed facility*

ACTIVITY

In your place of work or in an organisation of your choice produce a quick reference list of useful numbers. Know the key holders, who to call in case of broken windows, locks, doors, alarm system, memorise the police number and so on.

## PROGRESS CHECK

1 List the four main security hazards for organisations in sport and physical recreation

2 Why is the design and layout of the reception area so important?

3 Why is it important to record the findings of any security incident?

4 What are the main concerns when handling cash and credit cards?

5 Why is it a good idea to make regular checks on all promotional material?

# Dealing with accidents, injuries and emergencies

If you are working in sport and recreation you are very likely to encounter an accident or an emergency sooner rather than later. The severity of the injury will determine whether or not it can be dealt with at the facility rather than at hospital.

It is normal in an organisation to have several people who are trained in first aid. It is a legal requirement to have a trained first aider on the premises at all times and clear instructions on who and where they are and how they can be contacted. If you are not a trained first aider you will need to contact someone so trained to diagnose any action that needs to be taken.

## Dealing with injuries and signs of illness

Most people in sport and recreation have experienced or witnessed some kind of injury. This could be a minor injury, such as a small graze that can be treated on site, or a major injury that requires outside medical attention, such as a broken leg. The Health and Safety at Work Act extends to the duty to provide first aid (Health and Safety First Aid Regulations Act 1981) and states that an organisation must provide, depending on the size and nature of the organisation and its programme (e.g. holiday times are busier than normal term times) the following:

- first-aid equipment, including first aid boxes, a list of controls and their locations and supplementary equipment such as spine board and resuscitation kit
- a first-aid room – the regulations also specify the size, design and location
- first aiders (and any training programmes that should be provided). This includes a list of those people who have received a certificate from an authorised training body. Certificates are normally valid for only three years.

---

## REMEMBER

*If you are not qualified to handle first aid incidents get someone who is. Do not attempt to carry out actions you are not qualified to do.*

---

GOOD PRACTICE ▷ *When dealing with any accident or emergency, you can (and should)*

● *remain calm, speak slowly and reassuringly*
● *briefly assess the situation and decide if you can deal with it or need assistance*
● *identify any people with particular needs*
● *use the appropriate organisational procedures for the incident*
● *record the incident at the earliest appropriate time.*

**Figure 3.11** *Always be prepared to deal with an emergency*

## CONTENTS OF A FIRST AID BOX

| 1 | Guidance card | 6 | Medium-sized individually wrapped sterile unmedicated wound dressings 10 cm × 8 cm (4" × 3") approx |
|---|---|---|---|
| 20 | Individually wrapped sterile adhesive dressings (assorted sizes) | | |
| 2 | Sterile eye pads, with attachment | 2 | Large sterile individually wrapped unmedicated wound dressings 13 cm × 9 cm (5" × 3 1/2") approx |
| 6 | Individually wrapped triangular bandages | 3 | Extra large sterile individually wrapped unmedicated wound dressings 28 cm × 17.5 cm (11" × 7") approx |
| 6 | Safety pins | | |

### SUPPLEMENTARY EQUIPMENT

Scissors     Gloves     Ice pack
Tweezers     Cotton wool

### THINK HYGIENE

✚ British Red Cross

**Figure 3.12** *Recommended contents of a first-aid box*

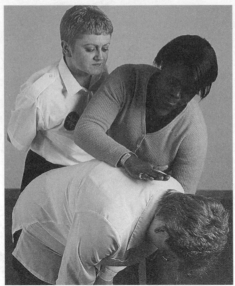

**Figure 3.13** *Keep up with first-aid courses*

© St John Ambulance

**Aims of a first aider**

The duties of someone administering first aid are to

- preserve life
- prevent the condition worsening
- promote recovery
- provide information to more qualified people (this could include history, symptoms and treatment).

**Responding to an injury**

Being able to respond to an injury can not only prevent further discomfort but may also save lives. The list below is intended to be general guidelines only. For specific cases (e.g. dehydration, burns) refer to the manuals produced by the British Red Cross or the St Johns' organisation.

- The first thing is to assess the situation and quickly and safely protect the casualty and any other person, including yourself, who may be at risk.
- Reassure and comfort the injured party. Children and people with special needs usually require more assurance than adults. This can be done by remaining calm and informing the person that positive action is taking place. As a general rule do not move the person or give him or her a drink, but do keep them warm.

GOOD PRACTICE ▷  *Find out where the nearest first-aid courses are and get yourself enrolled!*

- Find a first aider. If you are the only adult at hand send a responsible person to find one.
- Stay with the casualty. Try to reassure and ascertain any key information – age, how the injury occurred etc.

**Calling the emergency services**

The emergency services will require certain information. Knowing the kind of information they are likely to need in advance will speed up proceedings. After calling 999, they will ask:

- which service you require
- your telephone number and address
- the exact location of the incident
- information on the incident, specifically numbers involved, severity and type of injury
- miscellaneous factors such as no car access, wheelchair user involved, diabetic etc.

After the incident and the visit from the emergency services

- clean up
- resume normal service
- make the report.

## Following emergency procedures

It is normal for any organisation to have standard operating procedures for dealing with emergencies. These may be specific or general depending on the nature of the emergency. Typical procedures would cover fire, security incidents, missing persons, gas leaks, suspect parcels and lighting faults.

**Fire**

If a fire is reported by a customer and confirmed by a colleague the following steps should be taken:

- activate the nearest alarm
- call the fire brigade (see calling emergency services)
- inform the line manager and those with responsibility for security
- inform colleagues, including administration support
- assist the public by clearly informing them of the emergency procedure and location of the nearest exits
- extinguish the fire – but *only* after following the first five steps and if it is safe to do so
- ensure windows and doors are closed before leaving the building and help to contain the fire if it is safe to do so
- check the numbers of customers and employees to account for their safety.

**Missing persons**

It is common for small children to go missing or to be temporarily lost by a parent or guardian. If you find a lost child, always reassure him or her that they are safe and that their carer will be on their way. Try to find out as much information from the child as soon as is practical. This should include their name, address, phone number, type of car, place they last saw their carer and so on. Once this information has been gathered try to take their mind off the situation by keeping them occupied with a fun activity.

**Suspicious items/parcels**

In a sports facility bags, holdalls and boxes are commonplace. In today's climate there is a possibility that if a suspicious package or bag is not handled correctly it could result in injury and damage to the property. A suspicious item is anything which you feel is out of place or has been left unattended for some time. However foolish you may feel, it is better to follow your employer's standard procedure.

- Do not attempt to touch or move the item.
- Remain calm and report the matter immediately.
- Try to contact the potential owner through the public address system by giving a description of the item.
- If no one answers the call, contact the police.
- Record your actions and your reasons for considering the incident suspicious.

## Reporting accidents and incidents

The regulations relating to reporting accidents and incidents are covered under the Reporting of Injuries, Diseases and Dangerous Occurrences Regulations 1985 (RIDDOR).

RIDDOR basically allows:

- The Health and Safety Executive (the government body) to follow-up on reporting and check safety practices and operational procedures.
- A standardised report form (such as that shown in Figure 3.14) to be used.
- Officers from the Health and Safety Executive to advise organisations on prevention of further accident and illness.
- Investigation to prosecute, prohibit and make improvements where necessary.

**Minor accidents**

Accidents must be reported as soon as possible. They are usually recorded in an accident book and details would normally include:

- particulars of the person or persons involved (name, address, age, gender, etc.)
- date, time and place of accident
- description of the incident
- possible cause and action taken
- details of any witnesses
- further actions to be taken.

These reports are useful. Not only do they comply with legal requirements and insurance companies but they can also be used to find trends and target needs for training and operating procedures.

# Report of Accident to a Member of the Public

**I  Customer details**
a  Full name:
b  Home address:

c  Date of birth:          **d**  Age:
e  If a minor, full name of responsible person and relationship to child:

**2  Accident details**
a  Date of accident:          **b**  Time:
c  Exact location of accident:
d  Name and status of any witness to the accident:
e  Date and time the accident was first reported:
f  To whom was the accident first reported?
g  Full description of accident: (Include details of any machinery, plant equipment or substance involved):

h  Signature of person completing this form

**3  Injuries and treatment**
a  Nature and location of injury/injuries (state left or right side):

b  Type of treatment given:

c  Was an ambulance called?
d  Which hospital was the customer directed to?
e  Was advice to contact their GP given?
f  Treatment given by:

**4  Personnel use only**
a  Is the accident reportable to HSE?
b  If reportable, for which reason(s):
    Major injury/condition
    Over 3-day injury
    Dangerous occurrence
    Other (please specify)
c  Was the hospital contacted?
d  Signature of FLC representative (personnel department)

*Figure 3.14*  *Standard accident report form*

## Serious accidents

Serious accidents are those where the injured person has been sent to hospital. All serious accidents must be followed up and full details recorded. Any accident that resulted in an incapacity to work for more than three days must be reported to the Health and Safety Executive. Other types and occurrences that must be reported are those that cause

- fatality
- fractures, except those of the hands or feet
- amputation
- loss of sight
- loss of consciousness through lack of oxygen
- hospitalisation for more than 24 hours
- illness resulting from inhaling or absorbing a substance.

## Completing the report

There may be a person responsible for completing reports and processing them. If you were witness to an accident:

- keep the details for an incident report
- inform the personnel department that an accident form is being processed
- obtain statements from staff about the incident as soon as is practical
- take a copy of the accident form for the files
- do not disclose any information to unauthorised personnel.

## PROGRESS CHECK

1 Why is it important to have a first aider in the workplace?

2 Name five items that should be in a first aid box.

3 When calling the emergency services what kind of information would it be useful to know?

4 When must you report an incident to the Health and Safety Executive?

5 What is the process for dealing with a suspicious package?

## CASE STUDY

During a general fitness session at a health and fitness club the instructor sees a participant looking unsure on their feet and fall over. The instructor, a trained first aider, assesses the situation. The class is immediately asked to stop to avoid any further accidents and a known member of the class is sent to get assistance.

The fallen participant quickly awakes and it is discovered he ate shortly before exercising and fainted. He is now complaining of a pain in his arm where he must have fallen. The instructor makes sure the person and his arm are supported and his legs are raised above his head to allow blood to return to the head.

1 What further action does the instructor need to take?

2 What type of report should be completed if it is discovered the arm is broken? List the details that should go in it.

## KEY TERMS

*You need to know the meaning of
the following words and phrases.
Go back through the chapter to
make sure you understand.*

Civil law
Duty of care
Legislation
Policies
Safety programme

Criminal law
Hazards
Operating procedures
Risk assessment

# 4 Working with others

This chapter covers:
➤ Working effectively with other people
➤ Contributing to good practice in the team
➤ Supporting other people in their work
➤ Establishing positive working relationships with other organisations

Working in the service industry, whether you are coaching part time at weekends or an employee of a large leisure centre, you will inevitably come into contact with people: colleagues, managers, employees of other organisations or the general public. Developing a positive working relationship with such people, coupled with an effective customer care policy, informs others a lot about you and the organisation you work for.

Each person you work with will have their own needs and wants which may differ from, and sometimes conflict with, your own. Good 'people skills' come with hard work and an understanding of key issues such as the organisation's structure, working in groups and teams, communication, how to manage conflict and making decisions. Every person within an organisation has a role to play. It is the combination of these roles that can make the organisation a more cohesive unit and ultimately improve the likelihood of the organisation achieving its objectives.

## Working effectively with other people

You will be working with colleagues, possibly in a group or as a team. It is likely that the group will not always 'gel' and it is important to understand the structure of the organisation you are working in and the communication systems that are being used so that you can work effectively with other people.

### The organisation

This can take various forms – sole trader, partnership, limited company, local authority, charity, a voluntary group, club or society. The purpose of these organisations can be found generally in their mission statements or mottoes and, more deeply, in their objectives. It is the structure of the organisation, illustrated by the organisational chart, that can influence how effective the organisation is in achieving its objectives.

**ACTIVITY**

Obtain the mission statements of two organisations and compare them. What are the differences between them? What evidence can you find to suggest that the organisation is fulfilling its statement?

### The organisational structure

All organisations have objectives. Very often these are broken down more specifically to the area or department you may work in. The primary objective for an organisation may be to make a profit or to provide a service but secondary objectives that are something more specific, such as increasing the number of visitors who return, give something more tangible to work at on a daily basis.

Having an understanding of the structure of the organisation will help you not only to understand how it operates but also to help meet its objectives. A more formal organisation will have:

● different departments, such as Human Resources, Marketing and Finance

● a number of employees, with general and specific duties

● rules and procedures, to be followed by employees

● identifiable policies and procedures for decision making

● formal and informal communication methods.

Many informal organisations – usually smaller ones – tend not to have the above characteristics but are still very effective at achieving their objectives.

Knowing the basic structure of the organisation can help to identify lines of communication and levels of authority and responsibility.

### Organisational charts

The simplest way of identifying the structure of an organisation is by looking at the organisational chart. These can come in various designs but will normally identify

● departments

● employees' roles

● authority and responsibility

● communication lines.

Figure 4.1 illustrates an organisational chart. It is a pyramid structure, with departments clearly identified. At the top is obviously the person with the ultimate authority in the organisation. Authority is delegated to other named posts down the chart; this is shown by vertical lines which represent the chain of authority (when read from top to bottom) or the levels of accountability (if read from bottom to top). The chain of authority identifies who each person should contact if they have an issue they cannot deal with.

There are six senior managerial posts in this organisation, where the line managers have authority over a number of people in related areas of work (identified by horizontal lines). Management staff must know who is

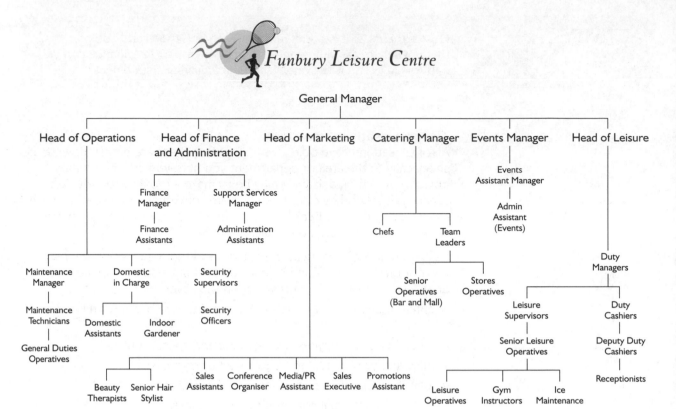

*Figure* **4.1**   *An organisational chart*

responsible for seeing that tasks are completed and such a chart helps to convey this information. It is unusual for personal names to be included on the chart; it shows the structure of an organisation, which should not be affected by changes in post holders.

The chart does not provide the whole picture, however. Working practices vary considerably and you may find yourself with extra responsibility. A structure that has too long a chain of command could take too long to make important decisions. An organisational structure that gives line managers large spans of control is becoming more popular because it gives people more responsibility and decision-making powers, thus making them more motivated.

GOOD PRACTICE ▷   *Ensure you know what all your responsibilities are and the people to whom you are accountable.*

### Roles

Each member of an organisation has a role and a function within that organisation. The role each person plays can be found formally in their job description. However, often unknowingly, we also categorise people according to our previous experience. We place people in these

**Figure 4.2** *As a trainee, you must learn quickly to select key information*

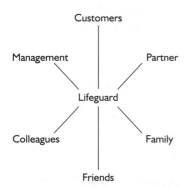

**Figure 4.3** *Each of these people sees the lifeguard in a different way and expects different things from him. It is likely that at times these expectations will conflict, causing problems for the lifeguard*

categories and expect them to behave in a certain way. As an example, a lifeguard occupies a number of roles, depending on who he or she is interacting with (Figure 4.3). At times the expectations of all these people will conflict, causing problems for the lifeguard.

## Communication systems

In Chapter 2 we briefly discussed the importance of good communication and the process of sending and receiving information. Put simply, you will work much more effectively with other people if you can pass on and receive information so that all parties understand it. Communicating well

- aids decision making
- increases the effectiveness of the organisation's systems
- increases the reputation of yourself and your organisation
- improves teamwork.

The method of communication you use will depend upon

- who you are communicating with
- where they are
- the speed with which you need to communicate
- the content of the message.

All organisations use a variety of communication methods.

### Formal communications

More formal methods of communication are usually written down, for example using e-mail, memos, reports, letters and faxes. When using written words to communicate use the following simple guides:

- Select the appropriate channel for the person you are communicating with and who they are. Remember to take confidentiality into account.
- Clearly address the communication and include the date and time it was sent. Some electronic systems do this automatically.

- Be concise – people are very busy and you do not want to waste their time reading unnecessary details.
- Check the style, syntax, spelling and grammar.

## Informal communication

Informal methods include unscheduled meetings, telephone conversations and 'picking up' information on the 'grapevine'. These methods tend to be mainly verbal and non-verbal communication rather than printed, as there is no need for evidence of the message being sent.

Non-verbal communication can convey as much information as what is actually being said. Much can be gained from observing:

- physical appearance, including personal hygiene, clothes/uniform and posture
- proximity – how close you are to a person and whether you are facing them or partially turned away
- facial expressions such as eye contact, smiling and looking downcast
- gestures, including head movement up and down (nodding in agreement) – leaning or sitting back are signs of being 'laid back'
- body contact, such as shaking hands and 'hi fives'.

Body language conveys messages which we do not always want to convey. For example, leaning against a wall whilst supposedly leading a children's activity session could give the parent the impression that you are apathetic, not paying attention or do not like your work. Such messages should be avoided at all cost.

## Verbal communication

You may speak to someone over the telephone, walkie talkie or face to face. These methods allow speedy conveyance of messages and an opportunity to ask for repetition or explanation of words not heard or understood. The way you say something will affect how the content of your message is received. The following can alter the message you send.

- Tone – different tones of voice can make you sound light hearted, depressed (deep voice), excited, urgent or enthusiastic.
- Volume – speaking softly sometimes will get people to listen more than shouting. This method is often used by people who work with children.
- Inflection – emphasis and stress may be placed on certain words and phrases.
- Speed – can show urgency and enthusiasm
- Accent – can often indicate where you are from.
- Use of jargon – this is the specialist language we use to communicate with others about a particular subject and is used in all organisations and groups. Those involved in sport and recreation have wonderful jargon.

Confirming that the message has been understood can help to ensure that all methods of communication are effective.

### REMEMBER

*Jargon should be used only by the people who understand it (as with an 'in' joke). Customers and other colleagues that do not use the jargon can feel confused and alienated by jargon they don't understand.*

## Groups and teams

An understanding of groups and teams is important. In our society we spend much of our time in groups, and perhaps teams, and for these to work effectively there must be some level of cohesiveness and inter-personal support.

### Groups

Members of a group have a common link. Groups may be formed to achieve specific tasks, for protection, companionship or a sense of belonging, and are based around relationships. If the group is to realise its full potential it is important to accept that the needs of the group itself must be met. These come under three headings:

- *Task need*, which ensures that there is a common purpose that holds the group together.
- *Preservation need*, which keeps the group functioning, avoiding too much conflict that may bring disharmony.
- *Individual need* – each person in the group may have separate needs, which must be recognised by the group. For example, two people may have difficulty in meeting, as they lack transport.

### Teams

Teams are similar to groups but the members are more dependent on each other to achieve shared goals and objectives. Sporting teams that share the workload and commitment have historically been very successful – for example, the greatest basketball player in the world, Michael Jordan, did not win the World Championships until a strong team, sharing and playing supportive roles, was formed.

Managers and owners have recognised the importance of teamwork and try to create it in the workplace. In-house training and external team-building exercises are all attempts to improve teamwork and increase the likelihood of the organisation fulfilling its goals. You are more likely to build a good team with the people with whom you immediately work. It is important to appreciate links between many areas and departments within an organisation and develop good working relationships with:

- cleaning staff
- kitchen staff
- administrators
- marketing and financial personnel.

Knowing your role and those of the people in your group, and communicating effectively, helps you to work well with others. If you are ever unsure about anything, ask a colleague for assistance. If you have committed yourself to someone, try not to let them down. Report any problems to colleagues and line managers.

## Dealing with conflict

Teams and groups are made up of individuals that have their own needs and wants, even though there may be a collective goal. However, conflict can arise from misinterpreted information or individuals having opposing needs and views. It can be difficult to be friends with everyone, but

── REMEMBER ──

*In times of conflict, pause
and try to see things from
the other person's
perspective!*

recognising and responding positively to conflict are essential aspects of working effectively with others.

## Recognising conflict

Factors that can lead to conflict can come from several sources, such as:

- poor working environment
- personal differences
- frustration
- unhealthy competition
- poor communication
- complaining culture.

These can impede the effectiveness of the team. Lack of agreement on objectives, information, authority, responsibility and decision making are all symptoms of an ineffective team.

## ACTIVITY

Draw your own role set to identify your role and the people who occupy various roles that affect you.

## Responding to conflict in the team

Conflict in a team may be temporary and emotional due to something that has upset an individual but it may be more serious if the person is unaware of the effect he or she is having on the team. People who are in a temporary emotional state generally should be given time to cool off before approaching them. More serious issues need to be discussed by the whole team to try to resolve them. Whatever the conflict, the following basic steps can help the effectiveness of any team.

- Keep conflict private. Conflict between colleagues should not be witnessed by the general public because it creates a negative impression of the organisation. Agree to meet at an appropriate time and place in order to air issues and solve problems.
- Do not let conflict affect your work. If the work of the organisation suffers because of conflict it reflects poorly on the organisation and on you.
- Refer problems to a mentor or line manager where issues cannot be solved within the team. Follow the organisation's procedures if formal grievance is involved.
- Compromise. Unfortunately, this is easier to say than do, but one person's willingness to compromise shows good teamwork and is often reciprocated.

## Negotiation

Sometimes a situation comes to the point where individuals/colleagues 'agree to disagree' and the only way to resolve problems involves some form of negotiation. This may be informal – asking a line manager to allow you to leave early if you carry out extra duties – or more formal – trying to change your roles and responsibilities, or those of the team.

## Characteristics of a good negotiator

Negotiation is a skill: people, issues and circumstances are always different. A good negotiator:

- has a quick mind to be able to respond to changing circumstances
- has unlimited patience and listens to others' points of view
- is able to conceal their own position, improving their bargaining position
- can ensure the trust of others and so improve relationships with other negotiators
- is knowledgeable – the more information you can have about the situation and circumstances being negotiated, the more informed your decisions will be.

Very few people have all the attributes necessary to be a good negotiator. In certain circumstances you can appoint a representative, such as a trades union member or sports agent to negotiate for you. The advantage of this is that the situation will be less personal if those involved in the dispute are not actually the ones negotiating.

## Negotiation strategy

Unfortunately, most situations are not suitable for an appointed negotiator and therefore you need an understanding of and a format for negotiation to help you achieve your aims.

- Collect as much relevant information as possible – hearsay is not enough. Facts and figures always look good and carry more weight.
- Prepare thoroughly – know the facts and consider your ideal situation (this is your start position) and an acceptable solution (your realistic position). The minimum solution is your 'walk away' situation, where terms offered cannot be accepted and a new approach has to be found in order to resolve the problem.
- Think of your strategy – your tactics. Include concessions you will allow and arguments you can use.
- Make your proposals, your opening bids, look for openings. Keep your statements brief and to the point.
- Implementation follows negotiation. Make sure agreements are documented and that all parties have a copy.

## PROGRESS CHECK

1. What is the purpose of an organisational chart?
2. Why is it so important to be able to receive and pass on information well?
3. What factors can affect how a verbal message may be interpreted? Provide examples.
4. What are the main differences between teams and groups?
5. How can you recognise conflict within a team?

# Contributing to good practice in the team

There are a number of positive steps you can take which can make the team, and your role within it, more effective. This can be achieved by making positive contributions to improve the team and being part of personal and team development.

## Making improvements

Being a member of a team does not in itself mean you are positively contributing to its success. A successful team has

- shared objectives
- good communications
- knowledge of each other's needs
- knowledge of each other's strengths and weaknesses
- good communication skills, including listening, and a high level of honesty
- flexibility and mutual support
- high motivation
- monitoring and evaluation systems.

It is often the style of the manager which has the greatest influence on the effectiveness of a team. An autocratic manager tends to issue directions without consultation and who does not use the team to solve problems. A democratic manager listens more and encourages the team members to develop ideas and solutions to problems.

Each individual member of the team cannot play all the roles within it. However, it is possible to play an influential role by making positive suggestions at suitable occasions and helping and supporting others around you.

### Providing and receiving suggestions

To initiate suggestions for improvement in areas of work, it is likely that you will already have gone through a decision-making process involving the following phases.

- Initial observation, to establish if there are areas which need improving – such as customer care or health and safety.
- Identifying the reason for the problem.
- Gathering all the relevant information so as to make a clear decision on possible solutions to the problem.
- Deciding on objectives (the things you want to achieve).
- Deciding on a solution after considering all the options.
- Presenting your ideas with supporting reasons and their benefits.

Identify the method of communication you are going to use and to whom you are going to send your message. Use a style that is positive and shows preparation. It can be very productive to find problems at work but even better to have thought about them and offered practical solutions. Always acknowledge time, money and safety in your solutions. An example is shown in Figure 4.4.

### Receiving solutions

Within a team it is usual for individuals to take on different roles based on their personality. There are those who encourage others, offer humour, create conflict and people who want to be leaders. If another team member has made a suggestion, whichever role you normally take, try to respond positively to their suggestions even if you do not initially agree with them. This shows willingness to be flexible and a good work ethic to improve teamwork.

You must be aware of standard operating procedures and the policies of the organisation (policies are statements on how an organisation intends to achieve its objectives). You should find policies on health and safety, equal opportunities, security and so on. You can make changes in practice in your chosen area of responsibility more simply than in those outside your working area. Use the correct channels of communication and keep colleagues informed of any changes.

### Delivering your suggestion

Providing suggestions at the right time and the right place are critical in whether they will be taken up – or even listened to. How much time a person has and the importance of the suggestion will also dictate how much time is given to the suggestion. Suggestions outside the area of the team's work are best made in writing (memo, letter or e-mail). Suggestions affecting the team are best made during team meetings.

*Funbury Leisure Centre*

**MEMORANDUM**
TO: Dave, Duty Officer    FROM: Rob
DATE: 17 November 1998
SUBJECT: Improving our communication to customers

I would like to offer a suggestion as to how we can improve our communication with our customers and improve the marketing of our programmes. The material costs will be £3.50 and I am prepared to make improvements in down periods or after completing my shift.

**The problem**
The noticeboard outside the sports hall has many notices on it but with no headings or order to them. This makes it difficult to find and present information and potential customers can be lost.

**The solution**
Split the noticeboard into headed sections and use coloured paper to identify each section – new notices, events, clubs and societies, results and so on. A well laid out noticeboard will communicate information effectively and will be easier to maintain.

I look forward to discussing this with you soon.

*Figure 4.4* A sample memorandum

## Meetings

These can be informal, where no real procedures are followed and nothing is recorded, or they can be formal, where a chair is appointed, procedures are followed and documents produced.

The function of a meeting could be to

- exchange views
- provide information
- negotiate
- to take democratic decisions
- solve problems
- evaluate and make recommendations.

The more formal the meeting the more likely it is to need an agenda. This is a programme of the subjects to be discussed at the meeting and the order in which they are to be discussed. The agenda is usually prepared by the secretary or chair. The items on an agenda will normally include the following:

- Introduction, place and time the meeting is being held.
- A list of the people who are attending the meeting.
- A record of the people who have sent apologies for their absence in advance.
- Minutes of previous meetings. Those invited to the meeting should have received a copy of these in advance of the meeting and have checked they are accurate.
- Matters arising as a result of previous action or issues that need to be discussed.
- Any other business – matters not submitted in advance but which need to be discussed by those present.
- Date of the next meeting.

The people attending the meeting should be given an opportunity in advance to submit items for inclusion in the meeting, either as matters arising or under 'any other business'.

Presenting suggestions at a team meeting is a good way of getting information across to the whole team at once. The team can exchange views and make a democratic decision. It also provides an opportunity to produce supporting evidence of your ideas in a simple, structured method.

## Personal and team development

People who have been most successful in their chosen area of work have often striven to develop themselves. Personal development involves assessing your own strengths and weaknesses and identifying methods and strategies to improve personal skills. In the work place the management will decide if development is to be done as a team or individually. This development can be achieved through education and training and is usually assessed and discussed at appraisals.

## Appraisals

Staff appraisals are used periodically by many organisations to exchange views on progress and development and to discuss any issues that an employee may want to raise. The purpose of appraisals is to

- review work done and discuss any changes to the existing job description
- discuss the employee's future aspirations
- identify ways of achieving any targets set
- discuss problems and find solutions
- identify an employee's weaknesses and discuss training and staff development.

The management also sees appraisals as an opportunity to improve communications, motivate staff, develop loyalty and help meet the organisation's goals. This 'improvement plan' will usually cover some of the items listed below.

- Technical and background knowledge of products and services, companies and markets.
- Management theory and techniques.
- Interpersonal skills, motivation, communication and leadership.
- Problem solving, computer skills, creativity and analytical skills.

There are many methods of staff appraisal. The most popular ones involve some aspect of grading against identified standards or criteria. Some organisations use a self-appraisal system before other appraisers become involved (Figure 4.5). This is a chart which can be used on a regular basis to indicate how a person is performing. Its use can also help in assessing strengths and weaknesses and help with motivation.

## Education

The appraisal may have identified a particular course of study which could aid your overall development. An education programme will not necessarily provide skills for a specific job but is seen by many managers as a way of developing mental, social and sometimes physical skills. The level of education is often an important item when job grades and salary structures are created.

There is a wide choice of course formats available:

- full time
- part time
- day release from work
- distance learning
- short course.

These options can be combined and there are many different types of course available.

- Courses designed for people who want to develop a career in sport and recreation but are unsure as to a specific area of work. These include courses such as sport studies and leisure studies.

# Funbury Leisure Centre

## SELF-APPRAISAL

Name: *D. Jones*

Post: *Pool Attendant*

Please ensure that you have read, and fully understood, the self-appraisal guidance notes before completing this appraisal.

| Standard/criteria | Excellent | Very good | Good | Average | Below average | Poor |
|---|---|---|---|---|---|---|
| 1. Punctuality | | ✓ | | | | |
| 2. Health and safety | | | ✓ | | | |
| 3. Appearance | | ✓ | | | | |
| 4. Customer care | | | ✓ | | | |
| 5. Communications | | | ✓ | | | |
| 6. Up to date with industry | | | ✓ | | | |
| 7. Use of initiative | | ✓ | | | | |
| 8. Problem solving | | ✓ | | | | |
| 9. Administration | ✓ | | | | | |
| 10. Adaptability to change | | ✓ | | | | |
| 11. Level of commitment | ✓ | | | | | |

Signed: *D. Jones*

Date: *17.3.98*

**Figure 4.5**  *A sample self-appraisal form*

- Courses aimed at a professional level and linked to specialist training. These include courses run by ILAM and ISRM.
- Vocational courses, such as governing body sports coaching qualifications and National Vocational Qualifications, which attempt to assess your competence at work.
- Academic courses, which have no relevance to a specific job but which are pursued for their own sake and personal development, such as a humanities degree.

Organisations differ as to the education and training they require of their staff, but there is no doubt that to become successful in our industry a sound educational background is essential.

### Training

Training is designed to provide a programme of activities aimed at acquiring the skills necessary to do a specific job. Many organisations are committed to a staff development programme which involves staff training – partially because government initiatives such as 'Investors in People' are now 'rewarding' organisations who support their employees.

Provision of training opportunities at work
- increases staff loyalty and lowers staff turnover
- reduces absenteeism
- improves provision of service
- increases efficiency and opportunity
- makes the work force more flexible
- identifies potential supervisors and managers.

Training also brings many benefits for the employee:
- improved job security
- possible wage increases – for example, someone with the Amateur Swimming Association Teacher's Certificate usually is on a higher wage scale than someone just supervising swimming with a Pool Life Bronze Award
- improved likelihood of promotion
- increased job satisfaction and thus increased motivation.

Training can be provided on the job or off the job – in the workplace or at a separate location, for example at a college. Many organisations use a combination. Team-building sessions have become very popular and can involve employees attending residential courses to perform a number of activities. These aim to develop good practice in the team by reflecting on the process of team tasks and demonstrating that working together to achieve a common goal is more effective than working as individuals.

## ACTIVITY

Working on your own, find out the specific training opportunities available at your workplace and from local providers and the relevance each may have in enabling you to achieve your career goals.

If you are to be involved in any training programme try to ensure that
- it forms part of your overall development plan
- you inform the instructor of your present level of knowledge and experience
- tasks are broken down (if required) to aid understanding
- you know why tasks are being performed in a particular way
- you see a demonstration
- you practise whilst receiving further instruction
- you make notes so you have points of reference later.

## REMEMBER

*Always keep a record of your training, whether it is 'in house' or external and whether it is certificated or not.*

**Motivating yourself**

Many researchers highlight the importance of having a 'positive mental attitude' but sometimes that 'get up and go' has 'got up and gone' and we find it hard to find the drive to work and be more successful. We can do much better when we are confident about ourselves and our situation. Confidence comes from experience, knowledge and success.

However, motivation is not just about feeling good. You may experience highs and lows during the working day, and how you feel and perform over a given period of time depends upon many factors. Listed below are factors that can affect a person's motivation at work, although you will find that some are more applicable to you than others:

- responsibility
- income levels
- conditions of work
- status
- job satisfaction
- promotion prospects
- success
- bonuses/perks
- working in a team
- autonomy
- recognition
- supportive environment
- flexibility.

These do not include personal factors that can also affect your motivation, such as your general health and safety at work.

**Motivating others**

Many of the motivational factors listed above depend upon the style of the managers. People tend to respond better when given recognition, autonomy, responsibility and opportunities for development.
Identifying what is important to the team, and together developing an action plan, can provide a focus for both the team and its individual members and help motivate everyone by promoting a sense of belonging and common purpose. Action plans normally list goals and ways of how to achieve these goals. Goals should be realistic and measurable. Ticking off items on a 'to do' list can be a simple pleasure and working together to achieve goals can be even more motivational. Goals can be work related or may simply be a series of social activities.

| ACTIVITY | List the factors that motivate people in order of importance for you. Then identify the factors you wish to change. Finally, create realistic goals and a strategy for how best you might achieve them. |
| --- | --- |

PROGRESS CHECK

1   What are the key stages in decision making if you want to initiate improvements at work?

2   What is the purpose of a meeting and why is it important to have an agenda?

3   What information would it be useful to have available if you are about to have an appraisal?

4   If you were a trainee on a training programme what would you try to ensure?

5   How could you improve the motivation of your team?

## CASE STUDY

At the Funbury Outdoor Adventure Centre there has been recent conflict between some members of staff. This is because some staff were returning late from 'field trips' and leaving equipment in poor condition and incorrectly stored in order to make up for lost time.

The staff decided to meet to discuss the issues and appointed someone to record and take minutes. The feeling of the staff is that they should work as a team and that all of them should have the time to perform their jobs. Nobody, it was agreed, wanted to compromise safety by not attending to the equipment correctly. Solutions to the problems were put forward and agreed – a rota would be developed for equipment responsibility.

However, the overall problem remained – outdoor conditions often meant that excursions took longer than planned, resulting in longer working hours. It was agreed to put the suggestions forward to management and try to negotiate for overtime or time in lieu for extra time worked.

1 What information would be useful to take into the meeting and why is it important to have a strategy clearly laid out?

2 What practical things can the staff team do to try to ensure they work effectively with each other?

## Supporting other people in their work

When working with other people giving and receiving support leads to a more cohesive and effective team and an increase in the quality of service. There are several ways you can support your colleagues, whether they are experienced or new and inexperienced. You also have responsibilities to create an environment and culture that reduces stress and practises equality.

### Providing support

This can involve offering appropriate help, being a good listener and presenting positive and constructive feedback.

#### Offering help

By offering to help a colleague you are providing positive support and could alleviate potential stressful situations. Your help could come in the form of:

- an explanation – for example, discussing why certain operating procedures are in place
- a demonstration – for example, of testing water quality in the swimming pool
- assistance – use opportunities to help colleagues to complete their tasks.

Owing to circumstances you might be unable to offer help promptly, but a knowledge of other sources of help, people and organisations who can assist can be just as effective. Try not to put people off – and ensure that the people to whom you refer your colleagues are dealing with the issue.

— REMEMBER —

*Before lending your sup-
port to a colleague ensure
you have addressed your
own problems.*

**Helping within limits**

All offers of help should try to meet the needs of other people whilst also ensuring that

- the person you're helping is working within the limits of their job role, and that you are not performing somebody else's function
- he or she is not taking on more responsibility than their job allows
- they are conforming to the organisation's standard operating procedures
- the legal requirements of health and safety and equal opportunities are being satisfied.

**Listening and advising**

The expression 'lending an ear' is used when someone listens to another person's problems. In some instances colleagues simply wish to express their views and just need someone to listen – listening is a good way of showing support. They might ask for your views and advice – once again you may help in achieving their objectives. However, on occasions your advice will conflict with their views: many people do not respond well in these situations – nor to receiving criticism.

GOOD PRACTICE ▷

*Give constructive criticism to colleagues who are not achieving agreed team goals. Comments should be made in a manner that stresses good practice and reinforces their self-confidence.*

## Stress

According to many researchers, people's stress levels are generally increasing, apparently due to a number of factors.

Under the Health and Safety at Work Act (see Chapter 3), employers have a duty of care to protect their employees' health. This commitment to employee welfare can also be found in the mission statements of many organisations and Quest for Investors in People. Many organisations recognise the importance of stress and attempt to minimise stress at work. They also encourage employees to recognise when they are stressed.

**Defining stress**

Stress is difficult to define. Generally speaking, it is the non-specific response of the body to any demand made upon it. Responses can be mental or physical and will vary from person to person. General health and personal situations can have a cumulative effect on stress levels. When these responses affect a person's comfort over a period of time the stress is said to be insidious and becomes more serious.

Stress, whether short lasting or long term, can affect

- health
- work performance
- absenteeism and need for sick leave
- motivation.

### Managing stress

People who are unusually harassed, abrupt or taking an increasing amount of time off work tend to be suffering from stress. Many organisations have systems for managing stress, including specialist support staff. However, individual staff members have a responsibility to themselves to identify and manage stress.

Whilst at work you can:

- try to develop a supportive and caring culture
- identify and take advantage of any opportunities for training in coping with and managing stress
- find out where to obtain confidential support
- explore recognised options for alleviating stress – e.g. exercise, sport and relaxation.

Once you have developed your awareness of stress try to recognise it in others. Try to modify your behaviour where it may be likely to cause stress to colleagues and invite them to pursue options to help manage their stress.

## Equal opportunities

It is highly likely that you will be working with people of different ages, gender, cultural backgrounds and abilities. Effective teamwork should start with the recognition that people are different and that we should treat others as we would like to be treated ourselves. This means working without prejudice and free from discrimination. Having a basic understanding of the law and using the appropriate language is a good start.

### Legislation

There are various pieces of legislation that provide a framework for equal opportunities covering equal pay, race relations, disability provision, sex discrimination and sexual harassment. These laws attempt to promote opportunity and equality for all employees, regardless of ethnic origin, gender, age and disability. These acts protect every individual against discrimination as:

- a person applying for a job
- an employee who is part or full time
- a customer.

Unlawful discrimination is defined in the acts as occurring in two ways:

- *direct discrimination* – where one person is treated less favourably than another because of their race or gender
- *indirect discrimination* – conditions that favour one gender or racial group more than another are applied to all, which cannot be justified.

**Figure 4.6** *Making others feel small may make you feel big, but is not good practice*

Sexual harassment is also covered under the Sex Discrimination Act (1976). Sexual harassment is often described as 'unwanted conduct of a sexual nature and which can affect the dignity of men and women at work'. It can happen to both men and women and is discriminatory.

It is worth noting that the sexes can be separated on the grounds of 'decency' – such as allowing 'women only' sessions at gyms and swimming pools. Private clubs are exempt from legislation on sexual discrimination, and hence clubs that exclude one gender can still exist.

All organisations should operate equal opportunities, grievance and disciplinary policies. The Commission for Racial Equality and the Equal Opportunities Commission are two government watchdogs who monitor and promote equality in the workplace.

**The use of language**
People can be offended by inappropriate language, although using the right word in context can still offend if it is out of date, as terms change quickly in our society.

Language is a positive tool, which, if used positively, can demonstrate

- respect
- understanding
- knowledge
- self-esteem
- value.

If used negatively it can

- be offensive and harmful
- belittle and embarrass
- insult
- show prejudice
- show stereotype.

Below is a brief explanation of some words or phrases that are often misunderstood.

- *Sex*. This refers to biological differences between men and women.
- *Gender*. This means more than simple sexual/biological differences – it refers to how society perceives what it is to be a man or a woman: cultural and social differences, including marital status, sexual orientation and family responsibility.
- *Girls/boys*. Persons over sixteen should be referred to as men or women.
- *Man*. This can be used inappropriately – e.g. 'man hours' instead of 'hours at work'.
- *Ethnic group*. This defines a social group with common colour, language, race and sometimes also religious beliefs.
- *Disability/special needs*. This phrase encompasses physical and mental restrictions but also includes learning and behavioural difficulties.

- *Age.* What is old to one person may be young to another. Again this can be used inappropriately – why say 'old-age pensioner' when 'pensioner' would suffice?
- *Class.* Identifies educational background and income.

---

GOOD PRACTICE ▷ *Discover the words and phrases with which your colleagues are comfortable.*

---

**Figure 4.7** *Everyone labels everyone else in different ways – risking seeing them as 'types' rather than people*

## PROGRESS CHECK

1 What are the best ways of offering help to a colleague who has difficulty setting upequipment?
2 Why is it important to be aware of stress in the workplace?
3 What are the different types of discrimination?
4 How can the same language be offensive to some people and harmless to others?
5 Provide three examples of how some words can be misinterpreted.

## Establishing positive working relationships with other organisations

In your organisation you are likely to have day-to-day contact with people from other organisations – contractors, sales representatives, competitors, inspectors, schools, local authority representatives, governing bodies, agencies and many more. A positive working relationship with another organisation can bring many benefits to all.

### Developing positive relationships

Positive relationships are built upon identification of needs and being able to satisfy them. Regular communication and sound planning and preparation will maintain positive working relationships.

**Building a database**

A good starting place is a database or index system of people and organisations with whom you come into contact. Information may come from letters, compliment slips, telephone messages and business cards. Creating a database or filing system with the following will enable you to find contacts by name or subject.

- Name of organisation
- Address
- Telephone number
- Fax number
- E-mail address
- Website address
- Type of business
- Contact name
- Contact's title/position
- Notes

A simple but effective database can act as a good reference point and also improve the efficiency of your external communication.

## Identifying sources of help

There are many organisations whose *raison d'être* is to support and develop other organisations and their members. There are also many organisations whose sole aim is to increase profits, but who feel they can ultimately do this by assisting you. A simple example is sponsorship. The following steps will help you to identify sources of help.

- Identify your objectives, which may be to obtain finance, equipment, free gifts, posters, banners – or simply information.
- Is help general or specific? Do you require help for the whole organisation?
- Are you restricted by finances? Can you afford to pay external consultants?
- Use existing known sources/contacts such as the library reference section, sports council, SPRITO, the Internet and ILAM.
- Create your own information library. Many organisations have fact sheets and organisational charts, telephone lists, e-mail addresses and Internet details. Extract useful information and disregard much of the sales promotion 'stuff'.
- Get to know key people. People are generally very busy but it is worth making note of those who have helped before.
- Make contact. This depends on the nature of the request – it will vary from a simple telephone call asking for addresses of potential partners to arranging a formal meeting to present a corporate sponsorship pack.

## Partnerships

Traditionally in a partnership two or more persons have ownership of an organisation. In sport and recreation the term partnership has come to mean co-operation of two or more organisations. Each has its own objectives but, through working together, they can improve the likelihood of meeting their goals. For example, a local community centre wanting to improve its role within the community may co-operate with a local college of further education who wants to expand education and their provision of training and education within the community.

Before deciding on any partnerships, you must be clear what you want to achieve and the organisations that can help you secure them.

### Defining your goals

In any partnership there will be give and take. This is why you must be clear on how a partnership can help achieve your goal. Ultimately, any suggestions you may have for partnerships should be in line with the organisation's goals. However, partnerships can be short term and aimed at meeting specific goals – for example, a commercial organisation may take an advertisement space in a school fayre programme.

It is essential to discover as much background information on the proposed partnership organisation as possible. Examine your goals and see if other organisations may be able to help you achieve them. A good example of partnership is seen with fast-food restaurants and cinemas. They work together by printing on the reverse of the cinema ticket a special offer to eat at the local fast food restaurant. The cinema and restaurant each attract more customers by offering more value to their customers.

GOOD PRACTICE ▷ *All formal partnerships will have a written agreement. Make sure you are aware of your duties within the contract and are clear about any offers and agreements that are in operation.*

## PROGRESS CHECK

1   What are the important parts of a database system?
2   Provide three examples of the steps you will need to take to identify sources of help.
3   What benefits are there to working with other organisations?
4   What are the key components and elements of a successful partnership?
5   Give two examples of successful partnership agreements in sport and recreation.

## CASE STUDY

Funbury community centre is planning to hold a large summer fayre and wants to develop partnerships with organisations that can help to make the day a success. It also wants to achieve the overall aims of the centre, which are to provide for the needs of the community.

The centre manager and staff met to 'brainstorm' ideas on the organisations that may be able to work with the centre. A list of local businesses was produced and a letter drafted asking for sponsorship for each of the stalls. Money raised could be put towards buying new equipment for the centre.

Funbury Leisure Centre was targeted – in return for use of their sports equipment on the day the centre would distribute the leisure centre's programme leaflets. The Outdoor Adventure Centre was also approached to see if they could offer their abseiling services and staff for free. This would help to promote the outdoor centre.

1   Make a list of the specific goals you would like to achieve with the partnership organisations

2   What other sources of help might be useful on the day?

## KEY TERMS

*You need to know the meaning of the following words and phrases. Go back through the chapter to make sure you understand.*

| | |
|---|---|
| Conflict | Decision making |
| Equal opportunities | Groups |
| Negotiation | Organisational chart |
| Partnerships | Staff appraisals |
| Stress | Teams |

# 5 Marketing yourself, your organisation and your activities

This chapter covers:
➤ Marketing in practice
➤ Promoting yourself and your organisation
➤ Promoting the benefits of sport and regular physical activity
➤ Marketing special events
➤ Evaluating marketing

In Chapter 2 we discussed the importance of understanding the needs of customers. The marketing process discovers what people want and need and provides services and products to match. Marketing has become more important as organisations realise that an effective marketing strategy can create awareness of your organisation, its products and services, attract new customers, retain existing customers and increase their spending. The more competition, the more important it is to discover exactly what people want and to have a clear strategy to attract their business.

It is essential to understand your market and how people buy products and services within it. By developing ways of promoting yourself, your organisation, special events, sport and exercise in general you can improve the way you promote and attract customers. All these methods should be evaluated to measure their effectiveness.

## Marketing in practice

It may be that your organisation has specific departments or personnel for marketing, or that all marketing is handled externally by an agency. It is your responsibility to have an understanding of the market you are working in, the strategies being used and how to undertake and process research findings.

### Understanding the market

The 'market' is the people who buy or potentially buy a product or service. This can be expressed in monetary terms; for example spending on leisure and sport in the UK is said to be over £120 billion. Organisations who sell products or services in that market try to capture as much of that money as possible. Their proportion of the total amount is known as their market share. It is important to know the market you are in. You can do this by examining your organisation's products, services and potential.

### Products and services

A product is often referred to as 'something that satisfies a desire'. This could be an hour's tennis or choosing a racquet to play with! Marketing specialists will attempt to demonstrate how much better their products are over any others. There are however, several differences between products and services and these can influence marketing (Table 5.1).

Table 5.1 *Differences between products and services*

| Products are: | Services are: |
|---|---|
| Tangible and are manufactured | Performed |
| Goods that can be moved to the customer | Fixed. The customer has to go where the services are being performed |
| Bought and then owned | Only owned temporarily; a moment in time at a venue |
| Goods that can be stored | Perishable – e.g. a squash court booking between 9 am and 10 am does not exist at 10.01 am or before 8.59 am |
| Easy to measure | Difficult to measure – e.g. quality |

Once you have identified the products and services, it is important to understand their benefits. These could include:

- new facilities
- cleanliness
- quality
- expertise
- convenience
- inexpensive/good value for money.

You should also understand what your unique selling point (USP) is. This is the main factor that differentiates you from the competition and gives you an advantage over it.

## ACTIVITY

Working on your own, identify the products and services in your organisation. Identify their main benefits and describe your unique selling point.

### Buyer behaviour

Having an appreciation of the process of buying will help you to meet the needs of your customers (and potential customers). All customers follow certain stages.

1. *Desire*. This is the initial need for a product or service. Desire could have been stimulated by many factors such as watching Wimbledon and wanting to play tennis or wanting an umbrella when it starts to rain.

2. *Examining the options*. This stage involves finding information on the options available and evaluating which one will best meet your desire. You need to know your products and services because potential customers enquire about your products and services at this stage.

3. *Choice*. The buyer now selects from the options available. If it is a product it will be a certain style, brand and or size; if it is a service it will involve time, location and other similar features.

It is important that the customer, having selected the product or service, is then satisfied with his or her choice. This will increase the likelihood of repeat orders and new customers.

### Market segmentation

This is the subdividing of a market into groups. The people within each group usually express similar patterns of values and buyer behaviour. By placing customers into groups based on common factors it will be possible to tailor your service and products to meet their needs. It is usual to segment markets by:

- gender – perhaps to offer women-only sessions
- location – perhaps promoting a local event by a leaflet drop using a certain post code in your community
- lifestyle – for example, offering a different price structure to the unemployed, people with families, etc.
- age – offering special activities for pensioners, assessing the need for crèche facilities, etc.

By segmenting the market you should be able to develop a strategy that can increase the number of customers and increase your market share.

---

REMEMBER

*Many organisations segment the market by buyer behaviour.*

---

## Marketing strategy

The overall marketing strategy is likely to be devised by senior management, although many organisations are using 'front-line' staff to feed back relevant information and you can make constructive contributions by forwarding them to the right personnel. Development of any marketing strategy involves analysis of the organisation, setting of objectives and developing the right marketing 'mix'.

### SWOT analysis

This is often performed in teams. It involves looking at the internal strengths and weaknesses of the organisation and explaining the opportunities and threats which exist externally. This helps in identifying what the organisation needs to do to develop in the marketplace. SWOT stands for:

- *Strengths*, which could include qualified and motivated staff, a good range and choice of programmes, good value of services and customer care
- *Weaknesses*, which could include poor or old facilities, lack of capital available for marketing, no car parking space
- *Opportunities* – perhaps a new housing estate is being built nearby, lottery funding is available, new events are being planned which could attract media and commercial support

● *Threats*, which might come from competition growing in the area or people having less disposable income due to increases in interest rates or recession.

This analysis is done systematically and must be updated regularly. It is a good idea to examine your individual strengths and weaknesses and explore possible opportunities for progression.

---

GOOD PRACTICE ▷    *It is a good idea to visit the competition – especially if they are successful. Try to analyse what it is that makes them successful and to bring some of that 'flavour' to your own organisation or workplace.*

---

**Figure 5.1** *Don't consider your facility to be an ivory tower – keep a good watch over the competition so you stay one step ahead!*

**Setting objectives**

All organisations will have objectives so that they can plan what needs to be achieved and measure their success. If you are working as part of a team trying to achieve objectives, ensure that they are

● specific, by ensuring that they relate to products, performance or services

● measurable, and that you know how they are to be measured

● attainable, so that they are realistic and hence motivating.

You should also monitor the objectives and feed back to your line managers if they are being met easily or are not achievable. Typical marketing objectives include:

● increase in sales/turnover (this could be measured by numbers of customers, memberships and visitors)

● increase in market share (this could include attracting more customers)

● increase in media exposure through advertising, or press releases

● diversification, by expanding into different services and markets – for example, Adidas diversified by producing toilet accessories as well as sports equipment.

**Marketing mix**

These are the variables that affect the relationship with the potential and actual customer. Traditionally known as the 'four Ps' – product, price, place and promotion – recently they have become the 'seven Ps' – people, physical evidence and process have been added.

● The *product* explores the range of products and services available and the quality of provision

● *Price* refers to the different levels of prices, discount, membership schemes and incentives. Prices are often reduced when demand is low

● Regarding the *place*, there is very often little choice in where activities are to be performed. However, one can have influence on the time activities are available – e.g. early morning sessions

● *Promotion* is aimed at attracting customers. Promotion is now more commonly expressed as 'marketing communication', which encompasses not only techniques of promotion but also how the overall image and brand is connected internally and externally to the organisation. Methods include advertising, public relations and personal selling – and are covered later in the chapter in more detail

- *People* refers to the customers, consumers and potential customers at whom the marketing strategy is aimed
- *Physical evidence* is the actual appearance of the environment where products and services are sold
- *Process* examines the experience of the consumer while purchasing the product or using the service.

The blend of the mix is important but it is most likely that *one* of the features (e.g. services being conveniently located) attracts the customer more than the others. Once again, as a 'front-line' employee you will receive direct feedback from customers on what they think of the cost of services and products and where and when activities are being run.

## Market research

This can take various forms and is essentially about gathering the information you will need to make better decisions about your strategy and the mix. Research can be structured and organised by external organisations or more *ad hoc*, being performed by individuals on a day-to-day basis.

### Primary research

This involves researching information in the 'field'. In the workplace most common methods include surveys and observation. Surveys can be undertaken face to face, or over the telephone. People often don't complete questionnaires and prizes and incentives are offered to encourage people to fill in the questionnaire. A lot of useful information can be gained simply from observation, such as watching youngsters enjoying an activity or checking to see if an aerobics class is too difficult for the participants. Observations can be made unobtrusively, using closed-circuit television – which is useful for security. It is important to know your customers' opinions and awareness of promotional material. Try to discover customers' preferences and what motivates them by asking questions, such as 'was everything all right?': this strategy can often provide a good 'feel' for what is happening in the workplace.

GOOD PRACTICE ▷

*Record all the information you receive from primary research. This can be fed back at team meetings or through internal communication systems.*

### Secondary research

This is using and interpreting information that already exists. Secondary research can often save time and money and is best used in association with primary research. There are many sources of secondary information that can be found within an organisation. For example:

- number of members/total/monthly
- number of visitors

**Figure 5.2** *Customer surveys are meant to be helpful!*

- sales figures
- postcodes, where members are located
- profiles of customers/segments.

Information can also be obtained externally, from censuses, annual reports, research organisations, governing bodies, etc. Most organisations order relevant journals and magazines, which provide a good source of information on issues and events in the industry. Use of the Internet and CD-ROMs is becoming very popular although ensure that, if you are 'surfing the net' at work, you have the permission of the line manager.

### Processing information

Once you have obtained information it is essential that it is recorded, either in qualitative form (views and opinions on information) or quantitative form (information represented in numbers and totals).

Any information you present – through writing in a report or orally at meetings – should be clear, accurate and complete. The information should be presented appropriately to the intended reader. Tables, graphs, bar charts, pie charts are good methods for comparing information and analysing trends. Ensure that you learn how to use the database (if your organisation uses one) effectively. Most database and spreadsheet packages enable users to create diagrams and charts.

Having gathered appropriate information and selected the appropriate style of presentation, you may be in a position to suggest changes to policy and practice. Your suggestions must be based on accurate information, and the practical implications. Try not to criticise colleagues, and deal with conflict in a calm and positive manner. The aim of any changes should be to achieve the objectives of the organisation.

1 Identify three differences between products and services, providing examples to support your answer.

2 What stages does a customer go through when buying a product or service?

3 Give examples of specific, measurable and attainable objectives.

4 What are the elements of the marketing mix?

5 How do primary and secondary research differ?

# Promoting yourself and your organisation

Promotion, put simply, is about communicating information to people about your services or products. This can be done using traditional promotional techniques, which usually are quite expensive. However, in your work within sport and recreation, you can produce and display material, use your own sales techniques and get your name and organisation well known at little cost.

## Contributing to promotion and service delivery

As well as being expected to know the services and products that are on offer and the environment you are working in, you may be asked to contribute to traditional promotional methods or to produce and display information.

### Promotional methods

Promotion can be beneficial to any organisation because it can

- be cost effective
- create awareness (e.g. of new schemes and programmes)
- persuade people to become customers
- encourage repeat business
- inform customers of the benefits of your product or service.

Traditional methods are often employed by specialist marketing personnel or senior management. These can include:

- advertising using television, radio, posters and the press
- direct mail (for example, sending promotional material direct to a defined target audience)
- public relations, cultivating relationships between the organisation and the media
- sales promotions, which offer temporary incentives (these are aimed at increasing the demand for the service or product)
- sponsorship, where organisations provide funding in return for some kind of publicity.

You must be aware of the promotional methods that your organisation is using, especially when dealing with members of the public who are, perhaps, responding to a promotion. This emphasises the importance of always having easy access to programmes and pricing structures and directing people to where they can acquire further information.

**ACTIVITY**

In pairs, try to find examples of promotional activities used by your competitors. In what promotional campaigns has your organisation been involved?

### Producing promotional material

It can be very cost effective to design and produce your own promotional material, which could be in the form of:

- posters
- leaflets
- fliers

all of which could be drawn freehand or designed and produced using a computer,

- electronic display board, which is more expensive but can often be subsidised by charging companies to advertise.

Use AIDA:

- awareness
- interest
- desire
- action

to produce your material. All of the information you produce should therefore

- use the organisation's logo on all material and, if possible in the organisation's colours
- include contact numbers and the name of someone to call for further information
- follow an approachable style, which considers colour, humour and involves the reader by using 'you' often
- be interesting, entertaining and not use long paragraphs
- be honest – you are compelled by law to be honest and truthful about the messages you are sending
- be carefully checked for style and syntax before it is made public.

Ensure you have permission to display a poster.

If you require more than one copy of a poster, a lot of the quality can be lost by using a poor printer or photocopier. It may be worth the small expense to have it properly copied and laminated – it will be longer lasting and more professional looking.

> **REMEMBER**
>
> *Always ensure you place posters in a prominent position.*

### Displaying promotional material

Once promotional material is ready it needs to be displayed and distributed. You should take the following points into account.

- Where is the material going to be located? Is it going to be displayed in house only or distributed in the community? Will it be 'lost' on the existing notice board or is it in a place where people will see it?

**Figure 5.3**  *Always display promotional material effectively*

- Safety is important, especially if you are using video or electronic display or billboards. Ensure they are not likely to cause an obstruction and that their use doesn't endanger staff or customers
- If you intend to leaflet existing customers, remember the infrequent users and send information to them directly
- Monitor your displays: check that posters are all visible and remove any which are out of date. Monitor levels of fliers and leaflets and refill when appropriate.

GOOD PRACTICE ▷   *Get someone not involved in the promotion to visit the organisation. Ask them if they notice the promotion and display, and to tell you what its good and bad features are.*

## Personal selling

You will often be called on to respond to enquiries from customers/potential customers. We have already established the importance of knowing your products and services. You should use this knowledge to encourage a customer to visit the facility or perhaps spend more whilst they are there. You are therefore involved in personal selling.

### Personality

Some organisations in the sport and recreation industry recruit only by measuring an applicant's personality because of the importance given to communicating with customers. You do not have to be an extrovert but you should be enthusiastic, friendly and willing to help others. People want to escape from their problems when pursuing sport and recreational activities. They want staff who are competent and confident at their work, which comes from experience and knowledge. Other qualities expected include honesty, reliability and trustworthiness.

### The selling process

You may be involved in some or all of the following selling processes.

- *Making contact*, which can involve approaching potential customers or fielding enquiries. After making initial contact you should introduce yourself and try to discover the needs of the customer. This initial stage may also involve finding out if existing customers require any of the other products or services you have on offer

- *Creating awareness* involves informing the customer of the types of products and services you have and the unique selling points of each

- *Developing a preference* is, perhaps, the most difficult part of the sale. It involves matching your products and services with the needs of the customer. Many different styles are used here, but believing in your products and services and communicating that belief effectively is a good start

- *Making an offer* once you have created a preference for your products. This could be used in conjunction with special promotions and should be in line with your organisation's guidelines and policies

- *Closing the sale* usually includes a commitment from the customer, which could be signing and paying for membership or simply buying some goggles

- *Post-sale follow-up* involves not only ensuring the customer is happy with his or her purchase but also having a system in place to offer true support – for example, staff being on hand to advise a new member on use of equipment during induction.

## CASE STUDY

The Outdoor Adventure Centre, north of Funbury, is looking to increase its number of visitors and users, especially between November and March. The centre manager invites the staff to be involved in a SWOT analysis of the centre. The findings are to be incorporated into the centre's marketing and development strategy.

Most of the staff agree that the strengths of the centre are its modern facilities, accommodation for large groups and the quality and experience of the staff. Its weaknesses are that it is not easily accessible, is poorly signposted and has poor-quality promotional leaflets. Opportunities, it was concluded, exist for attracting school and college users and businesses wanting team-building and decision-making activities. Competition is likely to come from other, similar, centres in neighbouring regions.

1    What actions would you suggest to address the findings of the SWOT analysis?

2    What secondary research would you undertake that would help to develop the marketing strategy of the centre?

## Networking

Networking is the development of useful contacts to assist you in your place of work. You can network on a regional, national or international basis, depending mainly on the technology available and the opportunity to meet people. You should always be aware of who you are meeting, the organisation they work for and their role within that organisation.

### Examining and maintaining existing contacts

Using the chapter headings in this book you could develop an indexed database of profiles of people and organisations (technical or professional people and volunteers) who can assist you and your organisation. Using your indexed database, you can examine any existing relationships you have and decide which need to be developed. Try to make time to contact these people and have a clear idea of what you are hoping to attain. Remember always to thank people for work they have done or information they have sent you. Always check whether there are any charges for information or advice, and if you use this information to acknowledge the source. Take time to keep in regular contact, for there can be nothing worse than contacting someone to whom you have not spoken for months and asking for a favour. In such cases try to have some information to offer by starting the conversation with 'Did you know?'

### Developing new contacts

You might have to go through an existing contact to find someone who can assist you. Try to find a name rather than just a telephone number – it can save you having to repeat your questions.

Developing new contacts is not just about finding specific people to assist you. It is also about putting names to your chart which may be useful in the future. Good places to meet new people are:

- conferences
- exhibitions
- seminars
- formal meetings
- relevant social events
- sporting events.

**Figure 5.4** *Keep your portfolio up to date and in good order for easy access*

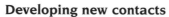

GOOD PRACTICE ▷ *Keep an up-to-date curriculum vitae and list of achievements in a portfolio in case you see an opportunity for personal development.*

Do not be afraid to introduce yourself and what you do – the person you're talking to could be looking for a contact within your organisation. It is not always possible to present business cards, but they are an excellent way of simply exchanging information. Treat yourself to a business card holder and always ask for a person's card. They are usually pleased to give them.

If you are not able to meet people face to face, you can use letters, fax and e-mail. Once again use a professional format (headed paper etc.), send letters of thanks and maintain contact with any new developments.

**Keeping a directory**
Log any new contacts into the database, and key information in the notes section. It is useful to always have a note of the last date of correspondence. Update your network chart and try to plan for ways in which important gaps can be filled – e.g. list contacts you have not yet developed.

## PROGRESS CHECK

1. What are the benefits of an effective promotional campaign?
2. What is the difference between advertising and public relations?
3. What does AIDA stand for and where would you use it?
4. Why is it important to monitor your promotional material?
5. How would you try to sell a product or service to a person making an enquiry about membership?
6. What is networking and where are the best places to develop contacts?

## Promoting sport and regular physical activity

It is also part of the sales role to know about the benefits of sport and regular exercise. You should be able to explain this to potential customers and work with existing customers to maintain their levels of activity – it is especially important to develop the confidence of newcomers for participation in their chosen activity. There are many organisations involved in the promotion of sport and regular physical activity. They are often willing to provide promotional material to use alongside your own promotion of your programmes and events.

## ACTIVITY

In pairs, identify organisations that are involved in promoting sport and exercise. Write a letter requesting promotional literature and information.

### Establishing and maintaining effective working relationships with participants

Clear written and spoken communication that shows understanding and support is the backbone of establishing and maintaining effective working relationships. Always be clear, accurate and non-judgemental. Over a period of time this will engender trust and enable you to assist participants to develop a routine, whilst ensuring that appropriate information is recorded.

REMEMBER

*By developing trust with and loyalty from the customer it is likely you will retain their custom and that they will be regular visitors.*

## Developing trust and loyalty

Trust and loyalty come with the time you take to demonstrate to the customer your

- professional approach
- knowledge of programmes and their content
- good ethics based on recognised and approved practice
- ability to monitor their needs, which may change depending on their circumstances
- respect for the confidentiality of their needs and details
- commitment by spending time explaining and demonstrating and making an effort to know all the participants' names and programmes.

These practices will make participants, whether individuals or groups, feel a part of the organisation. Try to make them feel like 'regulars', however infrequently they visit the facility. The ability to positively deal with a customer's problem or an unexpected situation will also develop trust and loyalty. Finally, honesty and reliability are two qualities everyone should have.

## Developing effective routines

This initially comes from discussions with the participants, discovering what they are wanting to achieve and what their limitations are. For example, a special needs group wanting to improve current physical activity for its members may be limited by time, money, transport and support staff. Discussing this and finding a routine that enables 'regular' physical activity, despite the limitations, will achieve the group's goals.

A routine might include a timetable of activities and times over a given period of time. It should clearly indicate the nature of the activity and the costs that will be incurred. A routine for a visitor to a health club might simply be aimed at improving fitness or reducing percentage of body fat. The important concept is to encourage people to develop a routine and hence make participation in sport and exercise a regular activity.

## Recording information

The initial agreed timetable of activities must be recorded and kept with the participant's personal details. Some organisations have the facility to use video tape of performances. This is a very effective method of showing previous performances, examining the technical and strategic aspects of the sport and looking at ways of making improvements. Less technical methods of recording information include index cards, which illustrate the proposed routine or type of programme, frequency, etc., and have a place to note down the actual programme done and the dates and times it took place. Recording information regularly enables you to measure success or failure and examine trends whilst also acting as a motivational tool. Always ensure you have recorded information accurately and legibly and that it is filed correctly. Confidential information should be secured.

## Promoting the benefits of regular exercise

By promoting the benefits of regular exercise to participants you are not only providing useful information but also encouraging them to continue to use your facilities. It makes good business sense to illustrate the benefits to customers – but then you must provide them with a programme of activities and sessions that will enable them to participate.

### Setting objectives

This involves slightly more than finding individual or group needs: it also involves clear identification of a participant's reasons for taking part and development of a clear strategy to work round any barriers.

Objectives should be measurable and attainable but challenging enough to motivate. Initially set objectives that can be easily obtained, thus showing success and achievement for the person following the programme. Try to provide, or have participants reward themselves with, a series of incentives to encourage them to continue exercising.

Try to ask open-ended questions that make the participant discuss the systems of reward, and be attentive to their responses. Having gathered all the necessary information, summarise the key elements. This summary should act as the basis for setting the objectives.

### Providing information

It is essential that the information you provide on the benefits of regular exercise is

- accurate
- well sourced, supported by the originator
- up-to-date
- detailed, not only providing accurate information but also identifying specific information such as work-out times and dates.

This will enable you to answer any questions raised by the participants. If you are unsure of an answer, find out as soon as possible. You should ask your line manager, a colleague or one of your known sources of help. Information on alternatives and ranges of exercises also needs to be discussed because different individuals respond to – or prefer to work with – different equipment or different methods.

Information can be given in a variety of ways – hand-written instructions, diagrams, demonstrations or verbal instructions. Find out which method each person prefers. This information should be produced in line with other similar material and display appropriate logos and awards. This adds to the overall professional approach.

### Developing a strategy

A strategy, similar to a routine, provides a programme of activities over the medium and long term. The difference is that a strategy is not simply about promoting regular activity; it is also about establishing an individual's most suitable method of achieving results over a longer period of time. You should clearly establish the participant's preferences for exercise and implement these in a varied and interesting programme. If the participant has been involved in the decision making, he or she is more likely to feel motivated to achieve set goals.

## Building confidence for participants

Many people start programmes with the best of intentions but are unable to sustain regular participation. Health and fitness clubs are full of members, the majority of whom do not work out regularly for many reasons, some of which can be controlled. Building the confidence of the participant by giving regular positive feedback, providing a positive social environment and having clear targets to aim for can help to sustain their involvement.

### Positive feedback

Try to use supportive words and phrases that encourage the participant – but not so often that it loses effect (although this is still better than not giving any encouragement at all). Positive feedback is also about discussing what is happening, such as explaining typical physiological responses during exercise.

Positive feedback can be given orally at the time of the activity and in a debriefing session at the end of the activity. Highlight the positive aspects and provide constructive criticism for the areas requiring improvement or change. Feedback can also be given in written form by regular reports or certificates of attainment/achievement.

### Developing a positive social environment

Some people are content to take part in physical activities on their own. However, most people choose to go to a club or leisure centre because they enjoy participating in sport and exercise with other people. They may form groups and friendships with others who have similar interests. However, you might wish to introduce people with similar levels of exercise to provide further motivation to exercise alongside other people by, for example, supporting a partner's weights when lifting.

New members should also be encouraged to meet people who are performing exercise with good technique. It is a good way of learning whilst also developing a friendly, caring environment.

Many organisations also provide a bar or cafe for customers to meet socially and initiate social events, outings, etc. Customers can meet in a relaxed social environment, which then helps them to get to know each other as well as the staff, and provides a supportive and enjoyable place to be when next they come to exercise.

### Offering incentives

Making the ambience and programme enjoyable in themselves is one way of motivating and building confidence for the participant. Many people respond well to goal-setting by rewarding themselves when they have achieved their goals. You can work with each participant to identify how and with what they can reward themselves (it might simply be buying themselves a special treat).

Your organisation might have its own nationally approved method of providing incentives; for example, the martial arts use grading and different belt colours to signify an approved level of competence. Presenting certificates of attendance or achievement to customers who achieve goals is also well received. Ideally, if finances allow, tangible incentives (e.g. T-shirts, bags or free services) are often most effective. All incentives help to achieve success and improve self-belief and confidence in maintaining regular physical activity.

---

## REMEMBER

*Always check organisational procedure to see that you are able to offer incentives to customers.*

---

# Marketing special events

Organisations are increasingly becoming involved in many types of special events – such as summer fayres, road races, swimming competitions. These events must be carefully selected and well structured and involve a lot of planning. You *might* be involved in these stages but will definitely be involved in the actual event itself. It is useful to understand the whole process and to recognise that your role is part of a team effort.

## Selecting an event

Special events can achieve many different objectives. They may develop from an initial inspiration or idea, but clear outcomes should be developed to identify what the organisation is trying to achieve. Working in the organisation, you may suggest ideas for events. Firstly, think about the implications for running the event, to see if it is feasible.

### Why have an event?

Any events that take place should be in line with the organisation's objectives. All objectives should be measurable and finance (as always) has a key role to play. Events can do the following:

- increase profit, or raise money for charity
- increase the number of visitors to the facility
- create awareness of the facility or a specific item
- gain publicity, possibly at low cost
- develop commercial liaisons
- develop partnerships
- involve communities and schools.

When setting the objectives of an event it is essential to determine how you would measure them to evaluate whether or not the event has been a success.

Some events become a regular occurrence and one main objective of a new event could be to establish it as a main part of the calendar. You should therefore see when is the most effective time for your event. Try to find out what is happening, both in the community and nationally, on your proposed dates so that you do not conflict with other well established events – yours should be the only event happening or a complement to existing ones.

**Proposing ideas**

Ideas for events may come through casual conversation or a more structured brainstorming session. If you have an idea write it down – you can add comments and further thoughts later as to whether it is feasible or not. Brainstorming, usually in meetings, involves people saying the first thing that comes into their heads. It can be a very useful way of generating ideas which may lead to a good proposal. Once the initial thoughts are written down they can be discussed in further detail or dismissed.

Ideas also come from reading about or visiting events in another community or organisation. You may be able to adapt the ideas slightly to suit your own needs. Consult members and visitors – they will be more likely to support the event if they have been involved in its conception.

**Feasibility**

Ask questions about timing, content, finance, objectives, resources and staffing. What are the implications for the existing activities and programmes offered? Can any problems and disruptions be overcome?

It is likely that several people and organisations (local authorities, the police, the accountants) will be involved in the feasibility phase. Written authorisation might be required, so it is essential to plan well in advance.

The feasibility stage should try to examine potential problems and offer solutions.

## The event structure

Having selected an event and decided it is feasible, you now have the task of putting the structures in place to ensure that it runs smoothly. Even a straightforward 16-person squash tournament has to have a clear programme of events, and administration and support systems are required. The staff roles and responsibilities should be clearly defined and there needs to be a solid financial base. A clear marketing structure will help to ensure that objectives are achieved.

**Programming, administration and support**

A programme identifies the course of the event – starting and finishing times and what should take place where and when. Ideally the event should have a start, middle and an end so as to welcome and thank people, present prizes etc. It is also a good idea to have a contingency plan for changes in circumstances, such as inclement weather.

Administration includes all secretarial and clerical requirements. It is usually best to have separate files for each event, including all the relevant paperwork, which can be referred to for planning future events and reviewing previous events. Using a recognised filing system will help to keep the paperwork in order. Administration also involves organisation of

- insurance
- tickets
- bills and invoices
- research findings

- budgets
- letters, memorandums and faxes.

Support may come from various sources, including volunteers and organisations that you may not usually work with. They may be responsible for catering, car parking, security and first aid.

### Staffing

Special events usually require more staff than normal – full and part-time staff, casual and contracted people and volunteers. You need to be clear of your role and responsibilities and with whom you will be working. An event is a good opportunity to meet new people and perhaps learn new skills. It is usual that an event will have a co-ordinator, who has delegated responsibilities to certain people. Make sure you know to whom you are responsible. It is important that, during the period leading up to the event, time is allocated for any extra preparation required over and above your normal duties.

### Marketing

The relationship of the seven Ps (see page 88) will determine the success of the event. The feasibility study has acted as the initial research and the event itself has dictated the product and the place. The price will depend on budgets and the objectives of the event, and will be set by senior management.

You may be involved in the promotion, which can include production of promotional material, ticketing and dealing with VIP guests.

Organisations are constantly looking for commercial sponsorship of events. Sponsors are often able to provide:

- financial support
- equipment
- prizes
- guest speakers.

The sponsor will expect something in return, usually publicity for their organisation. It is useful to know who the sponsors are and the individual representatives of the organisation, and to ensure their needs are being met.

### Budgets and finance

It is likely that you will have clear instructions as to the financial objectives of the event. Some events, such as open days, are not run at a profit if other objectives are sought. Open days invite people to look at the facilities, with a view perhaps of persuading visitors to become members. Whatever the objective, the budget must be kept to and all relevant financial transactions recorded. Events also often allow the opportunity for income from ticket sales, entrance fees, programmes, sales of food and drink, sponsorship etc. Many organisations will give individuals targets to aim for. Be clear of your role in terms of income and expenditure.

## Final planning

It is the attention to detail that will make an event successful. Once the structure is in place, final preparations will ensure the programme is in order. A checklist can be a useful method of ensuring everything has been done before the actual event.

### Preparation

A rehearsal is not always suitable or practicable. It is a good idea, however, to undertake as many checks – of equipment, security, health and safety – as possible. A rehearsal enables you to estimate final timings. It is always a good idea to confirm your role and responsibilities with your supervisor for the event. Ask questions if you are at all unsure and rehearse the parts for which you are responsible.

Usually, all the personnel involved will meet before the event. This is an opportunity for the organisers to give their final briefings and a chance for all staff to clarify their roles. It is usual that the contingency plan will be discussed and, wherever possible, rehearsed.

### Using a checklist

Each event should have its own checklist. This a comprehensive list of all the tasks that need to be undertaken, ideally with a time scale next to each. The tasks are not necessarily undertaken in chronological order; some will need to be done simultaneously. However, most can be produced in some logical order.

You should be able to produce a checklist within your role, thus ensuring all your tasks have been completed.

GOOD PRACTICE ▷ *Get into the habit of producing lists and keeping your own diary. This will help your time management and organisation.*

**Figure 5.5** *Get organised!*

103

## The actual event

As previously discussed, the event should have a clear start, middle and end. In a competition, the final race (match, game, etc.) and subsequent awards ceremony will be the conclusion. Success on the day will be down to the structure, planning and teamwork. During the event, customer care should be paramount and steps taken to ensure that all spectators and visitors enjoy themselves. Good timing is also a key to success and ensures you are following deadlines in the programme. If there are any problems during the event, try to solve any for which you have the authority, or quickly find your line manager and inform him or her of the situation.

> **REMEMBER**
>
> *Always remain calm and take positive action if problems arise – it creates an impression that the situation is being dealt with.*

---

**PROGRESS CHECK**

1  Name three benefits that can be achieved by holding an event.
2  What is brainstorming and when would you use it?
3  Why is it essential to have a clear event structure?
4  Why can it be beneficial to have a sponsor for an event?
5  What are the advantages of using a checklist for an event?
6  Provide five items for a 'day of an event' checklist.

---

# Evaluating marketing

It is essential that all marketing activities are evaluated and reviewed whilst the activities are in progress, so objectives can be measured and adjusted accordingly. A thorough evaluation should be completed after the marketing activities. When promoting yourself, your activities and sport and exercise, there are many techniques that can be used to measure effectiveness.

## Evaluating promotional techniques

The promotional techniques available to the organisation include direct mail, personal selling, public relations, advertising and sales promotion. It is likely that a combination of these techniques will be used and hence it would be useful to assess which ones were being most effective. It is important to note that effectiveness should be measured in conjunction with the objectives set. The following techniques can be used to provide useful information.

### Surveys

These, similar to surveys for customer care, can be written questions against a rating scale or choices to enable you to produce quantitative data at the end. Open-ended questions may also elicit useful information. Surveying customers about promotional techniques will raise questions regarding:

● where they heard about the facility/event/activity

● what they can recall about the activity

● what they thought of the activity.

### Counters

Counters (electronic, such as beams and turnstiles, or manual, in the form of tally counters) are used to count the number of visitors, users, enquiries etc. Some electronic devices measure how often a beam is broken, and not always how many people visit the facility. It is a good idea that, if manual systems are used, more than one person is counting to allow for human error, especially if the facility is busy. If you are manually counting, ensure that the entry point is streamed so that only one person can come through at a time.

### Coupons

Coupons are often distributed through retailers, door to door drops or in newspapers and magazines. They offer money off the price of services and activities and must be submitted upon payment. The effectiveness of a coupon campaign can be measured by the amount of coupons received and by the distribution medium (newspaper or magazine, for example).

### Accounts and sales

In general terms, the success of any promotions can be found in the organisation's accounts by examining the actual sales following a promotion. The more information available, the greater the analysis. Sales figures should be divided into repeat customers, new customers and the different classifications of customers (e.g. family, pensioner, off-peak, etc.). Accounts should include details of expenditure of the promotion and thus the cost-effectiveness of techniques can be measured.

### Editorial coverage

This is the amount of column space your organisation has in newspapers, magazines and journals – in the form of press releases put out by your organisation or articles written for the newspaper. The best way to evaluate this coverage is by comparing the amount of column space of the article with the cost of placing an advertisement of the same size in the paper. This gives a tangible figure to measure.

### Team feedback

After promotions and events it is a good idea to have a meeting of all personnel involved. All team members can feed back information on what they thought did, and what did not, work. Self appraisal and peer appraisal look more closely at individual performances. Always be willing to accept constructive criticism as it can lead to an improvement in performance. All parties should be invited to contribute suggestions for further progress.

### Group research

This can be useful to measure the effectiveness of advertising. Sales figures can provide some information but cannot always be directly attributed to advertising, unless coupons are used. Specific group research can provide more useful information, such as:

- public awareness of the organisation, its services, the specific adver-tisement

- recall, the extent to which individuals can remember details of any advertisements

- attitudes of interviewees to products, services and the organisation's overall image.

To be effective, group research should be undertaken constantly so that more detailed information is gained over a longer period.

## Reviewing your activities

Whether you have used an outside agency or undertaken marketing 'in house', reviews should be taken to assess its effectiveness. All research, strategy, promotions and events should have clear objectives, the attainment of which can be monitored. Changes may be needed if objectives are not being met and it is how we, as individuals and as a team, respond to change that can decide if objectives are to be achieved.

### Monitoring performance

This is the system of evaluating marketing techniques, such as market research, as they are being done. It looks at what has been achieved and what the overall outcomes are likely to be. Trends in responses, sales and information can be compared with the objectives of your marketing activities.

Any information should be given to the co-ordinator of the marketing activity, so that changes to strategy can be implemented if necessary.

### Adjusting marketing objectives

Your marketing objectives should be specific, realistic and measurable. If you undertake a marketing campaign, and then measure the results of the campaign, you may discover that some (or all) of the objectives have not been achieved. This can provide useful information but is likely to have a negative effect on motivation. Marketing objectives should be adjusted to take into account information received during monitoring. You should know what these objectives are and how they can be achieved.

### Responding to change

Change in general is inevitable, although it is often perceived negatively by individuals and teams. This is because we relate and respond better to systems and procedures with which we are familiar. In marketing campaigns, change occurs frequently. It is the responsibility of each individual and the team as a whole to react positively to these changes.

Response to change may involve altering information or cancelling activities on which you have spent time. Instead of looking at this as time wasted, reflect on the skills and knowledge you have gathered. You may be able to use these at a later date.

## PROGRESS CHECK

1 Why is it better to monitor performance continually rather than on completion of activities?

2 Why is change often viewed negatively and how should you respond to it?

3 What types of questions are you likely to find in a survey?

4 How can you measure the effectiveness of newspaper coverage?

5 Why is it a good idea to involve the team in reviewing marketing and promotion?

6 Identify the points that group research should reveal when measuring the effectiveness of advertising.

## CASE STUDY

An employee of Funbury Leisure Centre has had a good idea – to hold a road race in the summer. A feasibility study is undertaken, with each staff member gathering information regarding whether or not the race can go ahead. The local police force had some initial concerns but said that, with good organisation and planning, they would allow the race. The race would certainly achieve some of the centre's objectives of increasing public awareness of the centre, developing partnerships and possibly increasing the number of facilities at the centre. It was also deemed a good idea to involve the local community centre, schools and colleges, who might be able to assist in the organisation and management of the event.

1 What would be the benefits of having a sponsor, and how would you attract one?

2 How will you be able to measure whether or not the event has been a success?

3 In what way could the community centres, schools and colleges help to organise and run the event?

## KEY TERMS

You need to know the meaning of the following words and phrases. Go back through the chapter to make sure you understand

Feasibility
Marketing mix
Personal selling
Sponsorship
Unique selling point

Market segmentation
Networking
Primary and secondary research
SWOT analysis

# 6 Providing and maintaining facilities and equipment

This chapter covers:
➤ Selecting equipment
➤ Storing equipment
➤ Setting up and taking down equipment
➤ Maintaining and repairing equipment
➤ Maintaining facilities

The standard of the facilities and equipment of an organisation will have an important effect on the type and frequency of its customers. Most sporting and recreation activities require equipment, which is often provided by the organisation. Careful consideration must be given to selecting, purchasing and storing the equipment.

When customers hire equipment they expect it to be ready for use and in good, safe, functioning order when they arrive. Customers also expect a facility that is clean, hygienic and in working order. It is accepted that equipment breaks down, but action to remedy defects should be taken promptly.

Involvement in cleaning and tidying the facilities and checking and maintaining equipment is very often a major part of a typical day. You should be aware of what your responsibilities are in terms of maintenance and repairs. Most organisations have contracted specialists to clean and undertake repair and maintenance work – even, sometimes to change the light bulbs.

## Selecting equipment

The overall decision for selecting and purchasing equipment will be made by the management team. However, as the person using the equipment most often, you will have key information on the type of equipment required, and the quality of the equipment used. This information should be passed on to the management to aid their decision making.

### Determining needs

There are many different types of equipment, all of which have an expected life span that can be influenced by the frequency of use and how it is maintained. When selecting new equipment, you must assess the state of the existing equipment and predict the future needs of the organisation.

### Types of equipment

There are, generally speaking, two types of equipment – capital and expendable (this does not include emergency equipment, which needs to be regularly checked, and be in working order). *Capital* equipment is larger, permanent or fixed. This could include football posts, basketball backboards, seating and gymnastic apparatus. It is more durable and does not need replacing often. *Expendable* (or *consumable*) equipment includes smaller items such as shuttlecocks, balls, bats and racquets, which tend to need replacing regularly.

Some equipment is manually operated and some requires an independent power source. Manually operated equipment, such as the winches on a boat or weight-training equipment, usually has fewer technical maintenance needs than the powered equipment (such as a treadmill, or electronic scoreboard), which might require specialist assistance if it breaks down.

### Assessing current equipment

When determining equipment needs, you will obtain a lot of information by assessing the equipment currently in use. The amount of repairs and replacement required will depend on:

- frequency of use – hourly, weekly, once a year
- nature of use – recreational or competitive
- the age of the people using it – adults can often be more destructive than children, believe it or not!
- standard of equipment, which mainly includes its overall quality
- how it has been looked after
- ownership – a person who uses other people's equipment is less likely to look after it than if it was their own
- age of the equipment – this is especially important as items could still be under warranty.

You should have access to records on the manufacturer, the date and time each piece of equipment was purchased. This, coupled with the factors listed above, will provide a profile of the current equipment. It is useful to obtain product information on similar products from two or more manufacturers so that you can compare them and choose the type that appears best for your customers.

### Predicting future needs

Once you have a clear breakdown of all the current equipment you can begin to match this with the future requirements, in line with the resources of the organisation and, more specifically, the equipment budgets.

The booking sheets will allow you to predict future usage because they indicate what equipment is being used and by what specific groups. The time of the year and the seasons of individual sports will also indicate how much the equipment will be used. For example, some equipment (such as tennis racquets) will get more use in the summer periods, notably during the weeks immediately after the Wimbledon tournament. It is important to collect data from user groups (such as coaches), as they are often best able to predict their needs for their sport or activity.

> ── REMEMBER ──
>
> *Never attempt to repair equipment unless you have the skills or qualifications to do so.*

**ACTIVITY**

Select a sport within your organisation and carry out an equipment survey to identify the needs for the forthcoming year.

## Purchasing equipment

Most organisations will have systems for purchasing equipment and will use designated specialist suppliers. All organisations are concerned with finding the best value, irrespective of the specific features they want. The process of purchasing will have its own documentation system, which you must comply with.

### Quality vs. quantity

Quality should be the priority. It is often said 'you get what you pay for' – poor-quality equipment may initially be cheaper, but it is likely to need replacement more often. Safety is also a key factor and should never be compromised when purchasing equipment, although any purchases must be made within specified budgets. Quantity is another important consideration. This will be taken in conjunction with the assessment of future needs.

Purchasers should take into consideration whether to purchase individual items or in bulk. The amounts you buy affect the delivery price, and often the unit price because discounts are often available for bulk purchases. It can also be more cost effective to deal directly with the manufacturer than with individual retailers.

### Purchasing features

Equipment that has several uses is obviously more cost effective than specialist equipment. You often have to conform to the governing body's requirements, as many recommend different equipment, depending on the user – for example, soccer balls that are size 5 for adults and size 3 and 4 for children. The main features to be taken into consideration when purchasing equipment are:

- size, which is dependent upon the user (small, large, etc.)
- competition – it is important to know whether the item is to conform to official competition requirements or is for recreational use
- quantity – the amount to be ordered
- colour – many organisations want equipment which is intended to be permanent to fit into the decor of the facility or to be in corporate colours
- style – this again should be in line with the style of the organisation (modern, aesthetic, etc.)
- cost, which should take into consideration any discounts – but remember to include value added tax and transport and delivery costs
- codes – all products in the vendor's catalogue usually have a description and a product code number.

---
**REMEMBER**

*Before ordering always double check all the features of your order, to ensure they are correct.*

---

*Wherever possible, try to obtain samples of equipment for a trial period before taking the final purchase decisions.*

**Figure 6.1**   *Examine samples and assess them as soon as you can after receiving them*

### Purchasing documentation

Your organisation will have standard operating procedures for ordering equipment; these will normally be carried out by a designated person and processed through the accounts department. It is quite possible, however, that if you are involved in the selection of equipment you may have responsibility for initiating the purchasing process. It is important to pay attention to detail, ensuring that all paperwork is completed accurately. The first document to fill in is usually a purchase requisition form, which should be submitted well before you actually intend to use the equipment, to allow for payment and delivery time. This will ensure the equipment will arrive in time.

It is unlikely that you will be asked to deal with invoices, documents provided by the supplier requesting payment for the items ordered, which should correspond with the purchase requisition form and the delivery note. A delivery note is sent by the supplier with the goods, giving details of the items supplied. If you receive any goods check they correspond with the delivery note – you will generally be asked to sign the delivery note to confirm that all goods have been received.

GOOD PRACTICE ▷   *When receiving a delivery, ensure all goods are in working order and are undamaged before signing the delivery note.*

1   What are the two categories of equipment and what are their main features?

2   Identify three factors that influence the decision to repair or replace existing equipment.

3   Where would you obtain information about your future equipment needs?

4   What are the benefits of bulk buying?

5   Why is quality such an important factor in purchasing equipment?

**Figure 6.2**   *Check new stock against the delivery note as it's unloaded – that way you'll know immediately if something's not right*

## Storing equipment

Equipment should always be stored in a specially designed area. It should be kept dry, clean and tidy so that it remains in good working order and does not corrode. Storage conditions should correspond with the supplier's requirements – failure to follow their guidelines could affect any guarantees. Before storing any equipment you should assess your needs for space and security, and ensure you are familiar with your organisation's storage administration system.

### Assessing needs

Storage space is at a premium in most organisations. The constant change in equipment means that storage requirements should be monitored, taking into account full use of the space available, access to the storage area and relevant health, safety and security measures.

**Needs and space**

Start by making a list of all the equipment that needs to be stored. Consider

● the number of items

● the size and weight of each piece of equipment

● the shape of each item of equipment.

Next, think about the items that are used most regularly and those which are needed to quickly convert an area from one activity to another (e.g. from badminton to volleyball). The different requirements of the sporting seasons may mean that you will not need certain items for long periods – they could be moved to less easily accessible areas in the 'down' seasons. All of this means that the storage area will change throughout the year.

The storage area should be *fully* used – clever use of shelving and hanging hooks will help to maximise the space available. If you are using containers, ensure that they are easy to open.

## ACTIVITY

In pairs, make drawings of your existing storage area and discuss how each area can be fully utilised.

GOOD PRACTICE ▷ *Draw some designs to maximise your storage area and equipment. This will help to save time when it comes to storing equipment.*

### Health and safety

Entrances should remain clear and free from obstructions. This will help to avoid any problems that people trying to store or maintain equipment will experience – and all storage areas must conform to health and safety regulations for work equipment. The storage area should be kept neat and tidy, which avoids any unnecessary damage to equipment or harm to persons when items are being moved.

**Figure 6.3** *A tidy store room is one that's easy to use!*

Likewise, equipment should be stored in a way that will not be a hazard to anyone: heavy equipment should not be stored above head height, no equipment should be balanced on other items, stacking should not be so high that you have to reach and risk overbalancing, and no sharp edges should face outwards. Ensure that the correct lifting techniques are used to lift or move equipment, especially anything heavy.

**Security**

The cost of equipment makes it essential that all storage areas are kept secure. Storage areas are often accessed by many people and the following basic security system will be needed to keep equipment secure.

- Limit access to those people who need to be there.
- Ensure all documentation is completed accurately and promptly.
- Never leave keys lying around or in locks, or loan them to another person. If keys are lost, report the loss immediately, so a search can be made and the keys (and sometimes the locks) replaced if necessary. Visitors should never be allowed access to keys.
- Never leave an unlocked storage area unattended.
- Always lock the area when you leave the room, even if for only a short period of time.

## CASE STUDY

Funbury Community Centre decided to ask members of the local community what activities they would like to see at the centre. The response from the community was very good and questionnaires revealed that people were happy with the traditional activities but that retired folk would like sessions dedicated to board and card games. Parents of young children wanted a lunch club to be formed so that they could socialise and where, one day a week, they would not have to prepare lunch.

The board games were costed from various sources, taking into account quality and cost. Tables already at the centre could be adapted for cards and games by laying felt on the tables. The lunch club was formed by producing cost-effective meals and using the crèche facility. Leaflets were sent to the local community informing them of the changes and the new activities.

1   Put forward an argument for buying fewer good-quality products than more, cheaper, ones.

2   What actions can be taken to ensure that no game pieces or cards are lost from the board games?

3   What measures could you take to balance the amount of food required and the probable number of visitors?

## Administration

Part of storing equipment securely is to keep a well maintained administration system, which includes clearly identifying and categorising each piece of equipment and keeping accurate records for its issue and return. This will also help to keep the storage area tidy. All documentation must be completed promptly and accurately.

### Identifying equipment

Equipment should be marked as soon as it is obtained – marking on it a code by etching or using water-resistant or permanent markers. The logo, or initials of the organisation can be used in conjunction with a series of numbers corresponding to an inventory. If this system is used a date should be included to show the date the item was purchased. This helps in relation to warranties, and certain equipment needs replacing within a given time frame, so it will also help to know when an item needs to be replaced. Identification marks should not detract from the look or use of the equipment.

GOOD PRACTICE ▷  *Your local police force will offer good advice on identifying and subsequent storage of equipment.*

**Figure 6.4**  *Labelling equipment clearly helps to keep track of it*

### Categorising equipment

This can be done using a variety of methods, depending on your needs. Equipment can be stored under the following categories or headings:

- capital and perishable
- indoor and outdoor sports
- by specific sports – e.g. athletics, rugby, gymnastics
- clothing – e.g. bibs, gloves
- bats, balls
- technical/electronic equipment
- heavy/light equipment
- goals/nets
- winter/summer use
- climbing equipment.

Whatever the methods used, the categories should correspond to the codes used in the inventory. Clearly categorising equipment can enable specific needs analysis to be done and specific stock checks to be undertaken. Within the store cupboard categories should be clearly labelled using colour or diagrams to help illustrate where each item should be located.

### Keeping records

The inventory will be the master record of all the equipment held and will list the purchasing details and amounts of all categorised equipment. The store cupboard should contain a list of the items stored and their numbers – for example:

Footballs:     20

Netballs:      15

Basketballs:   12

When removing items from the store room, it is a good idea to check that the items listed correspond with the amount stated, taking into account any that have already been signed out. Signing equipment out and back in reduces the likelihood of equipment being stolen, by making individuals accountable for the equipment they use. When replacing stock make sure that the inventory is updated.

| PROGRESS CHECK | |
|---|---|
| **1** | List health and safety considerations of storing equipment. |
| **2** | Why is it not good practice to lend store room keys to unauthorised people? |
| **3** | How can you minimise the likelihood of equipment being stolen? |
| **4** | Explain the functions of an equipment inventory. |

# Setting up and taking down equipment

Customers expect facilities to be ready for use at the time they have booked it for. They may also need equipment to be assembled according to the regulations provided by the controlling bodies of the sport – e.g. the basketball ring for adults must be 10 feet from the floor. Very often the time between one activity finishing and another starting is very short. Careful planning and preparation following recommended guidelines will help to ensure that equipment is quickly and safely set up and taken down.

## Planning and preparation

It is important that you know the equipment and the programme of activities required for the shift you are working, and the needs of your users, before setting up any equipment. This will help you to assess whether it can be done individually or as part of a team.

### Knowing the equipment

As previously discussed, there are many types of equipment. The use of some equipment, such as that used by climbers, has significant health and safety implications, and you should know exactly how it is to be assembled. The manuals (where provided) for all items should be on file and referred to before assembling the equipment (climbing ropes, for example, have a log book describing their use). Equipment tends to change over time – for example, one volleyball post may tend to fit one hole better than another; some netball posts fit into certain bases more easily than others. Knowledge of the equipment comes from experience in using it. If you have not handled a piece of equipment before, find out from experienced colleagues the best and safest ways of assembling it.

### Knowing the programme of activities

When commencing your shift you should check on the programme of activities timetabled for that day. You should work out what equipment needs to be set up and at what time, and the needs of the users – they might require different articles during the session and certain equipment might need to be moved. Generally speaking, the more competitive the activity the more precisely the equipment should be set up.

It may be that after a few sessions it is evident that not all the participants are using all the equipment you have set up for them – finding this out from them will help you select equipment in the future.

GOOD PRACTICE ▷ *Have a trial run before setting up new equipment for customers. Be sure to record the time assembly takes and use the recommended guidelines provided by the manufacturer.*

**Figure 6.5** *A trial run will help you set up equipment efficiently*

GOOD PRACTICE ▷ *Keep communicating with your customers to verify that the equipment is set up as required and if they need all of it. This can help to save time in 'change overs' and will help to meet the needs of the customers.*

**Figure 6.6** *Make sure the equipment you've set up is what the customer wants*

### Staffing

Once you know how to assemble and dismantle the equipment required for the session you should work out whether you can do it alone or will need assistance. Items that must be assembled by a team, such as large seating stands, will probably require specific training to do so. Setting time aside to practise as a team will help to ensure that equipment is handled efficiently and safely.

As in all systems, there are quickest, safest and easiest ways of doing things. Experiment with colleagues to discover the different ways of setting up and taking down equipment, to find the best method for your team.

## ACTIVITY

In small groups select three items that need setting up and taking down on a regular basis. Suggest ways how it could be done more quickly, whilst maintaining safety.

## Using recommended guidelines

It is essential that you follow approved guidelines to set up equipment, in the interests of your personal safety and that of work colleagues and the people using it. You should be aware of health and safety issues and the approved guidelines, and should assess the state of the equipment before it is used.

### Health and safety requirements

All procedures for handling equipment should be followed to the letter in order to prevent a health and safety risk or hazard. For instance, when assembling inflatables all ropes, ties, moorings, platforms and areas of risk must be identified and a risk assessment undertaken before the customer is allowed to use them.

Once the equipment is assembled it should be left in safe surroundings, so that potentially hazardous situations are avoided. Equipment that requires supervision when being used should not be accessible to customers (especially children) until the appropriate staff are present. Appropriate lifting techniques should be used to move any equipment so as to avoid injury to people, fixtures and fittings.

### Manufacturers' and approved guidelines

The manufacturer will normally provide instructions for assembly and for lifting and storing their equipment. Be sure to check these guidelines before handling the equipment. Certain items are known as specialist equipment. Very often the governing body of the sport (and/or the Sports Council) will have full details recommending how to set up and take down this specialist equipment – for example, in trampolining there are recommendations for headroom height, checking all springs, straps and the bed before use, where to place the trampoline in a facility and where to place safety crash mats. Governing bodies also have details on the

> **REMEMBER**
>
> *The system you use should correspond to guidelines and recommendations set by your company, the suppliers or the manufacturers.*

118

dimensions of all types of equipment and playing areas. These are often dependent upon the age of the participant and the type of activity e.g. court dimensions are different for doubles badminton than singles, and hence more space needs to be allocated per court.

**Reporting damage**

Before any equipment is set up, during the process and once it is ready for use, it should be checked for

● damage to any working parts

● damage to the fabric

● missing parts

● failure to operate correctly.

Any damage you spot should be reported immediately and an assessment of whether it can be repaired on site made. If not, arrangements will have to be made for the equipment to be taken away and repaired. Damaged equipment should not be returned to the normal storage area unless it is clearly marked that it is not to be used.

Any equipment that is damaged or is deteriorating should be recorded on the appropriate forms. These forms can be used to determine the most cost-effective and best quality equipment when planning your purchasing requirements.

## PROGRESS CHECK

1   How can knowledge of the equipment and programme of activities help to assist you in setting up equipment?

2   How can you discover the best ways of setting up and taking down equipment?

3   What checks should you carry out when setting up equipment?

4   What should you do if you discovered equipment that was faulty, but only once you had set it up?

5   Why is it important to keep accurate records about damaged equipment?

# Maintaining and repairing equipment

Usually purchase of new equipment will include a contract for maintenance and repairs, which will detail any guarantees and list parts that are covered by warranty. It is usually the responsibility of the purchaser to carry out general maintenance and checks of the equipment. Minor repairs should be carried out in safe conditions and final checks carried out before equipment is put back in to use.

## Maintaining equipment

A sound understanding of the workings of your equipment (both manual and electrically powered) will help you identify any equipment that is

119

unsafe and must be removed. A schedule of regular maintenance will help to identify such equipment, although it may be that customer feedback has identified what is unsafe or not in working order.

### Maintenance schedules

A maintenance schedule is the regular examination and routine maintenance undertaken by the organisation. It should correspond with the manufacturer's guidelines and any other health and safety factors. A planned maintenance schedule will bring several benefits to the organisation – for example, it will:

- save money by preventing further damage
- help you evaluate your equipment and make better purchasing decisions
- provide a safe environment for all those using the equipment.

The schedule will normally break down into three areas:

1 Ongoing maintenance. This will include regularly checking equipment such as inflatables, emergency equipment and any equipment provided for customers' individual use – for example, making sure badminton racquets do not have any broken strings

2 Weekly checks. This will include checking equipment that needs less frequent maintenance – such as lockers, running machines and areas such as the car parks

3 Contracted maintenance will be necessary for certain equipment, as stated under a service agreement. This may be undertaken by specific staff in the organisation or by specialists from the manufacturer. Examples include maintenance of photocopiers and sunbeds.

Always be aware of the maintenance schedule and ensure that it is carried out with as little disruption as possible to normal activities. This may mean you have to examine the booking sheet so that you can plan when and where to carry out maintenance checks.

**Figure 6.7** *Keep customers informed about repairs*

### Identifying unsafe equipment

Equipment that is unsafe to use can sometimes be identified by simple observation. However, in the case of technical and powered equipment, this can only be done by testing the equipment – for example, an exercise cycle would need to be ridden and the options available tested during its use. In some situations you may need to work with a partner to ensure your own safety.

Having checked the equipment you must assess whether or not it requires maintenance. You must also decide whether any maintenance necessary can be carried out immediately by yourself or if a technical expert will have to be called.

### Removing and reporting unsafe equipment

Any equipment identified as unsafe must *not* be available for use by the customer. Damaged equipment that can be removed should be as soon and as safely as possible; equipment that cannot be moved easily, such as a multi gym, should be very clearly labelled as out of use (it could also be roped off). Try to replace equipment removed from use with an alternative as soon as possible. For example, an unsafe goalpost could be replaced by two cones. This is not ideal but means that the activity can still go ahead.

Whatever action is taken, it should be clearly and accurately recorded using the organisation's forms as soon as possible. This will ensure that decisions can be made, and repairs done, quickly.

---

GOOD PRACTICE ▷ *When placing 'out of order' or 'not in use' signs on equipment it is a good idea to inform customers when you expect it to be back in use.*

---

## Repairing equipment

The results of the maintenance checks will determine if repairs can be done within the facility or if the equipment needs to be sent to a specialist. Repair procedures will differ with the type of equipment used. Decisions will have to made as to whether components should be replaced, reconditioned or repaired. Any repair work should be carried out in safe conditions and the equipment tested before it is put back into use.

### Ensuring safe conditions

Before undertaking any repairs it is essential that all facilities and equipment are in a safe condition (e.g. unplugged from the mains, away from children) for servicing and repair.

- Make sure that the servicing and repair is within your ability and level of responsibility. If you are unsure, ask your line manager
- Do the work a safe distance away from any activities, and use signs where appropriate

- Ensure as little disruption to normal activities as possible
- Ensure the equipment is safe to repair. An obvious example includes switching off any power to the equipment before carrying out repairs
- Equipment that is awaiting repair should be placed in such a way that it does not block any exits and is not a hazard.

**Carrying out repairs**

All staff have a responsibility to themselves and their colleagues to adhere to instructions, guidelines and codes of practice for repairing equipment. Before commencing any repairs, ensure you have the right tools and materials for the job so that you don't have to leave the equipment unattended during repair.

Apportion an amount of time to carrying out the repair, so that your other duties and responsibilities are not neglected. If you encounter any problems during the repair you should immediately report them to your line manager. It may be that on closer examination the equipment is beyond repair or requires more technical investigation.

If equipment needs to be dismantled, keep a copy of the assembly plans to hand. Be sure to place all components (screws, bolts, etc.) in an orderly manner. You may need to use your own labelling system to ensure parts are replaced correctly. This also stops parts being lost or damaged during repair.

**Final checks and completing records**

Once the necessary repairs to the equipment have been made, it must be checked and tested to make sure that it is fully operational and safe before it is put back in its original place. If the repairs have been successful then the equipment should be put back into use as soon as possible and monitored closely to ensure there is no further breakdown. Replace equipment at a time that will cause as little disruption to activities as possible.

It is essential to keep clear and accurate records. It may be that within specified contracts there are several forms to complete, for example, a job status form, which identifies what equipment needs repairing and where it is located, must be signed to say exactly what repair work has been carried out and who has done it. It may be that an outside contractor is carrying out the repair. In all circumstances make sure that all the paperwork has been completed and signed by the appropriate people.

## PROGRESS CHECK

1 Who might be involved in carrying out repairs?
2 What are the advantages of a well planned maintenance schedule?
3 If a customer reported that the treadmill they were using kept speeding up and then stopping suddenly, what would you do?
4 What should you first ensure before undertaking basic repairs?
5 After completing repairs, what should you do before putting the equipment back into general use?

# Maintaining facilities

The facilities of any organisation (the buildings, purpose-built areas for sport, recreation and car parking, and other similar areas) are among its main assets. Neglect of maintenance and repairs can lead to failure in performing its function. It also provides a negative image of the organisation. The original quality of the facility, whether work is still under warranty and how modern the facility is can all have an effect on the level of maintenance and repair required. It is the responsibility of all employees to maintain and clean general and specific facilities.

## Cleaning the facilities

Cleaning will form part of your daily duties. Areas must be cleaned frequently, depending upon the number of users and visitors to the centre. Certain areas can become hazardous if not cleaned very regularly – e.g. wet areas. You should be aware of the equipment to be used and the rotas that will indicate

- what areas have to be cleaned
- how often cleaning has to be done
- by whom it should be done.

Cleaning contractors may be used for specialist areas.

### Cleaning and maintaining equipment

When using cleaning equipment, always ensure that you are conforming to the organisation's procedures and legal requirements, such as the Control of Substances Hazardous to Health Regulations, by wearing suitable clothing and using suitable equipment and materials.

You should first select equipment and materials that are appropriate to the area. Typical cleaning equipment will include:

- cloths and scouring pads
- buckets, mops and squeegees
- warning signs
- hose pipes
- ladders
- vacuum cleaner and extensions
- dust pan and brush
- brushes of various kinds for different surfaces and pools
- paint
- light bulbs
- varnish
- cleaning substances.

Your personal protective equipment will probably include:

- boots or protective covers for shoes
- gloves
- aprons and overalls
- goggles and face masks
- dusters and cloths.

---

REMEMBER

*Any equipment that is unsuitable for use or is damaged must be disposed of, reported and replaced in accordance with organisational procedures.*

---

ACTIVITY

In small groups suggest ways how you can make personal protective equipment more fashionable. You must not change the design if the change makes the equipment unsafe to use.

Equipment should always be stored safely and securely in a condition which is suitable for future use. Any equipment that is damaged or needs replacing should be disposed of and reported so replacements can be ordered promptly.

### Cleaning tasks

It is likely that before opening and closing every day, the same cleaning duties will be needed. However tedious these may be they should be performed to the standards of cleanliness and hygiene set by the organisation. Figure 6.8 illustrates the types of activities expected. If, during the day, an area of the facility is considered to be dirty, it should be cleaned straight away.

GOOD PRACTICE ▷ *Any time you walk through the facility, take a different route so that you can tidy up as you go.*

Any area that you feel should be added to the daily cleaning rota should be mentioned to the line manager. Several problems should be cleaned up promptly:

● rubbish and litter

● spillages

● breakages.

All items of waste should be disposed of safely and according to organisational procedures. Ensure that you know what they are, especially in terms of disposal and recycling.

### Cleaning rotas

Cleaning tasks are likely to be daily, weekly or monthly. Examples of daily and weekly rotas are shown in Figure 6.9.

All cleaning should be co-ordinated with planned activities, causing as little disruption as possible for customers. All rotas should be completed accurately and signed in the appropriate place. It is usual to find these rotas in the specific area to be cleaned so that the users can see them. This is to show that regular cleaning is occurring and when it was last done, thus giving a positive image to the customers.

### Lost property

Customers and staff may misplace or leave their property. It is likely that your organisation will have a procedure for dealing with this. You will be expected to record the following information:

# *Funbury Leisure Centre*

SATURDAY .......16.11.98.......

| Opening up duties | Completed by: | |
|---|---|---|
| • Pool test | KQ | |
| • Remove pool cover | KQ | |
| • Fill footbaths | | |
| • Swill yellow tiles and mop channels | JQ | |
| **Closing down duties** | **Ladies** | **Gents** |
| Toilet area: scrub floor, clean toilets, urinals, sinks and mirrors | JQ | DH |
| Showers/footbaths: scrub floor and clean drains | JQ | DH |
| Main area: scrub floor, clean drains and mirrors | JQ | DH |
| Landing: scrub floor and clean drains | JQ | DH |
| Disabled room: scrub floor, clean toilet, sink and mirror | DH | |
| Staff Room: wash pots and wipe surfaces | JQ | |
| Empty all bins | DH | |
| **Additional jobs** | **Completed By:** | |
| Sweep steps at entrance | JJ | |
| Clean pool hoist and chair | JJ | |
| Restock cleaning cupboard and tidy | JJ | |

| Changing area check/mop | 10am | 11am | Noon | 1pm | 3pm | 5pm | 7pm |
|---|---|---|---|---|---|---|---|
| Ladies | JQ | JQ | | | | | |
| Gents | DH | DH | | | | | |

**Figure 6.8** *Expected cleaning activities*

- a description of the item found
- the date and time it was discovered
- where it was discovered
- who discovered it
- the name and phone number of the owner if it is found with the item. He or she should be contacted as soon as possible.

All lost property should be recorded, accurately and with honesty, and placed in an allocated area. When enquiries are made concerning lost property, you should ask the enquirer to describe the item. If this description corresponds to the item you have, and the time and place where it was discovered, it can be returned to the owner, who should sign and date the record to show he or she has received the item.

## Cleaning and maintaining specific areas

Some areas are used more than others and need more attention, such as the car park, entrance and changing areas. These can have a great impact on the image and first impression of the facility and the organisation.

125

## Funbury Leisure Centre

**Cleaning rota week beginning** *9/9/99*

| | Monday | Tuesday | Wednesday | Thursday | Friday | Saturday | Sunday |
|---|---|---|---|---|---|---|---|
| **Opening up duties** | | | | | | | |
| • Pool test | Steve | Rachel | Jane | Chris | Steve | Jo | Jenny |
| • Remove pool cover | Steve | Rachel | Jane | Chris | Steve | Jo | Jenny |
| • Fill footbaths | Steve | Rachel | Jane | Chris | Steve | Jo | Jenny |
| • Swill yellow tiles and mop channels | Steve | Rachel | Jane | Chris | Steve | Jo | Jenny |
| **Closing down duties** | | | | | | | |
| Toilet area: scrub floor, clean toilets, urinals, sinks and mirrors | Claire | Simon | Brian | Sarah | John | Paul | Sue |
| Showers/footbaths: scrub floor and clean drains | Claire | Simon | Brian | Sarah | John | Paul | Sue |
| Main area: scrub floor, clean drains and mirrors | Claire | Simon | Brian | Sarah | John | Paul | Sue |
| Landing: scrub floor and clean drains | Simon | Brian | Claire | John | Paul | Jenny | Sue |
| Disabled room: scrub floor, clean toilet, sink and mirror | Simon | Brian | Claire | John | Paul | Jenny | Sue |
| Staff Room: wash pots and wipe surfaces | Simon | Brian | Claire | John | Paul | Jenny | Sue |
| Empty all bins | Simon | Brian | Claire | John | Paul | Jenny | Sue |
| **Additional jobs** | | | | | | | |
| Sweep steps at entrance | Rachel | Jane | Chris | Steve | Jo | Claire | Jenny |
| Clean pool hoist and chair | Rachel | Jane | Chris | Steve | Jo | Claire | Jenny |
| Restock cleaning cupboard and tidy | Rachel | Jane | Chris | Steve | Jo | Claire | Jenny |

**Figure 6.9** *Daily and weekly rotas help staff to manage their time efficiently*

## Public areas

A number of non-activity areas are accessible to the public – these are the areas most used in a facility and should be included on the cleaning rota.

● *Cafeterias* might be run by the organisation or through a franchise or contracted arrangement. This area might need more cleaning, depending upon the number of visitors. Tables should be cleaned as soon as people have left them, so as to create more space for new customers. This also maintains hygiene standards under the Food and Safety Act

● *Bars* are similar to cafeterias. Tables must be cleaned and wiped regularly and floors cleaned. Empty glasses should not be left on tables as they are unattractive to look at and can be broken easily

● *Corridors* should always be free from obstruction

● *Reception* and *entrance areas* need to be immaculate, especially if there is any glass on the doors

126

- *Vending areas* should have rubbish bins, which should be labelled according to their contents, for example cans. They should be emptied regularly
- *Changing rooms* need to be swept out and floors and surfaces (showers, tiles and drains) washed. Toilet paper and soap should always be available and hand- and hair-drying facilities should always be operational
- *Locker areas* need to be checked for rubbish and lock mechanisms cleaned so that they remain in working order.

### Non-public areas

These are areas not accessible to the public, and include the following:

- Staff toilets and changing rooms. These are the collective responsibility of all staff, and may have a specific rota for cleaning. Try to put all equipment and clothing in the appropriate places
- Offices often contain technical equipment such as computers. Care should be taken in cleaning this equipment, ensuring files and fittings are replaced after cleaning.
- The first-aid room should be cleaned immediately after use. Protective gloves should be used when cleaning up blood.

### Heating, lighting and ventilation

These will vary according to the age and type of the facility and must be maintained according to specific requirements, which may vary with the individual sport or activity that is taking place. Lighting systems should be kept clean and dust and dirt removed from protected guards and lamps. The covers and grills of heaters and ventilation equipment should also be cleaned.

### Car park

The size of the car park will depend upon the size of the facility, and will determine how much maintenance is required. Disabled parking should be near the entrance and clearly signposted. As the car park is probably the first part of the facility seen by visitors it should be kept clean and well maintained. There should be signs to inform the visitor exactly where to park, including special areas for disabled parking and coaches. Security lighting must be kept in working order, surfaces free from litter and individual spaces clearly marked (these may periodically need re-marking). If 'Pay and Display' machines are provided, they should be checked regularly to see they are in working order.

## Maintenance of sports facilities

Individual sports have their own equipment and maintenance requirements. However, many sports use the same facilities indoors and outdoors. Daily maintenance will help to preserve these surfaces and create a safe environment to play in.

---

### REMEMBER

*Always switch lights off when they are not required.*

---

GOOD PRACTICE ▷ *Contact the governing bodies of the sports you provide to obtain their recommended practices for maintenance of equipment and facilities. Keep these with your maintenance checklists.*

**Figure 6.10** *Look after the equipment!*

### Indoor areas

These include:

- sports halls
- squash courts
- health and fitness areas
- tennis courts
- indoor bowls areas.

Dust and dirt are probably the greatest daily maintenance concern. All of the areas listed above need to be swept, vacuum cleaned and mopped down – depending, obviously, on the type of surface. Ideally these tasks should be carried out when there are no customers about. If this is not possible, ensure that wires are not a hazard. Signs should be placed to indicate slippery surfaces and any spillages should be cleaned up immediately.

Court markings, unless inlaid, are either painted or taped. These gradually begin to fade or tear and peel. Taping is more expensive than paint but can be laid quickly and easily. Paint is inexpensive but really needs a specialist to create the right effect.

In areas which use mats – such as gymnastics, weight and exercise rooms – they must be in the right position. Any equipment not being used should be returned to its place.

### Outdoor areas

These include:

- grassy areas
- artificial turf
- tennis courts
- bowling greens
- play areas.

---

**REMEMBER**

*When marking out a court, always check the dimensions to ensure that the sizes of the sports areas are correct.*

---

128

Turf maintenance is often provided by specialists trained in horticulture. The condition of the soil and grass, mowing and watering needs careful attention to ensure the area is fit for use. Regular checks should be carried out to ensure that broken glass, litter and dog waste are removed from all areas. Artificial turf requires less maintenance but needs brushing to remove debris. Always read the supplier's instructions to ensure you are following their recommended maintenance practices. Very often machines are used to remove snow, sweep litter etc., and you should be well trained in their use before attempting to use one.

## CASE STUDY

In the fixed-equipment section of Funbury's Premier Health and Fitness Club, 'Funbody's', you notice that one of the bike ergometer pedals is broken and someone from the previous session has spilt their drink on the floor near the skipping area. This is the third time the bike's pedal has broken in a year and drinks are often being spilt, making the carpet look untidy.

Action is taken immediately so the next session can go ahead. The bike is removed as it has been agreed that it needs repairing by the supplier. This has been documented and the supplier is to collect the bike the following day. The spilt drink is cleared away and the surface, although marked, is safe for skipping and does not require a warning sign or roping off.

Following discussions with regular visitors it is agreed that drinks need to be available during workouts, but a designated area is to be created so it will not affect the decor of the workout area.

1  What forms are you likely to need to complete for the broken bike and how would you inform members where the bike is?

2  How can you ensure that members will use the designated area to take in fluid?

## PROGRESS CHECK

1  Before handling any cleaning equipment what should you ensure?

2  Certain cleaning duties should always be done promptly. What are these?

3  If somebody enquires about lost property what should you ask, to ensure that it belongs to them?

4  What type of maintenance is required in car parks?

5  When is the most appropriate time to clean a sports hall floor?

## KEY TERMS

*You need to know the meaning of the following words and phrases. Go back through the chapter to make sure you understand.*

Cleaning rotas
Guarantee
Maintenance schedule
Stock check

Delivery note
Inventory
Personal protective equipment

# 7 Programming

This chapter covers:
- ➤ Defining and achieving your objectives
- ➤ The features of a programme
- ➤ Changing your programme
- ➤ Taking bookings

The programme of any sport and recreation facility is basically the schedule of activities available for customers over a given period of time. This is designed by senior management, who have set objectives to achieve. It is important you understand that programming can be a complex process which must take into account the needs of specific user groups. Providing a balanced programme requires an understanding of the features of a programme and the ability to change it when necessary.

## Defining and achieving your objectives

A programme will reflect an organisation's *raison d'être*. Whether it is profit-driven or meets the needs of the community, your organisation will offer a programme that aims to achieve its goals. Very often the constraints (time, size of areas, flexibility of halls, etc.) are applicable to all centres and these must be taken into consideration when providing a schedule of activities for the different types of users. Even a 'men only' golf club has players of different ages and ability and will have different competitions throughout the year so that all members can be involved.

### Programme rationale
This is the logical process of determining what needs to be on offer for customers and should take into account the organisation's goals and the needs of users. By assessing current usage, an organisation can see if these objectives are being met.

### Achieving organisational goals
Most organisations want to achieve full capacity (maximum occupancy) for its activities. In this way it will achieve the more specific objectives that will aim to achieve goals such as:
- providing choice, flexibility and balance in the programmes
- maximising the use of facilities and resources
- reflecting the demand of current and potential users
- encouraging repeat customers.

131

You can help to ensure that organisational goals are being met by having a detailed knowledge of the programme. It is often produced in leaflet form or may be found on a booking sheet. Always have the programme available when you are talking to customers so that you are able to offer people the right programme.

### Meeting the needs of existing users

Very often you will be working in a facility that has members or regular users. They use the facilities because they are well located, have excellent equipment and so on. However, competition from other providers, fashions, new technology, improvements in ability, motivation all may require you to monitor the existing users to ensure that the programme continues to meet their needs.

GOOD PRACTICE ▷

*When surveying the opinions of existing customers be sure to include programming in the survey.*

**Figure 7.1** *Ask the customers relevant questions!*

Each user will have different objectives, depending on

- their age (child, youth or adult)
- whether they are competitive or recreational
- their reasons for using the facilities – for example, to improve their fitness or for leisure.

A simple example of changing needs is a woman who started aerobics beginners' classes to improve her fitness three months ago and who now feels the pace is too slow and wishes to go to a session with higher intensity.

### Assessing current usage

This can be done by using accounting ratios, such as number of users and space available, to provide some information that can be used as a comparison against previous times. You should be able to assess the programmes that are successful simply by looking at the booking sheets and identifying the numbers of users. However, it can be quite difficult to measure what facilities are not being maximised. For example, a sports hall may be booked every week for tennis but has the potential to attract 100 people if a circuit fitness session was offered.

Measuring and assessing current usage are therefore two different things. You must ensure that you keep clear and accurate records of the numbers of users and inform your line manager as soon as you can see that a programme is not attracting customers.

### Constraints to programming

Any organisation is restricted in the activities it can offer. Some of these restrictions, such as location, resources and competition, are difficult to alter but even these can be adapted to improve your programming. Having an understanding of what these constraints are will help you to plan an effective programme.

### Resources

All organisations and departments work to budgets and targets which greatly influence what programmes can be offered and at what price. Some activities, such as five-a-side football, will always be popular. However, a whole programme of football may alienate other people from visiting the centre, and hence affect projects in the long term. Subsidies and grants offered by other organisations, such as the governing bodies, may also dictate the programme design.

It is not ideal to run programmes that depend entirely on the financial support of others – if the finance is suddenly withdrawn the programme would have to be curtailed.

### Location and design

The location of the facility dictates its catchment area. It is the distance which people are willing to travel to visit your facility. The larger the facility or the more specialised it is, the further people will be willing to travel to use it. The number of visitors obviously affects the type and variety of programmes the facility can offer.

The local area of the facility can also affect the programming. Some people may not want to visit facilities in the evening. The actual age and design of the building will affect what activities can be offered – old gyms often have low roofs and beams and make some competitive sports such as badminton, volleyball or basketball impossible.

### Partnerships

It is likely that your facility has entered into partnership with another organisation. Examples include:

- sponsorship of a facility or activities
- compulsory, competitive, tendering contracts
- dual-use contract with a local school
- governing body, as a facility for excellence.

Partnership will bring some constraints to the programme design. You should be aware of any agreements with partners and the expectations of all parties. Representatives from the partnership organisations will visit the centre to ensure their contractual agreements are being fulfilled. Make an effort to know who they are so you can recognise them when they visit.

### Competition

Direct competition (which offers similar programmes) and indirect competition (offering alternative activities) can affect your programming. Very often facilities build reputations for being outstanding in certain activities, which can make them difficult to compete with. This is where your marketing strategy may need to be revised to offer incentives for visits to your facility. Perhaps you can complement the activities your competition is providing – for example, local health clubs that have several rowing machines may wish to take part in an annual competition at your health club. This could attract a good deal of publicity.

**Figure 7.2** *Being unaware of the local competition won't help your business*

*It is always useful to have copies of your local competitor's programme. This can help you to identify opportunities as well as predict direct competition.*

## Weather

We live in a climate that is both variable and unpredictable. This makes programming very difficult, especially programming of outdoor activities. Unexpected sunshine may also affect your indoor activities as people prefer to spend their time outside in good weather.

Most sports have specific seasons and participants are used to the weather associated with their sport. It may be that contingency plans are in place, especially where young children may be exposed to poor weather. This may involve leaving some indoor facilities free, so an indoor facility is available quickly if needed. Likewise, where appropriate, outdoor facilities should be used if there is an upturn in the weather.

**ACTIVITY**

In pairs, design a contingency plan for a general racquet session that is to be delivered to 28 12-year-old students on the two outdoor tennis courts. You have only one squash court available.

## Programming for specific groups

A programme should cater for specific groups, each of which will have their own needs and wants which must be clearly established before designing any programme.

### Education

Programmes that involve skill development or a formal structure for learning need specialist equipment and facilities, such as video equipment, white boards etc. The level of noise should be kept to a minimum during these programmes and they often require a high level of administration.

There will probably be a maximum number of participants allowed to enrol. It is often difficult to forecast the number of educational programmes such as coaching courses, first aid etc. The ones that are most popular (such as Football Association courses), should have waiting lists. It is a good idea to have a 'cut off' date for enrolment to allow sufficient time for cancellation and the possibility to re-programme the facility.

### Clubs

Clubs will often require regular and continuous usage of their booked facility. They often have diverse needs – for example, a sports hall may be used for cricket, and then for short tennis. Bookings tend to be in blocks and are usually seasonal. Clubs often have representatives, who are the people to deal with when confirming the booking. Clubs are often willing to take off-peak times, such as late evenings. Clubs frequently meet socially after their activities and ensuring that catering and bar facilities are available will provide a useful service and increase turnover.

## Special events

Special events are best programmed to run at the same time each year. For example, holding a particular road race on the first Saturday in April lets existing users know well in advance if their activities are to be affected. Special events often conflict with the needs of regular users and an element of 'goodwill' needs to be built into the programming as a way of expressing thanks to the regular users, whose programme may be affected. Goodwill may come in the form of:

- discount off the next booking
- complimentary tickets to the event
- complimentary drinks in the bar/cafe.

Whatever goodwill is offered, regular bookers should be notified well in advance and sent a letter of thanks after the event.

## Sports development

Governing bodies of sport have sport-development strategies to improve the number and quality of people playing their sport. Often block bookings of sport facilities are made for courses to develop the sport, from introductory classes for young people to excellence schools where the best young players in the area receive coaching. Any programming for young children needs to be in the 'twilight' hours, approximately between 4:00 and 6:30pm. Activities for older children can be programmed until 8:00 or 9:00pm. Very often the sports provide their own coaching staff and they should be familiar with your organisation's procedures regarding health and safety.

## Women only

Many providers of sport and recreation offer women the opportunity to participate in single-sex activities such as swimming, aerobics, keep fit and use of the fitness suites. Many of these programmes can be run during the day for women who do not go out to work. These sessions should be programmed, wherever possible, with child care and crèche facilities. Evening sessions for women at work should avoid the late evening. This is because many women do not wish to be visiting and leaving facilities late at night for reasons of personal security.

PROGRESS CHECK

1. Name three goals an organisation will want to achieve with its programming.
2. How can you assess the current usage of a facility?
3. What are the main constraints to programming? Support your answers with examples.
4. List three particular needs in programming women-only sessions.
5. What are the consequences of holding special events?

## CASE STUDY

Funbury Leisure Centre has decided to rearrange its off-peak programme to try to attract more users. Educational courses, special events and conferences are being targeted. There have been several letters of interest from organisations wishing to use the facility during the day for such reasons.

The regular daytime users will suffer a certain amount of disruption to their routine. A letter is written to these regulars informing them that they will be unable to use the facility on certain dates, due to special events. Alternative solutions are offered in the letter as goodwill. Unfortunately the bookings for an educational course go slowly, and the course has to be cancelled, highlighting the problem of making changes to programming.

1   Write a letter to existing users informing them that they will be unable to use the facility on a certain date because a special event is being held.

2   What course of action should be taken when sessions have to be cancelled?

## The features of a programme

Any programme will contain much the same features but it is how they are integrated and planned that will affect its success. The programme should take into account the different patterns and time zones available and combine these with the facilities and activities the organisation has to offer.

It is likely that the organisation's objectives can be achieved only by offering a balanced programme that has variety and flexibility as its main elements.

### The basic elements

Designing a programme is like putting a jigsaw together. You normally start by building the framework and often the rest will eventually fall into place. You must always establish your essential components early. Having a clear understanding of the basic elements of a programme will help to define your components.

**Activities**

These can be very varied, ranging from competitive sports to recreational and structured or unstructured activities. For example, squash courts can be programmed for ladder competitions or available for individual bookings. The sports hall can be programmed for a roller-skating session, or equipment made available for the users to decide what activities they do.

Activities can be categorised as mainstream (those which are popular) or not. Obvious examples include popular racquet sports such as tennis, badminton and squash and less popular ones such as lacrosse or racquet ball. When programming activities it is important to know the activities that are popular in your area and community, such as Rugby League in

### Funbury Leisure Centre

| | 9.30 / 10.00 am–11.00 / noon–1.00–2.00–3.00–4.00–5.00–6.00–7.00–8.00–9.00–10.00 / 10.30 | | | | | | |
|---|---|---|---|---|---|---|---|
| **Monday** | Casual Hire | | | Children's Badminton | Casual Hire | Short Mat Bowls | Block Bookings or Casual Hire |
| **Tuesday** | Casual Hire | | | Children's Basketball | Casual Hire | | Block Bookings or Casual Hire |
| **Wednesday** | 50+ Activities 9.30am–12.30pm including Badminton Table Tennis, Short Mat Bowls | Casual Hire | | | | | Block Bookings or Casual Hire |
| **Thursday** | Adult Badminton 9.30–11.15 Creche available | Casual Hire | Short Mat Bowls | Children's Football | Casual Hire | | Block Bookings or Casual Hire / Adult Coaching Course |
| **Friday** | Casual Hire | | | | | Netball Club | Block Bookings or Casual Hire |
| **Saturday** | Kids Fun Activities 9.30am–11.00am (4–8) 11.00am–12.30pm (9–15) | Children's Birthday Parties and Casual Hire | | | | | |
| **Sunday** | Casual Hire | Children's Birthday Parties and Casual Hire | | | | | |

**Figure 7.3**  A sample programme

the north of England. Unusual activities can also attract people, such as scuba diving for those wishing to go deep sea diving on holiday.

Activities can also be affected by trends, becoming more popular at certain times of the year – such as tennis during Wimbledon fortnight. Activities can also move in and out of fashion – such as skateboarding and line dancing.

GOOD PRACTICE ▷  *Stay aware of trends in sports and activities by reading appropriate magazines and journals.*

### Facilities
The facilities include the permanent fixtures – the building and its areas – and the equipment, which can be permanent or transportable. Some facilities are purpose built, such as a swimming pool, squash courts or halls with sprung wooden floors on which to play basketball or volleyball. However, a number of different activities can be performed in them. Many sports halls are designed for multi-purpose activities because they have concrete floors to allow most sports to be played and which allow

**Figure 7.4** *Keep up to date with the current trends in your business*

heavy vehicles to carry specialist equipment. Whatever the design, your equipment can change the nature and pattern of use of the facility. Some organisations are able to change sports hall seating and lighting in order to hold such events as snooker tournaments.

Your knowledge of the facilities and what can be done with them will ensure you get the best use out of them.

## ACTIVITY

List as many sport or recreation activities you think can be performed in:

- a squash court
- a swimming pool
- a tennis court.

### Services

Services include all the systems and operations which support the programme and the activities within it. Support from other organisations, such as the emergency services, is sometimes necessary before structuring special events that require a special licence.

The following essential services should be available for all programmed activities:

- changing and showering facilities
- toilet facilities
- emergency facilities – e.g. first-aid support
- water and refreshments.

The overall marketing campaign that accompanies the programme (information leaflets, etc.) can greatly affect the success of the programme. Perhaps the most important service is customer care, which is how employees and their systems care for the needs of their customers. A programme that does not include service support should not be offered.

### Staff

All programmes have staffing implications. The nature of the activity will often determine whether specialists or regular staff are required – for example, swimming instruction must be delivered by people who have a swimming teaching certificate as well as life-saving skills, whereas open roller-skating sessions require only someone to supervise. The numbers and ages of participants also determine how many members of staff are required.

It is important to know the skills that all full-time, part-time and casual staff have and what training they have received. Generally speaking, the more qualified and specialised someone is the more expensive their services will be. Look at the programmes your organisation offers and see what activities you are able to staff. This may involve the identification of training needs. The skills to lead and organise activities, work with young people or people with special needs are always in demand.

### Maintenance

All organisations will have a maintenance schedule. Daily tasks can be fitted into the programme of activities, by scheduling them for before and after use. However, some maintenance, such as repainting the gym, requires a longer time. All facilities have long-term maintenance schedules which should be built into any programming.

Many organisations are closed to the public at specific times of the year (often around Christmas and Easter) so that maintenance can take place.

Some activities, such as competitive five-a-side football or badminton, require regular cleaning of the floor before the activity commences, to avoid a dangerous surface. Time for this should be built into your programme.

## Patterns and time zones

The objectives of the organisation, the needs of the specific user groups and the elements of a programme will dictate the timing and pattern of use. Understanding the following factors will help to appreciate why certain activities happen at certain times and why some facilities are not in use.

### Time

The pattern of the programme is dictated by time. This initially involves the time at which the facility is open to the public. It is then split into the time allotted to the activities:

- hourly, such as bookings for a sports hall
- morning, afternoon or evening
- daily, weekly, monthly, annually
- mid-week or weekend
- school time, out of school sessions.

---

REMEMBER

*Always keep accurate and up-to-date information on file. Let management know if you have achieved any new qualifications.*

---

139

Time can be allocated in blocks, such as a 40-minute session for squash courts. Time should always be scheduled to allow for changeovers, maintenance or refreshments to be made available. The sport itself can also have an effect on time. Some sports may overrun allotted time – e.g. a hockey match that goes to extra time.

## Space

This is obviously dictated by the facility and its design, and by the activity. The space in some facilities can be changed by partitions or nets – for example, a sports hall can be divided by nets to allow cricket (batting and bowling) and table tennis to take place safely at the same time.

The sport and its participants also dictate the amount of space required. A tennis court, for example, requires a large amount of space and very few participants. However, short tennis for 8-year-old children can involve up to 16 people at the same time on one court. A tennis court area could also accommodate over 50 people doing fitness circuits.

## Seasons

You should understand the seasonal variations in your programme. Sports are seasonal, normally divided into winter and summer. It is important that the weather which usually accompanies the seasons is built into the programme to allow, for example, greater maintenance on football pitches in the winter, air conditioning to be available in the summer.

Holidays are another seasonal factor, and include bank holidays, summer, Easter, Christmas and spring. It is likely that families and schoolchildren will want to use the facility more during holiday periods, and this should be reflected in your programme.

## Peak/off-peak

Peak time refers to the time where most users want the facilities. For most providers this is between 5:00 and 10:00 pm on weekdays, and most of the day at weekends. Off-peak tends to be at other times, especially just before and after lunch.

How to sell off-peak or down time is the perennial problem of programmers. Many organisations target special groups, such as mothers and toddlers or schools, to fill their off-peak periods. During peak times, it is important that not too many visitors visit the centre as the quality of service can be affected. Maximum numbers allowed and 'first come, first served' systems are often found during this time.

## Wet/dry

Many organisations offer both wet and dry facilities. Wet facilities will include swimming pools, jacuzzis and saunas. Dry facilities would include all other facilities. Very often, wet and dry facilities could be programmed to complement each other – for example, gym and swim, workouts and saunas.

## Inside/outside

Activities will take place either inside or outside. This is often dependent on the season, the sport and the weather. Very often, when programming outdoor activities a contingency indoor plan is needed in case of adverse changes in the weather.

There tends to be more open space with outdoor activities, but natural light is available only at certain times of the year. It is likely that more outdoor programmes will have to be cancelled due to the weather and this should be accounted for in any budgets.

## Developing a balanced programme

A prominent feature of any successful programme is its balance – not only providing a variety of activities to a range of different user groups but also doing this within a flexible system which provides equity, reliability and continuity to all customers.

### Variety

It is important for organisations to offer a variety of products and services. This will increase choice and thus widen the potential market. Offer a choice of:

- activities and sports
- times available for use
- recreational and competitive activities
- casual or pre-booked use.

Variety is not about change (especially where a certain format is successful) but is about recognising that having a degree of flexibility may increase participation. A programme can be varied by inviting specialist staff to a training session, or, more specifically, offering members of a rugby team, who are working on their fitness, an opportunity to do aerobics.

Offering a variety of activities in the initial programme can be an effective way of determining the needs of the customers and can help in long-term planning.

### Flexibility

Flexibility in any programme can help to achieve variety and increase the usage of the facility. Flexibility is not just about being able to adapt fixtures and equipment: it is about planning in advance and predicting scenarios. Flexibility should also be adopted by staff. Many organisations send staff on activity training days to improve individual and team abilities to adapt to certain situations. You should always be adaptable, especially where problems arise.

However, the more flexible and adaptable a facility is, the more time and effort is required in changeovers and maintenance.

An organisation that has flexibility in both its facilities and employees can

- increase the usage of its facilities
- increase the number of visitors
- improve the image of the facility
- attract a wide range of partners and projects
- always have cover if staff are off sick
- deal with problems more effectively.

141

GOOD PRACTICE ▷ *Make sure you are familiar with your organisation's equal opportunities policy and the equivalent policies of key organisations such as the Sports Council and the relevant governing bodies of sport.*

### Equity

Many organisations, such as the Sports Council or local authorities, actively promote equal access for all. This can very often conflict with the organisation's goals of pursuing maximum occupancy and profit. Equity in programming is about being fair to your users. Resentment can be caused if it is perceived that certain groups and individuals are getting priority for times and bookings.

Procedures for booking should be made clear to all users before the booking is made. It is inevitable that peak times are in the greatest demand and that some people or groups will be disappointed. Equity should be evident in the service you provide for your customers. It should be the same high standard for all, irrespective of race, gender, class, age, ability and whether they are members, non-members or visitors.

### Reliability and continuity

Although flexibility and variety are essential parts of a balanced programme, too much flexibility and alteration to programmes can affect the regular participation enjoyed by the customer.

**Figure 7.5** *Facilities should be accessible to both men and women.*

Programmes need reliability built into them. It is important that club bookings and casual bookings can take place with the user knowing what is available and when. Continuity is also important, especially for those making club bookings – any future changes may affect the club's forthcoming fixtures. The level of dependability an organisation has is a feature that can be assessed as part of a customer care survey.

## PROGRESS CHECK

1 What are the different categories of activities?
2 What services are essential for all facilities?
3 Why can time be a difficult factor for programmers? Support your answer with examples.
4 What are the main components of a balanced programme?
5 Explain why reliability and continuity are important parts of a programme.

# Changing your programme

Programmes are constantly evolving to reflect changes in customer needs. These changes should be as a result of constant evaluation of the programme. By responding promptly to evaluations, programmes can be expanded and facilities and activities adapted to maintain the organisation's objectives. Once again, it is important to maintain a degree of continuity and inform customers of any changes as soon as possible.

## Evaluating your programme

There are so many features, variables and constraints to programmes that evaluation can be a difficult task. The key process is to obtain the right information before measuring its success. As in any evaluation, it is ideal to carry out some of it while the programme is running so that changes can be made to meet customer needs before the end, when changes will not be effective.

### Obtaining information

Information should be gathered on the whole process of putting a programme together. You should find out information on the following.

- The time spent putting the programme together
- The amount of people and supporting organisations involved
- The cost of putting a programme together
- The details of the programme itself – what happened during the programme
- Effectiveness of any marketing
- The occupancy figures, or total number of participants.

This information can be gathered through observation, customer surveys and booking sheets. You will constantly be receiving both quantitative and qualitative data and this should be gathered and recorded regularly. To make useful comparisons with previous programmes, use the same methods to gather and present information.

143

— REMEMBER —

*Evaluation should be regarded by the team and individuals as a positive process by which improvements are sought, and not as a process for apportioning blame.*

**Measuring success**

Success of a programme can often simply be measured by counting the number of participants involved or the income received. However, this will measure only two aspects of the outcome of the programme. The information gathered on the whole process of the programme should be measured against its objectives and those of the organisation as a whole. Be clear on the programme objectives and the methods by which you are going to measure its success.

Many programme objectives include specific targets, which can be motivational and require the co-operation of the whole team to ensure they are met. For example, to reach a target of 50 people in a new class needs careful marketing, staff involvement in personal selling, staff to prepare the equipment, and class instructors to work effectively to make the target achievable.

## Expanding your programme

Programmes which remain the same often become boring and outdated. New ideas and trends need to be followed to ensure demand remains high. You need to constantly look for new opportunities and be willing to try new ventures and to explore ways of maximising off-peak times.

**Experimenting**

Always be proactive in suggesting ways to improve the programme. This does not necessarily mean radical change, but adapting current programmes and activities. When presenting ideas, always be conscious of their advantages and possible disadvantages.

Very often, experiments should be offered as 'one-offs' or for a trial period to allow for a clear indication of their success. For example, a programme that includes a fitness circuit in the sports hall, once a week for an hour on an evening, could be changed by

- expanding the time to allow for more stretching and cooling down activities
- having later or earlier sessions, e.g. at lunch time or for people on the way home from work
- having introductory, intermediate and advanced workout sessions.

You may wish to experiment with opening times, running sample and taster sessions in holiday periods. All experiments should be carefully monitored and offered in such a way as to avoid disruption. If you cancel any sessions, be sure to erect notices as early as possible. Always try to provide people with alternative programmes.

**Developing partnerships**

People and organisations outside the facility might suggest changes to your programmes. These opportunities are often initiated from networking. Many clubs, such as tennis and cricket clubs, offer their members specialist coaching sessions, and trips to major events. These can still form part of your programme of activities and events.

You may wish to develop partnerships with organisations and providers that have complementary interests – e.g. you might be able to offer canoeing lessons in your pool and offer incentives to join the local canoe club, which is a good package for someone wishing to take up the sport.

Be clear in identifying the benefits of the partnership for

- the customer
- the organisation and
- the partner.

This should include the short, medium and long term.

## ACTIVITY

In small groups, select a sports facility you are familiar with and suggest a list of partners that may be suitable. You must outline the benefits to all concerned.

### Maximising off-peak times

This is often the primary concern of facility managers. You may wish to suggest ideas based on the aspects of experimentation and the development of partnerships. It is clearly a process that begins by exploring which individuals, clubs and organisations can access your facilities during the off-peak times:

- job seekers
- special-needs groups
- voluntary organisations
- staff that are not working
- housewives and house husbands
- professional sports organisations
- people who work flexi-time
- schools and educational institutions
- women on maternity leave
- pensioners.

It is useful to explore ways of adapting and modifying your facilities to perhaps to offer activities and services for which the facilities were not originally designed. For example, sports halls can become auction rooms, or used to house art exhibitions. All ideas should be forwarded to your line manager, with any financial and operational issues clearly identified.

## Renovating your facilities

Making any structural or internal changes to the building will be senior management's decision. It is often a lengthy process, which could require planning permission. Many organisations make structural changes in order to alter the programme and activities they can offer. You may be involved in assessing the activities, and invited to offer alternatives and present proposals.

### Assessing existing facilities

Assessment can be a complicated process, which examines different aspects of the facility including

- space
- occupancy figures for each area
- flexibility of the area (the number of activities that can be offered)
- costs, including general maintenance, repairs, etc.
- customer comments.

You must also consider how existing users may be affected by changes in the facility. There are certain considerations due to the property and the land – you must know whether or not the facility is a listed building, or if construction can take place without affecting the structure or design. Then there are more detailed programme and equipment factors to explore. These centre around assessing what equipment needs and costs would be involved, as well as fixtures and fitting requirements.

### Developing alternatives

All facilities can be renovated, but not all changes will directly affect your programme, and these areas can be eliminated from your assessment process. Facilities should be explored to see if they can be expanded, separated, partitioned and so on. It might be that structural changes cannot be made to certain areas, but that internal renovation can take place. For example, a squash court that is never used can be renovated as an aerobics studio, a snooker/pool room, a sun bed area etc. Each facility area should be examined to explore the range of alternative uses into which it could be converted and the potential demand for the new facility and programme.

All alternatives should be considered using a feasibility study. This uses the analysis of the existing facilities in conjunction with the needs of future programmes and the potential costs of change in terms of construction, equipment and disruption to present new programmes. Many organisations will involve specialists (engineers, architects, management and financial experts) at this stage.

### Presenting a proposal

Many forward-thinking organisations consult not only specialists but also their employees. This makes the employees feel part of the process and thus more motivated to assist in planning and preparing for change. If you have an opportunity to present your proposals to the management team, you should do so in a manner which shows effort, research, realism and attention to detail. Your proposal should *not* focus on economic, legal or political considerations but should acknowledge them to show you have given them some thought. The proposal *should* focus on the design, clearly outlining the areas to be changed and the advantages and disadvantages of each aspect of the proposal. Diagrams are the best way of illustrating your proposal. They should be clear and show before and after drawings.

PROGRESS CHECK

1 Where can you obtain information to help you evaluate your programme?

2 List at least five groups of people who may be able to access the facility during off-peak hours.

3 What are the considerations to be made before renovating your facilities?

4 What are the important components of a proposal?

# Taking bookings

Once all efforts have been made to create a positive first impression you must ensure that entry is controlled, people enrolled and bookings taken competently and efficiently. An accurate register of customers and numbers of visitors is essential under health and safety legislation. The point of entry must be monitored as a security precaution and to ensure there is no unauthorised access. Taking bookings and payments are key financial procedures which demand complete accuracy.

This suggests that you need to be able to perform several tasks simultaneously and have eyes in the back of your head. There are however, practical steps you can take to receive customers and visitors.

## Types of bookings

There are three types of bookings:

- block bookings
- club bookings
- individual bookings (including special events).

### Block bookings

A block booking refers to the securement of a facility at a regular time throughout a given period by an individual group. Typical block bookings will include a netball team requiring regular training on the Astroturf from 7:00 till 9:00 pm on Tuesdays throughout the season and alternate Saturdays from 10:00 am till noon to play home matches. It is usual to complete an advance hire form and to issue terms of hire. These usually centre on cancellation, notification for cancellation and subsequent charges. Block bookings enable organisations to plan programmes, improve budgeting, increase cash flow and use their staff efficiently. Block bookings are often given at a discounted rate but can have the detrimental effect of deterring potential new clients by being inflexible.

### Club bookings

For club bookings a representative of the club will confirm the use of facilities on its behalf. As many voluntary clubs can receive VAT-exempt rates it is usual to ask for a copy of the club's constitution. Therefore, the participants are often not the same people as the customers. The communication lines depend upon the club's representative, and cancellations and payments may require a system different from that used for block bookings. Payments for hire can be made weekly, monthly or annually when there is generally more commitment by both parties.

### Individual bookings

Individual bookings can come from anyone wishing to book a facility or an activity, whether existing customers or individuals booking for the first time. People may wish to book all the facilities for a special event, such as an exhibition. They will usually request a particular date and time and an efficient booking system is essential. Twenty-four hours is considered an acceptable cancellation time.

## Booking systems

Within any organisation there are systems for recording information. These may include using simple lists, standardised documents, computer software or large booking sheets.

### Manual systems

Manual systems for organisations with a range of facilities would normally appear in the form of booking sheets. These are large sheets of paper outlining the times and facilities that the organisation has available for hire. Most organisations would have a master booking sheet containing all the courses, block and club bookings and confirming the facilities that are booked in advance over a given period. The master will be updated annually, termly or seasonally and should be used for reference when completing the daily booking sheets. The information is then transferred from the master to the daily booking sheets. This will clearly indicate the facilities that are available for hire to individual customers, who would normally phone in to book up to seven days in advance.

There also needs to be a system listing the activities that are to take place. For example, it may be possible to divide an indoor sports hall into halves or thirds. This might be identified on a booking sheet by the number of badminton courts in each section. If a customer is booking half the sports hall the manual system should have space to record what activity is to be played because the hall needs to be prepared differently for five-a-side football or badminton. Sports assistants need a copy of the day's bookings so they can efficiently prepare the activity for the customer.

It is usual to use a simple coding system to highlight users, activities and facilities required. Block and club bookings could also be colour-coded. Here is a list of the codes commonly used:

A   =   Adult
J   =   Junior
SR   =   Special rate (this could be for pensioners, unemployed)
BB   =   Block booking
CB   =   Club booking
WH   =   Whole hall
HH   =   Half hall
TH   =   Third hall
SC   =   Squash court
BC   =   Badminton court
TN   =   Tennis
CK   =   Cricket

---

REMEMBER

*Record all information accurately and explain the conditions of bookings to first-time users.*

---

148

## SPORTS HALL

| | COURT 1 | COURT 2 | COURT 3 | COURT 4 | COURT 5 | COURT 6 |
|---|---|---|---|---|---|---|
| 10.00 AM | | | | | | |
| 11.00 AM | | | | | | |
| 12.00 NOON | | | | | | |
| 1.00 PM | MR BROWN  2 FUNBURY AVE  5-A-SIDE  TEL. 881966 | | | | | |
| 2.00 PM | | | | | | |
| 3.00 PM | | | | | | |
| 4.00 PM | KIDS CLUB ACTIVITIES | | | | | |
| 5.00 PM | KIDS CLUB ACTIVITIES | | | | | |
| 6.00 PM | FUNBURY TIGERS BASKETBALL CLUB | | | AEROBICS | | |
| 7.00 PM | Fletcher 21 Funbury Drive 878613 | | | | | |
| 8.00 PM | | | | | | |
| 9.00 PM | | | | | | |

## TENNIS CT

| | COURT 1 | COURT 2 |
|---|---|---|
| | | |
| | | |
| | REID  Fbry Call 878228 | |
| | TENNIS COACHING PROGRAMME | |
| | | |

## SQUASH COURTS

| | 1 | 2 | | 1 | 2 |
|---|---|---|---|---|---|
| 10.00 | | | 4.00 | | |
| 10.40 | | | 4.40 | | |
| 11.20 | | | 5.20 | PRIOR Fbry Call 878228 | |
| 12.00 | | | 6.00 | | |
| 12.40 | | | 6.40 | | |
| 1.20 | | | 7.20 | | |
| 2.00 | | | 8.00 | | |
| 2.40 | | | 8.40 | | |
| 3.20 | | | 9.20 | | |

NOTES

RECEPTIONIST

DUTY MANAGER

FUNBURY LEISURE CENTRE/BOOKING SHEET     DAY:               DATE:

**Figure 7.6**  Booking sheet

BL = Basketball
FB = Football
Membership:
FL = Full
FM = Family
OP = Off peak

The final item on a booking sheet is the number of participants. As an example, WH, BL × 10 simply means ten people have booked the whole hall to play basketball. Booking sheets can also be used as a method to balance finances as they are a clear system of identifying income.

Another manual system is the diary. This commences at the start of the financial year and is used for recording special events, cancellations and when maintenance is to be done. It is also a good idea to clearly indicate in the diary when the facility is to be closed.

Registers and waiting lists are perhaps the simplest forms of manual booking systems. They are most used when customers are enrolling for a course – for example, an Easter football course. The places available will be numbered and usually offered to previous customers first. Once all places are filled, further enquirers should be placed on the waiting list in case of cancellations or future courses. If the register is for children's activities extra information is required in the form of a registration card (Figure 7.7). This is kept with the person delivering the session. Under the Children's Act information on emergency contact, the child's doctor's

*Funbury Leisure Centre*

**Registration Card**

Family name: .................................... First name: ....................................
Date of birth: ....................................
School: ....................................
Address: ....................................
....................................
Phone no: ....................................
Emergency contact no: ....................................
Health problems: ....................................
Doctor's name and phone no: ....................................
Person collecting child: ....................................
Signature of parent/guardian ....................................

***Figure 7.7*** *Registration card*

name and address and the person collecting the child will all need to be identified. Registers are taken before and straight after the activity, once the child has been collected.

### Computerised systems

There are many sophisticated software programmes on the market which can integrate a customer database, a till and a booking sheet. They can be initiated by scanning a membership card or simply by keying in the customer's name and post code. This will then display other information including full address or facilities booked and any information updated. The system will also have the capability of printing out information. Only print out information which is to be sent out of the organisation – for example, confirmation of a club booking. Under the Data Protection Act, any system should be confidential and locked away when not required.

## Receiving and recording bookings

Bookings may be taken by telephone, answering machine, fax, e-mail, face to face or by post. Written requests are easier to record but do not give an opportunity to immediately confirm any item – and can sometimes be illegible. The writer may have omitted an important item. A request in writing does provide proof of booking but always remember to record on the letter the date you received it. The face-to-face and telephone methods for booking activities allow the person taking the booking an opportunity to collect all the necessary information. It is always a good idea to repeat the information to the customer to ensure that you have recorded it accurately.

### Using a checklist

Whatever system is in use you should have a checklist to ensure that all the information required is collated and recorded accurately. A typical list will contain the following:

- date facility required
- time required
- name of the person booking
- phone number of person booking
- number of people attending
- activity being booked
- running total of places left on programme
- membership number
- age (where appropriate)
- special requirements
- method of payment/receipt numbers
- any information the organisation needs to provide.

### Recording information

This information must be recorded accurately and legibly. Using a good pen and writing in print form are two simple methods of achieving clarity. If any information is found to be incorrect ensure that all relevant records and systems are updated. For example, a customer's address may have changed or a customer may no longer be a junior member.

---

**REMEMBER**

*It is a good idea to learn the abbreviations your organisation uses or keep a copy of them close at hand.*

---

## Filing information

All information must be filed and clearly labelled. There are many filing methods one can use – alphabetical order according to the sport or activity, or by clubs and members. Whatever system is to be used keep all files and information in sequence and if you remove any information leave a note stating where it is.

## PROGRESS CHECK

1  Explain, with examples, the main types of bookings.
2  What are the main forms used in manual booking systems?
3  What advantages do computerised systems have over manual systems?
4  What are the advantages of using checklists?
5  Why must all information be recorded and filed?

## CASE STUDY

Funbury Leisure Centre is running a range of activities during the school summer holidays. This is for expanding provision over the summer and is to have structured and unstructured activities. The programme follows an assessment of the existing facilities and surrounding grassland. The activities offered include soccer skills sessions, indoor and outdoor fun games, roller hockey, and a bouncy castle.

A manual booking system has been devised and codes created to identify the times and facilities required and the details of each person booked onto each activity.

1  What information needs to be recorded on the booking sheet? Devise a checklist to help you answer the question.

2  Why is it important to know how many children are coming to each activity and the total number visiting the centre?

## KEY TERMS

You need to know the meaning of the following words and phrases. Go back through the chapter to make sure you understand.

Balanced programme
Booking systems
Maintenance schedule
Programme patterns

Booking sheet
Equity
Peak/off-peak
Programming for specific groups

# 8 Finance, information and systems

This chapter covers:
➤ Business systems
➤ Financial control
➤ Office and reception organisation

In your job it is essential that you are familiar with the business systems of the organisation. You are unlikely to be involved in the issues around financing of the organisation, but a sound understanding of the systems and sources of information will help you maintain the organisation's objectives. You will also need to be familiar with office equipment and the most effective and efficient ways of undertaking administrative tasks.

## Business systems

All organisations have systems to help them achieve their goals and attain a level of quality and efficiency. Some organisations try to reach approved quality standards as a means of identifying their efficiency and effectiveness. All employees have to process information and 'deal with the paperwork' and there are usually systems in place to help speed up the process. Many organisations use computers to help store and process large quantities of information, and it is essential to know how to use the software to process information.

### Quality

In simple terms 'quality' is about providing a service well and, more importantly, to the standards expected by customers. Quality can now be externally measured by national and international standards. The organisation has to ensure that procedures are in place to maintain quality.

**Quality standards**

The International Standards Organisation (ISO), working on behalf of the British Standards Institute, has developed quality standards to measure how companies operate their systems; for example BSENISO 9000, more commonly known as ISO 9000, and Investors in People (IIP).

These standards are considered to be long-term strategies aimed at achieving a high-quality service, first time, every time. All members of staff should be involved in development to ensure they are aware of the organisation's quest for the quality standard. You will probably be involved in the following stages:

- Preparation for trying to discover customers' needs and understanding the concept of quality
- Planning how the level of quality will be achieved and maintained. This will be written as quality procedures and systems
- Implementing the systems, ensuring that staff training is continued where necessary
- Maintaining high quality by having an internal monitoring system as well as meeting standards set by external auditors.

Quality standards can help to improve the delivery of your service and some organisations prefer to work only with those who have attained these standards.

### Quality procedures

These are the statements of how the standards are to be attained. They will be recorded in a file and should be cross referenced to the standards file. You should be aware of the procedures that are relevant to your position – for example, the procedures on how to deal with customer complaints. The overall standard may be to respond to certain complaints within 48 hours, which will mean that procedures are likely to tell you how to record and respond to certain complaints in a given time scale. There might also be procedures on answering the phone within a certain number of rings and cleaning the facilities so many times a day.

GOOD PRACTICE ▷ *Familiarise yourself with the key procedures in your job and know how to reference procedures you use only occasionally.*

### Maintaining quality

Quality maintenance involves undertaking checks and inspections to ensure that the correct procedures are being followed. This should not just be a system of checking up, but should allow those involved in operating procedures to feed back to management on the efficiency and effectiveness of these procedures. Some organisations initiate 'quality groups', which are made up of employees and management, to discuss how quality can be maintained and improved.

If you have suggestions as to how procedures may be improved you should record and send them to the quality group. As programmes and services change so will procedures aimed at maintaining quality. This involvement of staff and management focusing on quality and customer needs is what many refer to as 'Total Quality Management'.

## Information processing

The purpose of any information processing system is to be able to use information to improve the quality of service and to help management in their decision making. This can often be done manually, using pen and paper and traditional filing systems, but it is becoming essential to be conversant with word processing, databases and spreadsheets.

**Figure 8.1** *Be familiar with key procedures of your job*

A computer system will enable you to input data, find and retrieve data and print it. This is a much quicker method of processing information than doing it manually.

**Word processing**

Word processing facilities are found on almost all computers and word processing has replaced typewriting. The capability of the software will depend upon its type but all word processing systems will enable you, once you have typed in the text, to:

- quickly make amendments to or delete text
- insert new text or move existing text into any desired position, including repositioning paragraphs
- print out, edit, or update stored data at any time
- write letters according to pre-programmed instructions, and personalise them using mail merge
- check spelling and grammar
- incorporate graphics and charts into documents
- use different styles (font, size, bold, underline, italic etc.).

You are most likely to use the word processor for:

- writing standard letters and documents where little context needs changing (e.g. thank you letters)
- updating reports, manuals and instructions
- responding to customer enquiries or complaints.

ACTIVITY

In pairs, design a letterhead and logo for Funbury Leisure Centre. Select the font and size to be used and where the address and telephone number of the organisation is to be located.

### Databases

Database software can be used to access a wide range of information quickly and accurately, which can help greatly in discovering information and making decisions. The type of information most likely to be stored in a database includes:

- customer details
- lists of stock items, including details on equipment
- details on training courses
- financial information, including income and expenditure.

All this information can be quickly retrieved or amended. The software asks you to select 'fields', which are the areas for the types of information you wish to input – for example, surname, forenames and age. The greatest advantages of a database are that it can automatically put records in any order you choose and that the data can be inserted into your word processing documents.

The database also enables you to extract certain combinations of information, such as names and addresses, or names and ages, for targeting certain groups.

GOOD PRACTICE ▷ *Before setting up a database try to decide the type of information you want it to produce. This will help you select the fields.*

**Figure 8.2** *Make sure your database is adaptable*

156

### Spreadsheets

Spreadsheets are used for processing numerical information. The most common uses in sport and recreation are for accounting. Using a spreadsheet will help you to forecast sales, membership break-even figures, as well as calculating total income and expenditure.

The main advantage is that you can change information – such as an admission price from £2.00 to £2.15 – and calculate possible income and break-even figures. You can then produce this information in graphic form, such as tables, and charts (these are always impressive when presenting information).

Many sportspeople use spreadsheets to store data on their performance. This can include personal details such as weight and body fat percentage and outcome details such as time taken to run a certain distance, metres thrown or goals scored. This can then be incorporated into an action plan and records.

## PROGRESS CHECK

1  What is ISO 9000?

2  Identify procedures of how organisations can maintain the quality of the services they offer.

3  Describe five features of word-processing systems.

4  Identify two examples where you may wish to use a spreadsheet.

5  What should you do before starting a database?

## CASE STUDY

Funbody's Health and Fitness Centre is trying to achieve ISO 9000. To do this the management has to prove that quality procedures are in place and that they can be maintained. One of the systems is information processing. The organisation must demonstrate, for example, that the database on club members is accurate and that procedures conform to the Data Protection Act.

The management has created quality standards and procedures to follow when entering information or retrieving it from the members' database. The quality, standards and procedures files are located in the club's main office. Staff are to be involved in a training day to ensure that the procedures are clearly explained and demonstrated and regular quality checks are to be undertaken to ensure that they are being followed. All members have been informed by direct mail about their rights under the Data Protection Act.

1  Why is it important that all staff follow the same standards and procedures?

2  What information on the database should be made available to members if they wish to see it?

# Financial control

In all organisations there are individuals who have the responsibility for preparing and interpreting financial information, known as financial and management accounting. It is likely that you will be part of a department or section who are working to a budget, prepared by the financial manager. It is good practice to be able to recognise where financial information can be found and where funding comes from.

## Handling data

Most organisations have computer systems and employees are often expected to be able to take bookings, deal with memberships, receive money and issue receipts. This will all involve inputting data, retrieving data and then printing it out.

### Inputting data

You should have received training on the type of software and systems that you will be using. You should always be prepared to back up the information to a floppy disk. This will be shown as a different 'drive' on your computer. On most computers the drives are labelled by letters – e.g. C is the hard drive and the floppy will be a different letter, often A.

You should frequently save information as you input it, and should back it up regularly to prevent data being lost. All information is kept in files and it is important to label (name) each file in such a way that it clearly identifies its content – for example, 'File: members details', which should also have the date on. This name should also be written on the floppy disk (Figure 8.3).

Take time to input data, because mistakes are caused by the person inputting the information, *not* the computer.

---

GOOD PRACTICE ▷ *If you are involved in entering a lot of data a basic typing course will help to save time and avoid mistakes.*

---

**Figure 8.3** *The contents of a floppy disk should be clearly marked on it, or how will anyone know what's on the disk?*

### Finding and retrieving data

A major part of working with computers is being able to locate and retrieve data that has been stored. Naming the file is critical in finding correct information.

To retrieve data you should be able to move the cursor into the file or enter the file name you are looking for. Very often information will be retrieved by entering a person's name or their membership number. If you are searching for information in databases, you can enter the 'field' you are interested in (such as address or gender) to find details associated with that field.

When entering a common name, such as Smith, you might find several examples, and you should be able to make further searches to find the person you are looking for. If you need to find information in order to update it, always save to the hard disk and then back up onto floppy.

**Figure 8.4** *If you have to enter a lot of data you'd better learn to type!*

Some systems retrieve data by a swipe card. You should always check the details on the card and screen with the person who gave you the card.

### Printing information
All computers have the facility to print information that is on the screen. Before printing information be sure to check that

- the data on the screen (including spelling, grammar, total amounts) is correct
- you need to print it – what is it to be used for? Could you save paper by keeping it on disk?
- you are using the correct quality and colour of paper – should you be using letterheaded paper?
- the type of font and print size is standard and in line with the organisation's approved practice
- the printer is on and that the paper has been placed correctly to avoid jamming
- the layout is correct – that it is printing the size and orientation you require.

If there are any problems with the equipment you should report them immediately and put up a sign stating it is out of use.

## Budgets

Budgeting is planning finances over a given period of time. By allocating budgets to specific departments and for specific items, the management are, in theory, more able to control the financial spends. There are several types of budget and ways of controlling them.

### The purpose of a budget
The main purpose of a budget is to help meet the organisation's objectives. Budgets are stated in financial terms and aim to ensure that businesses spend their money in a controlled manner. Managers apportion money to departments over a given period of time, usually a year. This may also be broken down month by month. It is then possible to know how much is being spent, by whom and when. This aids management in making effective plans, and to forecast what will happen in the future.

If the manager sees that a budget is inaccurate or the money is being spent too quickly, changes can be made to spending patterns or the budget altered. You should be aware of the budgets that operate in your work place. There are normally codes apportioned to each budget to ensure that money spent is being taken from the right budget.

### Types of budget
It is likely that a number of budgets will affect you in your place of work. Budgets are likely to be apportioned to:

- expenses, such as travelling costs incurred in attending a conference
- cleaning, including equipment and materials
- stationery, such as paper, files, pens and other office stationery
- marketing, which may have money available for artwork, posters, direct mail and advertising

- staffing, which could include numbers of full and part-time staff, overtime paid and rates of pay
- sales – projected income from sales of equipment (e.g. squash balls) or services (e.g use of halls).

An important budget is the sales budget, which will be used as a base for forecasting likely sales in a particular time period. This will help to identify the results of marketing strategies and trends in participation and memberships. It is likely that you will be working towards sales targets. This will be a statement of how many sales (e.g. numbers of new members) need to be achieved. All these figures will be seen in the sales budget.

### Budgetary control

There is little point in setting targets and budgets unless they are monitored and controlled. At the end of each control period (probably monthly) managers will have information allowing them to compare budgeted and actual figures. Any significant variances are likely to be investigated further, and necessary actions taken. The review period can be a stressful time for all those working to tight targets and budgets. It is essential to be aware of the targets expected of you, and to be clear on how you can best achieve them.

## Sources of information

All organisations record their financial transactions. This is for tax purposes, and used by managers to assess the financial situation of the organisation. Financial information is found in various forms – such as invoices, till receipts and cheques. It is the job of an accountant to prepare the financial accounts. These will normally consist of the cash flow statement, profit and loss account and the balance sheet. You should be able to extract key information from these statements to help assess the type of organisation and the financial state it is in.

### Cash flow statement

Cash flow means the movement of money into and out of the business. This is usually detailed monthly and totalled annually. This cash flow statement is important to businesses as it monitors how much cash is needed for the organisation to function. There are some times in the year where cash inputs exceed cash outputs – for example, school holidays for leisure centres or just after Christmas for health clubs. The management should be able to calculate how much money needs to be put aside from these periods for the times of the year that are less busy and when outgoings exceed income.

### Profit and loss account

This statement compares the expenses incurred by an organisation with the income generated through sales and grants. Some organisations attempt to generate more income than expenditure, and this figure is known as the profit. Organisations working in the public sector are required to produce statements of accounts which include details on income and expenditure. The profit and loss statement will contain the following terms.

- Sales, which is the amount received for your services or products, such as 'squash balls 200 at £1.20 each'
- Cost of sales, the costs incurred by the organisation in generating these sales. This is usually labour and purchase of equipment – e.g. 'squash balls 200 at 80p each' – but can include overheads, which are items indirectly attributable to costs incurred in sales and which include heating, lighting and telephone
- Other income, which could be grants or fundraisers
- Gross profit, which is arrived at by subtracting cost of sales from sales
- Net profit, which is the profit left after interest and tax are paid.

### The balance sheet

The balance statement provides information of the assets, liabilities and capital that the organisation has at a given time. You should be able to look at an organisation's balance sheet and ascertain its financial position. The important terms are assets and liabilities.

- *Assets* include all the items that are of value to the organisation. These can be either fixed or current, depending on how easily they can be converted into cash. The premises is a fixed asset and the amount of stock you have a current asset
- *Liabilities* are the amounts which the organisation owes. Long-term liabilities could include loans or mortgages; short-term liabilities may include outstanding invoices, or tax payable.

---

ACTIVITY

Working in a small group go to your local library and obtain the financial statements of several sport and recreation organisations. Write a small summary of the profit and loss and balance sheet statements and compare them. Decide which organisation is in the strongest financial position.

---

## Sources of funding

All organisations try to supplement their income by exploring other sources of funding. Several organisations have responsibility for distributing funds to individuals and organisations involved in sport. However, there are often strict criteria that must be met before funds can be allocated. Allocation will be determined by the aims and objectives of those distributing funds.

### Central and local government and the Lottery

The sports councils of the home countries are the main central government's arm for allocating funds. It is also the responsibility of the sports councils to distribute the funds for sport via the Lottery Sports Fund (LSF). Funding is available for many projects, especially those that will bring benefits to the whole community.

The sports councils will allocate funds to help projects that are in line with their objectives and the LSF for elite sports persons. To discover if you are eligible for a grant phone the LSF or the governing bodies of sport.

Local authorities often have development officers who aim to develop sports participation in their community. They may provide funding for educational courses, equipment and facilities. Other schemes may be available through the local leisure services department.

### Governing bodies and foundations

Several foundations have been set up to support sports projects and sportspeople pursuing excellence. These include the following.

- The Foundation for Sport and the Arts, which has been set up by football pools promoters
- The Sports Aid Foundation, which grants aid to elite sportspeople
- Sports matches, where finding a business sponsor is rewarded by the government matching the contribution of the business (up to a certain amount)
- The various governing bodies of sport have their own schemes aimed at developing their sport. Support can sometimes be in the form of cash, but very often is provided through equipment, coaching or facilities.

### Fundraising

Fundraising is the most popular method within the voluntary sector of raising extra funds. This involves organisations starting projects involving family, friends and the community to raise money. Examples include:

- jumble sales
- sponsored events such as walks, runs, bed races, 24-hour pool events
- car washes
- fayres, including bring-and-buy or summer fayres
- coffee mornings, luncheons
- sports dinners
- race nights.

Fundraising activities are most suitable at certain times of the year, for example jumble sales before Christmas and outdoor fayres in the summer. Sports dinners are always popular.

---

REMEMBER

*Before putting on a fundraising event, check on the activities going on in your area for anything which may put people off coming – such as a local team's cup final.*

---

GOOD PRACTICE ▷

*Whenever you are involved in a fundraising event, try to explore ways of developing 'secondary spends', such as inviting participants and visitors to buy raffle tickets or purchase refreshments.*

---

**Figure 8.5** *Secondary attractions enhance everyone's enjoyment*

# Office and reception organisation

All sport and recreation facilities have areas in which money is received and administration records and procedures are dealt with – probably at reception and in the office. It is often left to the staff to organise these areas in such a way so as to efficiently deal with the duties to hand. This can be done using a system known as 'organisation and methods' and by using technological equipment.

## Planning and organising the office and reception

All employees will have some responsibility for office work, even though mostly it will be dealt with by specialist staff, such as receptionists or secretaries. You should be clear about your responsibilities and the layout of the office and reception areas. Very often there is little space to work with, but it should be planned to meet its objectives.

### Objectives

These will depend on the functions of the area and responsibilities of the people that need to use it. There will be priority for security of finances and information, access and exit. Areas will be needed to store keys, and possibly equipment such as megaphone and first-aid kit.

It is important to consider the functions of the area – such as typing and answering the phone – and to have objectives for reducing noise from people and machinery. The office in many organisations is also used by staff as a recreation or rest area. Objectives need to be agreed by all members of staff as to how to combine administrative duties with the requirements of those wishing to use the space to take breaks.

### Layout

Once the objectives are agreed, the actual layout of each area can be decided. At reception the layout should take into account security of finances as well as the ability to perform the duties required – for example, dealing with customers and answering the phone. You should have all the information you need within arm's reach and a chair that will be comfortable and supportive.

The office layout should use natural light as much as possible. Machines, such as photocopiers, should be kept in a separate area because of the noise. There should be a place for notices so staff can exchange messages and receive important information from employers and unions. Desks, chairs and filing cabinets should be carefully positioned to allow people to work and process information easily. The aesthetics of the office can be improved by using colour and plants, making it a more pleasant place to work in.

## Organisation and methods

This has traditionally been the process used by office managers to review administrative practices with a view to making them more efficient and economical. However, many people working in sport and recreation use organisation and methods to examine all their procedures and systems and to assist them in improving working practices.

### The purpose of organisation and methods

The overriding objective is to improve efficiency and effectiveness and, wherever possible, to make savings. This can be achieved by

- ensuring that communication methods are clear and the correct message is being received within the required time
- ensuring that working practices are the most economical (for example, avoiding duplication of tasks)
- having clear policies on environmental concerns (such as use of paper and recycling)
- examining the way jobs are performed (such as filling envelopes for direct mail or deciding whether putting something on a notice board is more effective than issuing a memorandum)
- evaluating equipment to ensure it is being used optimally
- examining the relationship between equipment and individuals (ergonomics) to ensure that safe practices are being used.

This last point is very important; it can help to ensure that staff are avoiding practices that adversely affect their general health and well being.

164

### Work measurement methods

You can take any task at work, such as preparing information for direct mail, and ask questions about how to improve the efficiency and effectiveness. For example:

- Who is going to be involved in the task and what are their requirements – for example, is the person left-handed?
- What is the purpose of the task?
- When is it to be achieved by?
- How is it going to be done?

Having asked these questions you can work with a colleague who can observe and record how the task is completed. You will need to record information such as time taken and mistakes that have occurred.

A successful method is to 'trial and error' several ways of performing tasks to see which one best meets your objectives of efficiency, effectiveness and safety.

GOOD PRACTICE ▷ *When measuring work methods always have the appropriate equipment to hand, including a stopwatch, clipboard and clicker. Using a video to record work methods is also a useful method to help analyse work practices.*

### Responding to organisation and methods

Sometimes organisations may ask external teams to examine working practices. This often concerns employees as they feel they are being scrutinised and that they may lose their jobs. It is essential that employees are involved in the process and that they work with management to agreed objectives. Very often, changes in practices can

**Figure 8.6** *Always have the appropriate equipment to hand for what you're measuring*

help to improve systems of work and safety. If you have any suggestions for improvements, give them to your line manager with an explanation of the benefits.

## Using technological equipment

Technological advances are such that equipment used to exchange information is changing almost daily. We are often expected to be able to use computers and operate other equipment such as fax machines, photocopiers and mobile communications. There are procedures to follow with all equipment, especially to safeguard against damage.

### Preventing damage

Damage to equipment can mean the loss of key information and the need to revert to manual (and often slower) methods of communicating. It is essential to follow the manual for all equipment that you will be using.

Damage to equipment can be avoided by keeping food and drink away from it. Drinks should never be placed near a computer. Equipment should also generally be kept away from areas of extreme temperature, such as radiators, and sinks.

If you are ever unsure of where to locate equipment you should contact the suppliers or manufacturers, who should be able to advise you.

### The facsimile (fax) machine

This machine can scan or read images on a piece of paper and, through a series of electronic signals, send an identical copy to another fax machine, which will then print out the image onto paper.

Very often the fax is part of a telephone and may have the same number, although it could be a separate machine with a different number. The fax machine usually has the facility to confirm whether the message that has been sent has been received. The original document remains with the sender as a reference.

Most media organisations, including radio stations and newspapers, sometimes ask for items such as press releases to be faxed to them. Many organisations have a standard layout for fax transmissions which includes a note of how many pages are being sent. Most machines automatically record the date and time the fax was sent. An added feature of many fax machines is that they can be used to photocopy.

### Photocopiers

These machines transfer images from one piece of paper, using powder or toner and a heat process, onto another piece of paper. Copiers can take different sizes of paper and copy onto white or coloured paper or onto acetate.

Most copiers are designed for specific purposes – such as high-speed copiers designed for leaflets or items that are used frequently. Photocopying can often be expensive and mistakes should be avoided by carefully selecting the amount of copies and size of paper you require.

Sometimes, if many copies are required, it is actually cheaper to have them printed. This can be easily researched by asking for quotes from local printers.

**Figure 8.7** *Modern office equipment includes photocopiers, fax machines and computers*

### Mobile communication systems

These systems include two-way radios and paging systems. The radio pager is used by many people and attaches to their belt. You can radio or telephone a pager number and leave a number or a message. Many systems allow short messages to be left, which the receiver reads on a small screen. On receiving the message the pager will bleep or vibrate to inform the recipient that they have a message.

Two-way radios operate on local frequencies so that individuals within a certain distance can be contacted. This allows people to be in contact on large sites and to be in two-way communication out 'in the field' where perhaps there are no telephones.

### The Internet

This system of communication is available through computers, and using it you can access information from external organisations. Each organisation needs its own individual website address – for example, www.Funleis.ac.uk

### E-mail

It is possible to write messages and send them through a computer via the telephone line. You will have some of the basic facilities of word processing and very often 'attachments' and pictures or images can be sent if you have additional equipment (such as scanners) to capture the information. Individuals can have their own e-mail addresses, such as FunLeis@Leeds.ac.uk

---

**REMEMBER**

*When using a two-way radio you must wait for the other person to finish transmitting before you respond.*

---

## ACTIVITY

Working on your own, research and list five World Wide Web addresses for sport and recreation organisations. Compare them with the addresses the rest of the group find and compile a useful directory.

---

## CASE STUDY

The management of Funbury Outdoor Adventure Centre have decided to review working practices in their office and reception areas. This is in response to the growth in the centre's business, installation of new equipment (computers, photocopiers, faxes and radio system), and to the fact there are a number of new part-time and full-time staff. A meeting of all staff is called so they can undertake an organisation and methods study to improve internal communication and ensure that all equipment is being used correctly. Many messages are not being passed on, especially as there is no visible record in the office area for staff to see who is out of the centre, where and for how long (although this is recorded in the booking sheets in the manager's office).

Staff are put into small teams to analyse and measure (where appropriate) how they can best access and use the office and to offer solutions for improvement to communication within the centre.

1    What suggestions would you make to improve internal communication and ensure that the staff get messages?

2    Why is it important that centre staff know how best to use the new equipment?

167

## PROGRESS CHECK

1 Why is it important to spend time deciding the layout of an office or reception area?

2 What is the main purpose of organisation and methods?

3 What are the key questions to ask when trying to improve the efficiency and effectiveness of a task?

4 How can you prevent damage to technological equipment?

5 Provide examples of when it would be useful to send a fax, e-mail or use a photocopier

## KEY TERMS

*You need to know the meaning of the following words and phrases. Go back through the chapter to make sure you understand.*

Business systems
Financial and budgetary control
Gross and net profit
Quality standards and procedures
Word processing

Database
Fundraising
Organisation and methods
Spreadsheet

# 9 Working with children (sports leadership)

This chapter covers:
➤ Meeting the needs of children
➤ Planning and preparing to lead activities
➤ Conducting and evaluating your activity
➤ Protecting children and yourself

It is inevitable that, working in sport and recreation, you will work with children. This can be a difficult task that requires many skills, including organisation, planning and patience. However, it can also be very rewarding work as you can have a positive effect on a child's development.

Children are in need of protection from abuse and potential injury and those working with children need to employ precautions to safeguard themselves from difficult situations. This is one consideration of many when attempting to meet the needs of children. By developing your own skills in working with groups you can run effective and enjoyable activities.

Even though this chapter focuses on working with children a sports leader may work with elderly people or with people with special needs. Many of the principles outlined in this chapter will also apply to these groups.

## Meeting the needs of children

No one child is the same and, like adults, they all have individual needs that have to be addressed. There are, however, many common factors to the way children develop. Very often sports and activities have been adapted to assist in their development and to achieve success in their chosen sport or activity. It is likely that, within a group of children and during an activity, you will have a range of special needs and emotions to deal with. This can be accentuated in a sporting activity.

### Child development

It is important to have an understanding of the basic principles of a child's development. This includes physical and psychological factors. Very often the environment that the activity is played in can have an effect on the child's behaviour.

## Physical development

Children obviously grow at different rates, but particularly in early childhood and again during adolescence. This can result in children having apparently disproportionately sized arms, legs and heads, depending on their age. Children of similar age may be completely different physically. Girls and boys differ in the ages at which they have growth spurts and when they reach full adult height. Boys have their final growth spurt around 14, girls nearer 11 or 12; girls reach their full adult height at around 15 but boys not until they are 17 or 18.

Puberty is the stage of sexual development, and the age at which it occurs can vary. Puberty can have emotional effects on children. The strength and weight of children also vary at this stage.

The change in a child's growth (including height, weight, effects of puberty and strength) mean that you will have to take all of these factors into consideration when working with children. It is a good idea, when running activities, to:

- be aware of the physical differences between children and their different growth stages
- try to support those children who look clumsy and uncoordinated
- group children according to height and weight – for example, to make evenly sized groups
- try to encourage children to be aware of differences and to respect them
- be aware of the temperature – children are more vulnerable to extremes of heat and cold than adults
- ensure that children are taking plenty of fluids because they are prone to dehydration
- ensure that they know where the toilets are
- be aware of a child's limits.

> **REMEMBER**
>
> *Never push a child to extremes of exertion and always follow approved practices of exercise.*

## Helping children to learn

Changes in physical development, coupled with the fact that their body's systems have not fully developed, are just two reasons why a child might find it difficult to learn skills. The influences of the home, school and peers can also affect a child's willingness to learn. This is not just about skill development but the ability to understand concepts, rules and structures of activities.

Generally speaking, children learn very quickly as they often have no fear of injury or failure and learn by trial and error. They tend to be good copiers. These factors often depend on their confidence levels and who they listen to – perhaps a parent or a certain teacher.

Some practical steps you can take to help a child learn:

- Help individuals to understand by trying different methods, including demonstration and trial and error
- KISS: Keep It Simple and Small! Do not try to do too much, too quickly
- Ensure success; structure the activity or your feedback to ensure that children feel they have improved or been successful
- Use language that they can understand.

**Developing a positive environment**

As well as making activities fun, creating a positive environment will ensure the children want to continue to participate. You can make the environment more positive by:

- developing activities that stress teamwork
- not emphasising winners and losers – everyone will be aware of who has won and lost
- finding positive things to say to all participants
- never insulting or humiliating a child
- trying to encourage the quick learners to help the slow developers
- teaching children ethics
- offering support to any children who need it
- showing and praising examples of good behaviour and ethics.

These practical tips can also be employed when children are involved in competition. As a leader or coach you have the opportunity to reinforce and focus on positive aspects, and this creates an environment which children want to be a part of.

## Dealing with behavioural issues

The different needs of children, linked to their development, also influence their behaviour. Most people involved in running activities for children will have to deal with children whose behaviour is unacceptable, and who become very emotional about winning and losing. Very often, some behavioural issues can be avoided by improving teamwork.

**Inappropriate behaviour**

It can be difficult for some children to understand what bad behaviour is, if such behaviour elsewhere is condoned. It is important, therefore, to establish as early as possible exactly what you expect from the children involved in your programmes. For example, swimming pools often have clear signs and diagrams about conditions of use of the pool, and you could use a similar method to help children understand what is expected from them. Signs that could be used as a reminder are shown in Figure 9.1.

Ideally, have the children devise and draw the posters; this will encourage them to observe the rules. You are an important role model and therefore you should set an example of the kind of behaviour you expect. Children respond better to clear guidelines and to a person who exerts a positive manner in ensuring that rules are adhered to.

The following ideas will also help in dealing with unacceptable behaviour:

- emphasise and reward good behaviour
- keep groups active – do not spend a lot of time in giving too many instructions, feedback etc.

---

REMEMBER

*Above all else, the most important aspects are to make activities enjoyable and safe.*

---

171

**Figure 9.1**   *Imaginative signs will remind children of good behaviour*

- vary the activities, so the children are less likely to get bored
- give children responsibility – for example, make someone responsible for collecting equipment, or captaining a side.

### Winning and losing

When an activity involves competition there will inevitably be winners and losers. It is important to recognise how children respond to winning and losing. Winners can get over excited, 'cocky', tease others, and even bored if they win all the time. Losers may show emotional outbursts, tears or tantrums. They might want to avoid further competition and even to give up participating. Some children accept both winning and losing with grace.

If responses to success and failure are dealt with efficiently, competition can be very beneficial. It is always a good idea to:

- highlight the positive aspects of individuals who won – but more especially of those who lost
- never place emphasis on the score – children realise who has won
- set extra challenges for those who are constantly successful
- even-out teams and groups in terms of ability, size etc.
- encourage 'sportsmanship' and fair play, especially shaking hands after the game
- offer encouragement and realistic goals for those not achieving
- condition activities so that losing is not continuous
- celebrate effort over attainment.

### Improving teamwork

The advantages of teamwork apply as much to children as they do to adults. However, teamwork is often a very difficult concept for a child to understand. It is something that has to be constantly encouraged. There are many activities that do not involve competition but are based around the co-operation of all those taking part in trying to achieve preset goals. In order to make teamwork a greater part of your activities you can

- give children individual tasks and ensure each child understands the importance of the role of each member of the team
- clearly explain the activity, the rules and purpose of the game
- keep the rules and responsibilities simple and the size of the teams small.

| ACTIVITY | Devise an activity that will help children develop the concept of teamwork. Draw diagrams to help illustrate your idea. |
|---|---|

## Adapting sports and activities

We often find ourselves working in an adult environment, where the facilities, such as sports halls, and equipment, such as soccer goals, are too large and not always suitable for children. Some children are better developed and more able than others and tend to monopolise a sport or activity. You can adapt the rules and equipment to ensure that your objectives are achieved. Conditioning the game also can help to ensure everyone's participation.

**Changing the rules**

The first thing to know is the rules of the sport or activity so that you can change them if necessary. The safety of the children should be the primary objective, although enjoyment is important. Follow these general principles:

- keep physical contact to a minimum, such as no tackling in rugby
- reduce the playing time of the activity, making shorter periods. This will allow you to make further changes as required
- change the rules to ensure there is more success, such as awarding points for attempts on goal or basket as well as for goal, or basket, scored. You could also change the measures of success and failure – for example, in cricket you might allow a person to continue to bat after he or she has been bowled out
- reduce the size of the playing area. This can help to reduce fatigue and improve your control over the players
- reduce the numbers of people in a team.

REMEMBER

*It is likely that you will make mistakes, but use these to improve your ability to work with children.*

GOOD PRACTICE ▷ *Contact the governing body of your chosen sport and ask for their adapted rules for children and the suggested equipment to use.*

**Figure 9.2**  *Make sure the equipment is adapted to the needs of the users*

## Using the right equipment

Much equipment is designed for adults (handles of racquets, weight and size of balls), although most sports do have equipment for children. This is usually softer, smaller and lighter than that which adults use. Using the right equipment is not only safer but can also help to teach children the right technique when you move on to coaching.

Once again, the key to success is in choosing the right equipment. Children should be able to hit objects, kick, throw and catch in accordance with their chosen activity. The speed of the game can also be reduced, when required, by using specialist balls such as those made of foam. There are many activities that can be played using the following equipment, which should be part of any organisation's store room:

- bean bags
- hula hoops
- coils
- range of balls – soft, medium, large, tennis etc.
- bibs
- cones, discs, markers
- baskets, boxes, containers
- adjustable nets and posts
- racquets (such as short tennis), rounders bats
- chalk.

## Conditioning the activity

It is likely that, even after changing the rules and selecting the right equipment, you are not achieving your goals, such as success or involvement of all those taking part. This is where you can 'condition' the game. This means imposing your own rules and conditions, all the time, or some of the time or directed only at some of the children. For example, two talented boys playing five-a-side football may be monopolising the ball and scoring at will, and the other children are not enjoying the game. You could condition the game to ensure that the two boys are put on opposing teams and restricted to one half of the pitch. This allows other participants, if they wish, to have the ball in the other half and makes it more competitive for the more talented boys. Conditions can be put on anything, depending on your goals. If you want to develop teamwork, points can be awarded for passes and/or encouragement.

## PROGRESS CHECK

1   What are the main differences in physical development between boys and girls?

2   What are the main influences on how children learn?

3   Identify five methods for developing a positive environment when putting on activities for children.

4   How can you remind children about how to behave?

5   List three ideas that will help children cope with winning or losing.

6   What does 'conditioning' an activity mean? Provide two examples to help illustrate your answer.

## CASE STUDY

The Saturday morning open activity session at Funbury Leisure Centre involves 25 8–11-year-old children. Two sports leaders are running the one-hour session. During the bench ball game (a mixture of basketball and netball), which is usually the children's favourite game, it is noticed that one child shows unacceptable outbursts when he loses the ball. The session is also being affected by two children's domination of the game because they are more developed and skilful than the other participants.

One sports leader takes the child who is showing outbursts and discovers he is very competitive and does not like losing. The leader emphasises that the session is fun based and points out all the positive aspects of the child's performance as well as explaining that even the greatest players lose. On returning back to the game the child loses possession of the ball. He does not show any outbursts and the leader praises the child.

The leaders change the rules of the game for the next match, putting the two strong players on opposing sides and restricting their movement to one side of the court. This allows them to compete against each other and allows the other participants to play in the same game but have the freedom to find space, should they wish, away from the dominant players.

1   What other options are there for the leaders to condition the game?
2   How should they finish the activity so no one leaves feeling they have failed?

## Planning and preparing to lead activities

Whether you are coaching or leading activities for children it is likely to be in groups. Many governing bodies and local authorities have suggested ratios for leaders and numbers of participants, depending on the activity, ages of the children and the facility. Groups of 15–25 are not uncommon. Good planning and preparation and a knowledge of the variety of sports and activities at your disposal will ensure you plan a safe, fluent and flexible programme. There are also practical steps that can be taken to avoid injury.

### Planning and preparation

Time spent on planning and preparation is always time well spent. It involves gathering as much information as possible on who you will be working with and the facilities you will be using. You can then try to set objectives and choose equipment and a plan to meet these objectives.

**Knowing your personnel**

Sometimes the people coming to the activity will be unknown to you but you should be able to find out who is going to take part in the activities from booking sheets and application forms. The types of information you should know about the participants include:

- age
- ability
- experience
- special needs
- reason for participating
- gender
- total numbers.

This information will help you to plan and prepare activities to suit the children's needs. The key information is how many people are participating and their ages: knowing this, you can ensure safe practice by having suitable facilities and members of staff. If you are unable to find all of this information in advance you should discover it as soon as is possible. This may involve communicating with parents and guardians, who are usually paying for their child's participation and have their interests at heart.

**Facilities and equipment**

Even though facilities are booked in advance, they should be checked before use. You must know exactly what facilities you have and their size. You should carry out a safety check before use and eliminate any hazards. If there are any problems or if you note some damage you should report it immediately. You should also explore how flexible the facilities are, such as how many areas and courts can be made. It is essential to know the procedures for dealing with changes in the weather, and any other procedures specific to the organisation.

It is also essential to know exactly what equipment you will require and to check what equipment is available. Be specific – know exactly the numbers and type of equipment you are going to have. You *must* have a clipboard and pen, whistle and watch.

**Figure 9.3** *Be familiar with the facility in which you're working – for example, know where the fire exits are!*

GOOD PRACTICE ▷ *If you have never previously used the facilities and equipment, take a visit to the facility and familiarise yourself with it, especially the positions of fire exits and evacuation procedures.*

## Preparing notes and session plans

This involves taking your information about the participants, equipment and the facilities and making notes outlining what activities you are going to run in the time you have available. The session plan should allow for flexibility and is to be used only as a guide. If an activity is going well and being enjoyed by the group, you may want to continue with it, even though your allotted time has elapsed.

It is worth using a pre-printed form (Figure 9.4) to make comments and evaluate the activity, so you know what parts were successful. File it and use it as a reference for future use.

Have your session plan on a clipboard so you can refer to it and write comments on it easily.

### Sports and activities

To be able to run activities and to improvise you need to develop your knowledge of a range of sports and activities. This can also help to gain the respect of children if you know the rules and personalities of traditional sports. Having a reserve of adapted games will help make improvisation appear as if you have planned in advance.

*Funbury Leisure Centre*

**Activity List**

Date: ........................................ Time: ........................................

Length of activity: ........................................

Group size: ........................................ Age range: ........................................

Any special needs: ........................................

Equipment needed: ........................................

Warm up: ........................................

Activities – comments: ........................................
........................................

Feedback: ........................................

Changes for next time: ........................................

**Figure 9.4** *Activity list*

**Traditional sports**

There are many sports which form the basis of our teaching curriculum and receive most exposure through the media:

- athletics
- badminton
- basketball
- cricket
- football
- hockey
- netball
- rugby
- swimming
- tennis.

These are likely to be the most popular activities.

The governing bodies of these sports have policies aimed at developing participation for children, and have adapted their rules and equipment to suit children's needs. They also provide an opportunity for leaders to develop skills in leading activities in their chosen sport. These are often called Leaders' Awards and provide a stepping stone to coaching awards. Some of the sports tend to be more popular for girls and boys – for example, netball for the former and rugby for the latter.

All of these sports can be enjoyed by both boys and girls and can be used to develop teamwork, co-ordination, and skill. When running general activities for children, avoid staying with one or two of the popular sports, unless that has been specifically requested. Other sports, such as

- kabadi
- water polo
- korfball
- roller hockey
- handball
- baseball

can also be fun and exciting and have the advantage of being different and challenging.

**Games and improvised sports**

Improvised sports are games which have less formalised rules and are enjoyed by children from an early age. Games such as 'Tag', 'Simon Says' and 'Relays' are popular everywhere and have different names depending on the part of the country in which they are played. It is important to develop a 'bank' of these games. Many can be used as part of a warm up or cool down. They can also be adapted to include some elements of the traditional sports. As an example, in 'Relays' each team has to take it in turns to run to a given point and return for their next team mate to go. Adapt 'Relays' to a sport by making participants footballers dribbling a ball to a given point, or hockey players using a hockey stick and ball.

**ACTIVITY**

Improvise an activity using a traditional sport that will help to increase the likelihood of scoring and thus bring greater success for children.

**Developing your knowledge**

It is important to develop an understanding of sports and the teams and personalities involved with them. This can be done through reading information from governing bodies and reading and watching the media.

You can also learn by observing others. Have a notebook and pen handy to record games and activities. These notes can then be typed up and filed under appropriate headings such as warm up, stretches and team games. You should also include diagrams to help illustrate how the games are played.

GOOD PRACTICE ▷ *Observe somebody leading activities, then approach them to ask further questions as to variances and adaptations on the games and activities you have seen.*

## Preventing injury

The general health and safety procedures discussed in Chapter 3 should be followed when running activities for children. You should constantly be assessing risks and removing any hazards. There are, however, other practical steps to follow to ensure injury is prevented as far as reasonably possible. This involves performing a warm up and cool down, monitoring the activity and ensuring that children do not suffer overuse injuries.

**Warming up and cooling down**

Before warming up, each child should be checked to see if he or she is wearing clothing and footwear suitable for the activity. Participants should not be wearing jewellery, such as watches, or chewing gum.

Children and adults should warm up before taking part in sport or recreation. A warm up is simply the preparation of our bodies for more rigorous exercise. More specifically, it

- prepares our energy systems for exercise
- warms the muscles, making them more flexible and less prone to injury
- prepares us mentally for the forthcoming activities.

The warm up should commence with gentle exercise that raises the body temperature. These exercises should be in line with the principles of working with children – sending children on long runs around the facility is certainly inappropriate. There are many activities that can involve a gradual increase in body temperature where you are in control, such as 'Simon says'. Once the heart rate is higher, some stretching work can begin. Children tend to be more flexible than adults, but stretching not only prepares the specific muscles for exercise but also teaches children

---

**— REMEMBER —**

*Always be ready to listen and learn from others who are successful.*

---

179

good habits. When leading the stretch, stand so that everyone can see you, and go round the group ensuring good practice. Initially, stretches should be slow and held at a position where muscle tension can be felt. Hold for a few seconds, release and repeat.

Before the session is completed, a cool down should be performed by each person. This helps to prevent soreness, which often occurs after physical activity. The format of the cool down can follow the same routine as the warm up, but in reverse. It should therefore include stretching and reduction of the heart rate to its resting pulse rate. Cooling down also provides an ideal opportunity to feed back and provide information to the group.

## ACTIVITY

Devise a safe and fun warm up for a group of children of mixed age and gender.

GOOD PRACTICE ▷ *Ensure that no bouncing occurs during stretching until a thorough warm up and static stretches have been performed.*

---

**REMEMBER**

*At no time should you ever leave the group unattended or without a suitable ratio of supervisors to children.*

**Monitoring the activities and the children**

You will have selected the facility, the area, the equipment and the activities that are suitable for your group. However, during the activities many changes can occur that may affect the safety of the participants – for example:

- the weather may change, becoming too cold, wet or sunny
- the playing surface may alter, making it unsafe to play on
- behaviour becomes unruly or uncontrollably aggressive
- the participants may behave in a way detrimental to their development or making injury likely.

It is important to keep your concentration for the duration of the programme. You should monitor the children to see how they are coping with the session. If the temperature is too high, plenty of breaks should be given to allow children to replace lost fluids.

GOOD PRACTICE ▷ *Should any child suffer an injury during the session, make all the children sit where they are. This ensures that no further incidents can occur whilst you are attending to the injured person.*

180

**Figure 9.5**  *Don't neglect a class, even if a child is injured*

### Overuse injuries

It is the responsibility of all those working with children to be aware of the possibility of overuse injuries. Such injuries are found in players who over-exercise specific parts of their body. You might simply be supervising a swimming session and recognise a child who comes twice a day to practise with a team (remember, this is not about preventing children from participating or enjoying themselves but ensuring that they do not injure themselves in the long term). The appropriate action is to communicate with the parents, supervisors, teachers and coaches to ensure that the child follows a safe programme. Possible signs of overuse injuries are:

● stiffness or aching, which has come on gradually throughout the activity

● pain when certain actions are performed

● tenderness in the affected area

● a recurrent problem.

If you think that a child is exhibiting symptoms you should inform the parent/guardian and seek medical advice.

## PROGRESS CHECK

1   Identify two methods for starting and stopping a group.

2   Why is it important to take care when selecting teams?

3   What information should you ideally have about your participants before your activities commence?

4   What are the advantages of producing notes and plans for your sessions?

5   Why is it important to warm up and cool down before activities commence?

# Conducting and evaluating your activity

Planning and preparation, as we have discussed, are the keys to success of running activities. Organisation and control of the group are also important. The activities should be well structured but allow for flexibility. An evaluation will provide you with a useful source of information, so as to make improvements for the future.

## Organisation and control

Working with groups of children can be fun and rewarding but at the same time very demanding. By being organised and having control of the group you will be able to run the activity much more smoothly and successfully. This organisation stems from the ability to start and stop the group, selecting the teams and being able to communicate effectively.

### Starting and stopping the group

It is important to be able to stop and start group activities so you can communicate information when you start the session and give further information as and when you want during the session. Stop the group only when you have something important to say. When you work with a group, you should stand in a position where everyone can see you and where you can see them (Figure 9.6). The group should be in front of you and, if you are outside, do not let the group look into the sun or face other activities. Always make sure you are heard and do not keep the group together for too long, especially if the weather is poor.

You can use a command or an action, and should tell the children in advance exactly what it means. For example, putting an arm in the air could mean 'stop what you are doing and come in close to the leader'. Always using phrases like 'you have five seconds to come into me' which can work very well, especially in your first session. You can stop the group by using phrases such as 'Stop and stand still' or 'Thank you, look and listen'. A whistle can also be used effectively but should not be used in isolation, as it can become very impersonal.

### Selecting teams

Having uneven teams can greatly influence the outcome of your activities. It can lead to the problems previously discussed in constantly winning and losing. Also, many children want to be in the same team as their friends. The key thing is to be flexible and willing to make changes when required, and not to make individuals feel inadequate or penalise them for achieving.

It is probably not a good idea to let children pick their own teams on a regular basis. It can be especially bad for the last person to be picked. Selecting teams by height can be a useful way. Get all the children to organise themselves in order of height and to stand between two points or along a line, then count the total number of participants and divide by the number of teams you require. The tallest is in team one, the next in team two and so on. The last team is allotted two children and then you place individuals in reverse order through the teams until you reach team number one. This can be done quickly and without any fuss. Explain to the children why you are selecting teams this way. Another good way of selecting teams could be by shoe size. For general games and activities,

> ## REMEMBER
>
> *Always ensure you can be heard by asking a question of a person at the back of the group.*

**Figure 9.6**   *Make sure all the class can see you*

selecting by the colour of their tops or by their house number (e.g. odd and even) demonstrates equality.

### Effective communication

It is important to have good and clear methods of communication to control the group and to issue instructions. All communications should be given with authority. It can be effective to involve children in decision making but, generally, instructions need to be given by the leader.

You should speak slowly and see if children understand by observation rather than by asking 'Do you understand?'. However, asking children questions can be a great way of developing their discovery and team skills – for example, 'can you show five ways of balancing without standing on two feet?'

It is important to communicate in a variety of ways, using different signs, signals and voice tones. All information should be conveyed with a positive attitude and with enthusiasm. Being well presented and showing you are organised communicates positive statements about you. You should also be willing to listen to others.

**ACTIVITY**

Working with a small group, and without talking or writing, try to organise a group into a single line with the person with the lowest house number at the front and the highest number at the back.

## Delivering the activity

Each activity requires a beginning, middle and an end. You have to keep to your schedule and get the balance between competition and participation. During the session you also have responsibility for motivating and encouraging others.

### Beginning, middle and end

Having a clear structure to your activity not only helps you manage your time well but also enables you to control the intensity of the session. The beginning can be used for your warm up and for giving instructions whilst the children are stretching. Select groups and begin the activities. The main part of your session is the activity itself. This is where children are likely to be most excited and enjoying their participation. Time should be left at the end for a 'cool down': this also provides an opportunity for feedback to and from the participants.

Timekeeping is important. You should apportion time for administration duties, such as registering in and out, or handing out prizes. The beginning and end of your session have less flexibility than the middle. This is to allow you an opportunity to extend successful activities or shorten and change ones that are not working as well.

### Competition and participation

Depending on the nature of the group, the activities will involve forms of teamwork and competition. The important aspect, however, is participation. Children have enrolled on your programme to take part in the activities offered. This means that the main part of your session must involve all the children. Some competitions, such as knockout, will exclude children who are not successful.

Careful consideration must be given to the competitive element. Winners and losers should be given an equal amount of participation time. This is not to say there should never be a final, but if participation is the key one-off finals should be infrequently held. The level of enjoyment is often higher for the children who are able to participate in the final. Where children are waiting for their turn, simple tasks can be set to maintain their level of interest, such as individual ball skills or throwing and catching. This should take place at a safe distance from the main activity. People watching could also be encouraged to join in by cheering and encouraging all participants.

### Improvisation

Effective communication, control and organisation are the foundations for delivering a successful session. However, improvisation is a quality that all those working in sport and recreation need to develop. Improvisation is about responding to changes to your plans caused by:

- facilities being double-booked and having a reduced or different space to work in
- increases or decreases in the number of participants
- equipment being inappropriate, unavailable or damaged
- the ability of the participants differing from that for which you had planned
- activities that are not being enjoyed by the children.

184

The ability to improvise comes from experience of working with children and the knowledge of activities and games. It is also about how you react to changes in circumstances. Never panic or let the children think you have lost control. A key to success is keeping children active. Be willing to change quickly and with authority.

## ACTIVITY

Working in pairs, design an activity for a group of 15 10-year-old children. You have a small sports hall, three empty drinks bottles, three bean bags and one toilet roll.

### Evaluation and feedback

During the session you will constantly be making observations as to what is successful and what requires change. However, after the activity you should apportion time to reflect and evaluate what happened and make changes accordingly. Very often it is not possible to evaluate straight after an activity but think about the good and bad parts. Jot them down and expand on them later at a more convenient time.

**Evaluating the activity and yourself**

This has to be done alongside the set objectives, which should include:

- making the activity safe
- making it fun
- involving everyone.

No two sessions will ever run exactly the same way, even if the same children are involved. This is why you should never base changes on one session, unless they are necessary for safety reasons. In evaluating your activity, you should not only ask yourself whether it was successful but should also consider how you could adapt or improve it. Try to involve the participants and get their feedback on the parts they liked or disliked. If they dislike the warm up, you might need to explain to them its purpose and involve them more in leading or designing what is being done.

It is always a good idea to discuss your activities with a colleague. This shares good and bad practice and lets someone else see what you are doing from another perspective. You could invite colleagues to watch you lead activities, and allow time to feedback and discuss it with you. You should also reflect on the role you played in the activity. Ask yourself the following questions:

- Was I prepared and planned?
- Did I stick to the plan?
- If not, why not?
- Was I able to adapt to situations that arose?
- Did I communicate effectively? For example, did the children respond to my instructions and actions?
- Was my knowledge appropriate and up to date?

### Making changes

Following evaluation you should be prepared to make changes where appropriate. Even activities and sessions that are successful should be changed to ensure variety and prevent boredom.

Making changes will benefit both you and the children. It helps to prevent sessions becoming stale and predictable, and maintains enthusiasm. The principles and structure of your activities can remain the same but, if you are working with the same children, you could vary your warm up, main activities or cool-down period. This may simply involve adding new stretches to the warm up, or allowing the children some unstructured time to create their own fun. This 'planned recreation' is also very important.

### Providing feedback to participants

At the beginning and end of a session, you may wish to give feedback to participants on positive or negative aspects, or simply to explain why you are making changes. If you are providing feedback, always finish on a positive note, so the group leaves with this foremost in their minds. It is always a good idea to review what the group has done even if it was an unstructured activity. Children always appreciate it when you show you have taken an interest in what they have been doing.

## CASE STUDY

The Saturday morning activity sessions for children of 12 years old and over have always been popular and have included traditional sports such as cricket, rugby, hockey and tennis. The sessions are to be expanded to attract children aged 5–11. This means that leaders will have to adapt these sports and improvise to suit the age group.

After contacting the relevant governing bodies, you have received information and specific equipment, such as special racquets for short tennis, arrives in time for the first session. The session goes well but there is a huge gap between the abilities of the participants. The leaders meet soon after the session and evaluate the feedback they have received, the activities offered and their role.

1   How can the session be organised to allow beginners and those more able to participate fully and enjoy the session in safety?

2   Why is it important to evaluate the session immediately and to continue to monitor and evaluate further sessions?

## PROGRESS CHECK

1   What are the main general activities of the beginning, middle and end of your session?

2   Why is the skill of 'improvisation' so important when working with children?

3   How, and why, should you develop your knowledge of sports?

4   Why is it good practice to evaluate your sessions?

5   When is it appropriate to make changes to your activities?

# Protecting children and yourself

It is the responsibility of all those working with children to protect them from abuse. There are many types of abuse and it is important to be able to recognise the signs, and know what action to take if you suspect it is occurring. You must also examine your own practice and avoid any situation that might be misinterpreted as being abusive. There is no need to become paranoid but it is important to raise your awareness of the welfare of the children you are working with.

## Protecting children from abuse

To deal safely and effectively with possible concerns about child abuse, you must know your responsibilities under the Children's Act 1989. Develop your knowledge of supporting agencies and organisations to enable you to understand the types of abuse, and know how to report and respond to a child's disclosure of it.

### The Children's Act 1989

This came into force in 1991 and has the care and upbringing of children as its main focus. As well as families, the act applies to people working in the voluntary, public and commercial sectors, including recreational services. The Act puts duties upon local authorities to hold a register of all activities for children under the age of 8 where

- activities are supervised
- (and) activities are held on their premises
- (and) last over two hours
- (and) take place more than six times a year
- (and) are inspected at least once per year.

The register includes the nature, location and quality of the activities. For employees leading activities the implications are that the authority has to be satisfied with all the people it employs to work with children. The authority must assess the suitability of its employees to ensure they are a 'fit' person. This assessment includes

- previous experience
- relevant qualifications and/or training
- ability to provide safe and consistent care
- knowledge of and attitude towards multicultural issues
- commitment to treat all children as individuals and with equal concern
- physical health
- mental stability, integrity and flexibility
- criminal history involving children.

### Signs and types of abuse

Abuse can mean different things to different children. A child may be hurt or neglected and may not realise that what is happening to them is abuse. Very often the abuser is known to the child. The main forms of abuse are listed below.

- *Physical abuse*: adults physically hurt or injure children. This may involve hitting, shaking and biting. Providing alcohol and drugs to children is classified as physical abuse. Physical abuse can often leave signs, such as bruising and red marks

187

- *Sexual abuse*: children are persuaded or forced into sexual acts for adults' gratification. Showing and encouraging children to look at pornographic material is also considered sexual abuse. Evidence of this may be very difficult to detect by observation alone
- *Emotional abuse*: children are not given any love or affection. It also covers children who are constantly shouted at, threatened, or made to feel rejected. Signs can include changes in personality where a child appears to be more nervous and withdrawn than usual
- *Neglect*: adults fail to meet a child's basic needs such as food, clothing, or cleanliness. Signs of neglect can often be very difficult to detect and it is important that conclusions are not made before more facts are discovered.

It is important to note that there are other forms of abuse, which are less common but none the less serious. These include:

- educational neglect
- Munchausen by proxy
- failure to thrive
- psychological abuse
- organised abuse.

Recognising abuse is difficult, especially as children tend to receive cuts and bruises in everyday behaviour – e.g. through sport. However, you should be aware of changes in behaviour which are unusual for the child or a child of that age in their development, such as:

- aggressive behaviour
- precocious sexual behaviour or knowledge
- a fear of adults or other children
- loss of weight and/or general eating problems
- difficulty in concentrating
- being withdrawn.

### Responding to a child's disclosure of abuse

One of the main ways you may discover abuse of a child is by the child partly or completely telling you. You must listen to the child and take him or her seriously. It is important you respond promptly and calmly to any information given. You should let the child know that you will have to inform appropriate people, and tell him or her that these people will provide help and support. You may be able to find out more information by talking sensitively with the child, but keep questions to a minimum and do not ask leading questions. Do not make promises you cannot keep and try to communicate with the child at his or her pace.

GOOD PRACTICE ▷     *When dealing with a child disclosing information on abuse, always offer reassurance and do not apportion blame.*

### Reporting signs of possible abuse

If you suspect that a child is being abused you must take action quickly to report the information, as well as any signs and indicators of possible abuse, including dates and times.

- Keep calm and do not take hasty actions
- Record the dialogue between you and the child immediately. This should include the time and date and should be signed
- Inform your line manager, as soon as possible, who will take further action
- Do not discuss the matter with any other individual

---

**ACTIVITY**

In small groups discuss the advantages and disadvantages of ensuring all those working with children have training in counselling skills.

---

## Avoiding difficult situations

We are in a society where some practices and procedures that were once approved are now thought by some people to be inappropriate – such as supporting children on gymnastic equipment or assisting young children to get changed. It is important to take precautions to safeguard yourself, by avoiding risky situations, working with individuals or dealing with children who are over-affectionate.

### Working in safe situations

You must always work in safe situations with children (such as never working alone with a child); this not only puts the needs of the child first but takes into account your needs. Never leave yourself open to accusations of abuse. Many sporting organisations provide guidelines for safe practice when working with children. Avoid unnecessary contact with children and look to parents for support when children need personal assistance. Try to avoid working alone with children and, whenever possible, work with a colleague when taking children's activities.

### Working one-to-one

Inevitably there will be times when you have to work individually with a child. This may arise from a need to give feedback about his or her performance or behaviour. You should always make sure that

- this is done within sight of other people, and preferably within earshot
- another adult is present
- the language used is appropriate and cannot be misinterpreted
- no contact is made with the child that can be misinterpreted.

If you need to improve technique with a child try to use demonstrations first. Any contact with a child should be impersonal and in the presence of others.

> **REMEMBER**
>
> *When dealing with children who are informing you of possible abuse confidentiality is essential, apart from informing your line manager immediately.*

### Dealing with affectionate children

Sometimes you will be faced with a child (usually of the opposite gender) who has a crush on you or sees you as a 'hero' figure. This may initially be quite flattering but can easily lead to difficult situations. It is always a good idea not to handle the situation alone. Inform someone else of the situation such as the child's parents or a colleague. Do not encourage the child. Try to alternate with other colleagues in taking the activities.

It should still be a goal of all those working with children to earn their respect and trust.

## PROGRESS CHECK

1  What are the main implications of the Children's Act for those working with children?

2  What are the main types of abuse and how can they be recognised?

3  If a child informs you that he or she is being abused, what should you do?

4  When working one to one with a child, what should you first make sure of?

5  What action can you take with a child who is showing undue affection for you?

## KEY TERMS

*You need to know the meaning of the following words and phrases. Go back through the chapter to make sure you understand.*

Child development

Conditioning the activity

Feedback

Monitoring activities

The Children's Act

Child protection

Evaluation

Improvisation

Overuse injuries

# 10 Sports coaching

This chapter covers:
➤ The role of the coach
➤ Preparing for coaching sessions
➤ Conducting coaching sessions
➤ Looking after your athletes

People become coaches for various reasons, but everyone should have the same goal – to help people become better performers in their sport, in a safe environment. Whether you are coaching small children on a part-time basis or coaching a Sunday league men's hockey team, as a coach you are in a position of responsibility and are able to influence the people you coach. It should therefore be your goal to develop athletes who comply with the principles of good ethical practice.

Coaching is similar to leadership and involves a lot of the principles outlined in Chapter 9. However, there is more intervention in the sessions and planning becomes more detailed and long term. A sports coach also requires more skill and knowledge of a particular sport and an ability to gain the best performance from the athletes.

## The role of the coach

A coach is a role model who can socially, morally, emotionally and technically influence the people he or she is coaching, especially the young. The role of a coach is changing constantly to meet the needs of the team or individuals. Being able to communicate, analyse, solve problems and evaluate performance are just some of the 'key skills' required for a successful coach. The more knowledge a coach has, the better the decisions he or she will be able to make when using their skills.

The role of any coach begins with setting good examples of behaviour and attitude. Very often a coach has to be multidisciplined and play different roles for different people. He or she should also be trying to encourage athletes to develop their own learning.

### Being a role model

A coach is in a position of responsibility, with the ability to affect the behaviour of participants, especially young children, who are more easily influenced by successful sportsmen and women whom they may wish to emulate. Perhaps unknowingly, a coach acts as a role model and how you act and what you say may be copied by others. Even adults will respond better to coaches who present themselves in a positive manner.

Coaches have their own individual styles but all should
- look the part – wear the appropriate clothing and use the right equipment
- be well presented and smart
- be a good timekeeper, which involves starting and finishing on time
- always appear enthusiastic – groups always respond well to coaches who are obviously enjoying their work
- keep any vices, such as smoking, out of sight of children. Cigarette smoke can often be smelt on the breath and clothes and gives a very negative impression
- use language appropriate for the age group, including good manners.

Being a positive role model is not about being a perfect individual, but about having a set of sound principles on which to develop your own style and personality in your coaching.

---

**ACTIVITY**   Working in pairs, discuss each other's style and personality and offer practical suggestions on how they may improve.

---

## The changing role

The role of a coach is to improve performance through a programme of safe and structured practices. To do this effectively you must create a positive environment in order to try to identify and meet the needs of individuals. This can often be achieved through planning and preparation and the ability to communicate effectively with your participants.

It is the responsibility of the coach not only to be a positive role model but also to develop good ethical practice. Coaches should
- obtain recognised coaching qualifications
- promote fair play and respect other players, competitors and officials
- follow standard and approved practice, covering safe practice. Always make the safety of participants a priority
- develop participants to become good winners and good losers.

---

GOOD PRACTICE ▷   *Develop links with specialists who may be able to help you – such as physiotherapists, dietitians, other coaches and officials.*

---

**Figure 10.1** *The expert in everything*

The role of the coach is constantly changing. To keep up with new techniques and developments a coach also has to be a student and a scientist. Because you must keep good records and comply with legal duties, you also have to be an administrator and understand the law. Very often athletes come to a coach for advice and support and you feel like a social worker, but you should always be a friend. You should always seek other sources of help to assist you.

## Developing self-learning

The coach cannot be with the team or individuals 24 hours a day, 7 days a week. Part-time coaches may see their athletes only once or twice a week, for an hour at a time. This makes improving performance very difficult. The coach should encourage the performer to take responsibility for his or her own actions and to develop goals. This can be extended to include self learning. By discussing with the performer what you hope to achieve and how you are going to do it, he or she can understand the basis of self learning. For example, athletes can be taught how to practise well, warm up and cool down properly, to recognise major faults and so on. This enables them to maintain their programme when the coach is not in attendance.

It is important therefore to encourage individuals to take on responsibility. Ask questions about their performance and make them reflect and comment on the positive and negative aspects. This will also help to develop good communication with your performers and create a learning environment.

## Knowledge that a coach requires

Most successful coaches continue to look for more knowledge to improve their coaching. It is essential to have knowledge of the most up-to-date rules and regulations of the game, and the ethics of the sport and of coaching in general. It is also essential to understand the basic technical and tactical aspects of the game. People who also have a sound understanding of the science of their sport usually have a greater advantage.

193

### Technique and skill

It is essential that any coach understands the basic techniques used in the sport. This is how the fundamental movements are optionally performed. Skill is said to be the 'application of technique under pressure'. An example is a hockey player learning sound stick control, dribbling round cones. He may show good technique but when faced with real opponents he has more to think about as the environment around him is constantly changing. The coach must be able to provide clear and technically accurate explanations to enable performers to understand the techniques to be used. It is also essential to be able to recognise errors and offer technically correct solutions.

The coach not only needs to understand the techniques of the sport but must also have the knowledge of the range of methods of how to improve an athlete's performance. This is discussed further on page 208.

### Tactics

Coaching to improve performance can be truly measured only by playing against an opponent. This tests the performer's technique and skill. Success involves many other factors, such as motivation and decision-making by officials. Tactics and a game strategy can also have a major influence on success.

The coach may want knowledge of the opponents, the environment and the officials to formulate tactics and a strategy to beat the opposition, such as:

- systems for attacking and defending
- set situations, e.g. line out in rugby, or the serve in badminton
- tempo of the game: fast, slow, as it develops
- positional play: players on a team or areas of the playing area.

Even in individual sports such as swimming and gymnastics, coaches will look to employ tactics depending on their performer, the environment and the opposition.

## ACTIVITY

In small groups observe a sport of your choice. Try to identify the tactics that were used by both competitors or teams. Half of the group should examine the systems of defending and the other half the systems of attacking.

### Sports science

This is often more the realm of an advanced coach. He or she will try to develop their knowledge of scientific influences on performance, such as:

- anatomy and physiology, which include the skeleton, joints and muscles and the heart and respiratory system
- biomechanics, which looks at the mechanics of movement
- exercise physiology, including energy, exercise and fitness
- psychology, which examines the learning of skills and individual differences.

Even an advanced coach would not expect to be an expert in all of the above, but a knowledge of the basic fundamentals is important at all levels of coaching.

All these aspects are often no substitute for fitness or skill but can allow players to reach their full potential. In some sports there is a small margin between winning and losing and good application of sports science may be the difference that is needed to win.

## Skills required of a coach

In many sports there are successful coaches who have not played to the same level they are coaching. However, they are a success because they have developed their knowledge and have the ability to communicate effectively with their performers. The coach also needs to develop an ability to analyse the performers and solve problems. This can often be achieved through the process of evaluation.

### Communication

Good coaches are good communicators, not just in transferring knowledge to participants but in developing interpersonal skills and maintaining relationships. In previous chapters we have examined the methods and principles of communicating which are needed in the coaching environment. A coach must be able to

- gain control of the group
- provide clear instructions
- develop two-way communication methods with performers, checking that players understand by asking questions
- give feedback on performances
- motivate the performers
- understand the needs of the performers.

Effective communication is often found in positive, supportive environments where athletes can be involved in the decision-making process and are able to handle the pressures that may be put on them.

### Analysing and problem solving

Even at foundation level coaches analyse and attempt to solve problems. This may be something as simple as finding out why a child cannot hit a tennis ball or why your Sunday league football team cannot defend well from a corner.

The ability to analyse a problem is a skill that is heavily dependent on knowledge and gathering of information. This enables you to assess the strengths and weaknesses of your performers as well as those of the opposition. There are many methods available to coaches, in addition to their ability to observe at first hand. Use of technical machinery, such as a video, and testing equipment, such as a speed gun, provides more detailed information.

The use of statistics must also be acknowledged as an important part of a coach's skill to analyse situations. Statistics provide raw data on measurable aspects of the game. However, they do not provide the whole story and must not be used in isolation. A team that has had more possession of the ball, has made fewer errors and spent more time in their opponents' half, may still be losing. Statistics, used correctly, can help to analyse performances. The skill of the coach is to recognise problem areas and offer solutions.

> **REMEMBER**
> *Statistics must be used in conjunction with other methods of measuring performance such as participant feedback.*

**Evaluating**

Evaluation is best done against a set of objectives. As a coach you should reflect on each coaching session that you take, and have specific goals for each session. You can then use the following evaluation criteria to assess each session:

- Were the objectives for the session met?
- If not, why not? What can be done differently in the future?
- Were the performers motivated, intense, positive, supportive and did they use teamwork (where appropriate)?
- How did the player perform?
- How did you perform as the coach?
- Which methods and instructions worked?
- Which part of the session did not work?
- What analysis may be useful for comparisons, previous and future?
- What improvements have been made?
- What are the views of the athletes?

*Funbury Leisure Centre*

**Evaluation**

Session: ............ Time: ............ Coach: ............

Group details: ............

Equipment used: ............

Key objectives:

1. ............
2. ............
3. ............

Safety objective met: yes/no

If not, why not: ............

Organisation ............ Rating 1–5

Player's performance ............

Instructions/demonstrations ............

Communication ............

Analysis ............

Individual needs met ............

Team needs met ............

Enjoyment of session ............

Comments for future: ............

***Figure* 10.2** *Evaluation form*

Recording such details on an evaluation form (Figure 10.2) will help the coach to make an overall evaluation, from which he or she must be able to construct suggestions and agree areas and methods for improving further performance.

## CASE STUDY

Funbody's Club runs a fitness circuit, which incorporates free weights, ergometers and multigym equipment. An instructor runs the session and attempts to improve individual techniques as well as helping participants achieve their own pre-agreed exercise and fitness goals.

The instructor provides clear instructions on how to use the equipment and perform exercises with good and safe technique. Demonstrations are used to communicate this effectively. Each session is followed by an analysis of any problems and a review that goals are being achieved.

1  What important qualities and knowledge should the instructor have?

2  How can the instructor develop self-learning in the participants, so that they can help to monitor their own performances?

## PROGRESS CHECK

1  What are the key aspects to being a positive role model?

2  Why is the role of the coach constantly changing?

3  Why should it be the goal of all coaches to develop self-learning by participants?

4  How do technique, skill and tactics differ? Give examples.

5  List five examples of the criteria to be used in evaluating coaching sessions.

# Preparing for coaching sessions

The initial stages of preparation for coaching sessions have the same components as preparation for conducting activities. A coach needs to ensure that the facilities, equipment and safety factors have all been checked (see Chapter 9). Planning for coaching sessions differs slightly because the objectives of the participants are more specific and the information, plans and preparation are more detailed.

## Collecting and analysing information

Information that can help prepare your coaching sessions will come from various sources. You may have received information on forthcoming opponents or received the latest league statistics. This type of information is critical to help meet the needs of the performer(s) and develop a strategy.

## Collecting information

It is most important to make sure information is correctly sourced and dated (this will help to establish authenticity and show whether it is up to date). It should also be as comprehensive as the sources will allow. Essential information (such as the strengths and weaknesses of opponents) should be confirmed. Through networking you can develop regular sources of information. Scouts are employed by full-time organisations to obtain information on opponents, but there are many sources of information open to all coaches.

Perhaps the best source of information is your evaluation of previous sessions. It can help to create your action plans. All information you receive on performers should be correctly handled – this means treating certain information with confidentiality. The performers themselves are a key source of information. They can tell you if they are tired, injured or not being tested enough.

## The needs of the athletes

When you are working with a number of participants, whether they are a team or not, each has individual needs regarding his or her performance. These needs can be identified by discussion with each member of the group and should, therefore, be accurately defined and consistent with any information previously collected. Within any group ability will be mixed and therefore a range of needs must be assessed. Some performers will have better technical ability, some may have more experience than others. These needs should be recorded accurately; they will form the basis of your coaching plans.

For coaches who are responsible for a team, the needs of the team as a whole must be established. These may include the need to:

- develop an understanding of the roles of individuals within a team
- develop the ability of the team to work together
- create positive relationships between members of the team
- deal with conflict in the team
- develop trust and respect for each other
- develop clear lines of communication within the team and with the coach and administrators.

## Identifying your coaching needs

You must be able to examine your strengths and weaknesses, which again can form part of your coaching plan. It may be that you are unable to meet all the needs of the performers and have to obtain further skills or knowledge or use the expertise of other individuals. A lot of specific support material is available from governing body coach education departments and, more specifically, representative bodies such as the National Coaching Foundation. Very often, bringing in a specialist such as a dietitian is not only very informative but also a welcome change to the normal session.

## Producing coaching documentation

Teaching plans are documents that clearly outline what is to be coached, to whom and when. The plans reflect the needs of the performers and are set against agreed goals. All information can be contained in log books and further action plans developed. Once this information is recorded, the coach will be able to develop a strategy for success.

> **REMEMBER**
>
> *Be realistic with action plans! Take into account the time, equipment, facilities, the athletes you have and the competition you will be facing.*

**Producing plans**

The coaching plan should address the objectives, which could be short, medium or long term. The objectives should be prioritised and in a logical sequence: for example, developing sound technique before creating a complex system of play. Producing a coaching plan will help to achieve your objectives. You must take into consideration the following:

- plans, which are based on the information previously collected.
- a series of activities that will meet the needs of the participants in the time available and with the resources you have at your disposal
- all plans should comply with health and safety legislation and the welfare of the participants
- your plans should have a degree of flexibility to enable you to build or change activities based on previous sessions
- your plans should take into account the ability of the athletes and enable them to maximise their potential. The plans should be based around the season of the sport and should take into account the specific needs of off season, pre-season and mid season.

*Funbury Leisure Centre*

**Coaching Plan**

Session: ........................ No. participating: ........................

Date: ........................ Time: ........................ Duration: ........................

Group details: ........................

Equipment required: ........................

Facilities required: ........................

Safety considerations: ........................

Session objectives:

1. ........................
2. ........................
3. ........................

**Structure** **Time**

Warm up: ........................

Main content: ........................

Cool down: ........................

Comments: ........................

***Figure* 10.3** *Coaching plan*

ACTIVITY Produce a short-term coaching plan for athletes in your chosen sport. You should clearly identify the standard of the athletes and the time of the season.

### Creating and using log books

A log book can be used to record and evaluate a participant's progress. Whereas the action plan is for the coach, the log book should be maintained by the performer. It contains a breakdown of all activities undertaken and an evaluation of and reflection on their performance. It is best used initially by the coach and performer together to set goals – either a short-term goal or a long-term goal such as a national championship competition.

The log book then becomes a systematic diary of events that record what the individual did, when and how well. Grading schemes can be used as well as qualitative feedback. The coach can use his or her action plans in conjunction with information recorded in the log book. The athlete reflects on the activity and the performance and records the findings. This also helps performers develop self-learning.

## Preparing athletes

Once you have collected all the necessary and relevant information and produced your coaching plans, you need to prepare the athletes, not physically for activities but by taking steps to ensure that behaviour in the group will be appropriate. You will also have to receive the group, make arrangements and give instructions for forthcoming sessions. Relaying this in detail will help athletes prepare mentally for their activities and ensure they are in the right place at the right time.

### Code of conduct

A code of conduct is an agreed series of statements outlining the do's and don'ts of behaviour during coaching sessions and competition. The most approved method of developing a code of conduct is to let the participants create their own. They will then feel they have ownership of it and are more likely to keep to the statements about their conduct. The coach can encourage participants to include:

- personal ethics, where they respect themselves by looking after their bodies and taking responsibility for their own actions
- sports ethics, respecting the rules, officials and administration of their sport
- sports equity, where fairness and equality is encouraged, irrespective of age, gender, race or disability.

Once the code of conduct has been created it should be signed by all those involved (athletes *and* coaches) and placed in a position where it can be clearly seen.

### Receiving participants for the first time

It is essential that, when first meeting the participants, you are punctual and well presented. Try to put them at ease by making them feel

> **REMEMBER**
>
> *Log books are best used for serious performers who are working towards specific goals and are mature enough to cope with success or failure.*

welcome, and sure that they will be well looked after. Introduce yourself and provide a little background on how you came to be their coach.

Make an effort to get to know as many names, as early as possible, when you take the register.

GOOD PRACTICE ▷ *Use word association to help remember names: for example, by taking the first name of the participant and picturing a prominent sports person of a similar name.*

**Figure 10.4** *Try to learn everyone's name as soon as you can*

Check to see that all participants are fit, able to take part and are dressed accordingly. This includes wearing appropriate footwear and clothing and not wearing anything that may harm others or themselves, such as watches, bracelets or earrings. Give participants all the information they need before commencing the session. You also want to obtain as much information as possible about the athletes, which will centre around their level of experience. You are then set to physically and mentally prepare them for their activities.

**Making arrangements**

This builds upon the planning and preparation discussed in Chapter 9, and reinforces the importance of ensuring that the arrangements for coaching sessions are as agreed. It is always worthwhile confirming that reservations of the facilities are in order and that you have all the necessary equipment and space for the activity to take place.

Ensure that all the administration and paperwork is correct and all health and safety checks have been carried out. Your arrangements for the coaching session should aim to involve all the athletes. Any participant whose particular requirements cannot be met should be referred to a competent person. For example, if you are organising a beginners' rugby team and a teenager has exceptional talent you may want to introduce him or her to a more advanced team and coach.

GOOD PRACTICE ▷ *Always carry a spare whistle, pen and stopwatch in your bag as all may fail to work when you require them.*

**Figure 10.5** *Keep spare equipment to hand – your usuals might go wrong*

One of the essential features of coaching is ensuring that all the athletes receive the necessary information about future arrangements. It is a good idea to provide a training schedule, which includes fixtures, and lists

- date
- activity (e.g. training or fixture)
- equipment required (e.g. indoor shoes)
- venue
- time (start and finish)
- place to meet.

## PROGRESS CHECK

1 Why is it important to identify your own coaching needs?

2 What are the main components of a coaching plan?

3 What are the key aspects to a code of conduct? Provide examples.

4 What should you do when receiving participants for the first time?

5 What information should be provided in a training schedule?

## Conducting coaching sessions

Planning and preparation are very important parts of coaching, but it is very often the content of the session and the method of the coach that can improve performance. Each coach has his or her own style and ways for improving skill. All coaches should end a session in a way that prepares themselves and their athletes for future or follow-on sessions.

## Coaching methods

Each coach will develop a style that represents their personality. Many successful coaches believe they have many styles to meet the needs of athletes and changes in circumstances. Recognising the need for change and the importance of focusing your services on a central theme are essential for all coaches.

### Coaching style

A coach will often change style, depending upon the nature of the group and the individuals being coached. However, coaches still retain a preferred style in coaching their sport. The two extreme styles of coaching are:

- the autocratic style, where all the decisions are made by the coach without consultation with the athletes
- the democratic style, where the athlete has the greater say in decisions about programme and goals.

Both styles have advantages and disadvantages and can be used successfully in different circumstances. For example, it is hard to keep control of 16-year-old students using solely democratic styles. Many coaches like to have a feeling of control and fail to understand the principles of encouraging athletes to take on responsibility for themselves.

Whichever style you choose, you should show enthusiasm and commitment to the activity, to the athletes and to the chosen sport.

### Establishing a theme

It is very difficult for any participant to receive coaching and advice on many aspects of performance simultaneously. It is also difficult, when faced with limited time, to coach just one technique per training session. Establishing a theme is about having a focus for the session. This can be incorporated in the warm up and cool down as well as in the main activities. For example, a coach of a basketball team may wish to focus on effective communication and involve warming up, the main activity and cooling down, where players have to relate information to each other. This could be instructions, feedback and encouragement.

The theme should be explained to the participants before the session starts. Even though the theme is the main focus, it is good practice to reinforce important techniques and overall strategy. The theme should be explained (how you want it practised in a conditioned game). This places further emphasis on the theme.

### Regularity and change

It is important to have a structure to the activity where athletes know what is to be expected from them and that they are prepared for the session. However, it is also essential that you do not keep the same structure and content in every session because you risk losing the interest of the group, adversely affecting their motivation.

Changing your sessions not only keeps the motivation of the athletes but also shows that you are putting thought and effort into preparation and planning. Many coaches, for one training session only, may change the elected sport for something else, such as making rugby players take a

---

**REMEMBER**

*Being intense often shows a level of commitment, but always be in control of what you say and do.*

---

dance class. The coach is still working on key aspects of fitness but is also creating a fun environment and a positive change from the cold and rain outside.

## Developing skill

In trying to develop skills in performers it is essential to plan well and recognise that individuals learn at different paces. Some athletes will also learn better from some instructional techniques than others. There are many methods of developing skills and the essential techniques of success, whole–part–whole, maintaining quality, and demonstrations are essential methods for any coach to use.

### Success and quality

In developing skills, especially new ones, individuals have to piece together different patterns and movements in the correct sequence. These often have to be learnt and taught in different stages. It is important to emphasise that each movement and technique is performed correctly to increase the likelihood of long-term success. There are, of course, exceptions, athletes who develop the skills simultaneously, but such people are the minority. It can also be difficult to change poor technique, especially if someone has got used to their style and is having a degree of success with it. It is important to assess this individually and ascertain whether or not this person will be able to develop more difficult skills in the long term.

The difficulty in teaching new skills is that there is very often little success. It is important to adjust goals for individuals and set more specific attainable targets. For example, teaching an overhead serve in tennis can be difficult, and success in terms of landing over the net in the correct area is, initially, unlikely. Simpler targets, such as hitting it into a larger area than normal, can be met and the targets made more difficult as the server progresses.

It is also important not to progress onto new skills until the existing techniques can be performed correctly. Praising good quality, even if the outcome is unsuccessful, is one of the keys to developing skill.

### Whole–part–whole

One method of ensuring quality and success is to use the whole–part–whole technique. This involves coaching all the skills to be performed at once, breaking the skills down into individual parts and then performing them simultaneously. This can be done with individual techniques as well as with more general ones, such as playing a whole game, then isolating a skill to practise, and then playing a whole game again. A specific movement, such as kicking a football, can be taught this way. Ask the player to kick the ball (the whole), then you can look at the parts.

- *Preparation*, which is how they prepare to kick the ball: the approach, angle and positioning of feet and body
- *Action*, which is the specific phase of making contact with the ball, such as the position of the foot on the ball
- *Completion*, which is the end phase, such as the follow through and completion of the movement.

Once these individual parts have been practised and performed with success they can be put together as one again (the whole).

This method allows individuals to see their competence at the start and then, by breaking down the whole movement, deliver specific coaching points to ensure that when the whole movement is performed again it is more likely to be successful.

### Demonstrating

Some individuals find it difficult to learn from instructions and a demonstration can help them to visualise the skill to be performed. Demonstration can be used at different times, especially when using the whole–part–whole method.

It is essential to demonstrate technically correctly. It is always better if the coach does it, as this can help develop respect and a positive relationship with your athletes. If you are unable to demonstrate, select someone who is of the required standard. Having selected the demonstrator, you must position your athletes in such a way that they can clearly see the skill. If your athletes are facing you, they will see the opposite of what you are performing. It may thus be better to face away from them. Specific views can be sought, such as a side view, which can be used to observe specific techniques such as where the non-striking foot is being placed on a soccer kick.

Perhaps the most important aspect of demonstrating is to perform the technique correctly. Very often you may demonstrate and not achieve the correct outcome, such as with a tennis serve which finishes in the net. You must leave a clear picture in the minds of the onlookers of exactly what they should be aiming to achieve.

> --- REMEMBER ---
>
> *Ensure all your participants are in a clear position to observe your demonstrations and that they are paying attention: a picture paints a thousand words!*

---

**ACTIVITY**

Demonstrate a technique for your chosen sport in front of the group. Allow time to plan for any equipment required and the steps to take in order to make the demonstration effective.

**Figure 10.6** *Develop your skills so you can demonstrate effectively*

205

*Learn to develop skills and techniques in your chosen sport so you are able to demonstrate effectively. Ask other competent coaches to feed back on your performance.*

### Repetition

The more you practise a skill the better you can become at it. However, practising skills incorrectly will result in you performing them incorrectly. Once you have achieved a certain level in a technique or skill it must be practised so it becomes a permanent skill. This, again, is dependent on planning, ensuring that the session allows for repetition of skills.

Very often athletes need good support from others to practise and repeat skills. They will need

- servers and feeders, for example, who supply the balls to be hit, or caught
- 'gofers' – people who go and retrieve balls, etc.
- supportive colleagues who allow time to practise.

Having planned to allow practise it is essential that the skill is repeated enough times for it to become learnt, but not so much that fatigue causes incorrect technique.

## Ending coaching sessions

There is still a lot of work for a coach to do at the end of a coaching session. You have to exchange information with the participants and provide feedback. You have to clear up any equipment and evaluate the session to see if there are any changes required to your action plan.

### Finishing on a positive note

During the session you will have given feedback to the athletes on their performance. Some comments will have been encouraging, others less so. It is important to give all the participants the feeling that they have achieved something from the session. They need to be motivated in order to want to return to the next session.

It is a good idea, even when working with individuals in a club, to cool down together. During stretching is an ideal opportunity to focus the athletes on their goals and reiterate the main coaching points of the session. Highlight examples of good performance and their outcomes. It is essential that, whatever activities you end the session with, they are safe and effective. This means leaving ample time for a proper cool down and, if it is a late session, sufficient time to shower and change.

### Before departure

All the equipment that has been used should be dismantled and put away, following safe procedures and organisational procedures for storage. If any equipment has been damaged during the session this should be recorded and reported using the appropriate forms. The playing environment should be left suitable for future use.

It is also a good idea to have bags/containers for equipment set out so that they can all be counted in before people leave. A missing ball can be

> **REMEMBER**
>
> *Practise does not make it perfect, it makes it permanent.*

easily found with everyone searching for it. Bibs, balls, bats and all equipment should be collated so that they are ready for use at the next session.

Always use the participants to help collect and carry in equipment. They should not, however, be allowed to carry equipment that might be unsafe. The store room should also remain out of bounds.

GOOD PRACTICE ▷ *During a cool-down jog, it is a good idea to allow participants to collect any light equipment from the practice area and bring it to a central place (e.g. in front of the store cupboard).*

**Figure 10.7** *Use your class to help you clear up*

### Exchanging information
Information exchange starts with providing an opportunity for any participants to feed back on the session. Constructive feedback should also be recorded in their log books and action plans may be changed if the needs of athletes are not being met. You should inform participants of any key aspects of the game they should work on, or any preparation they can do before the next session.

This is also the time to inform the participants of the time, location and the theme of the next session; this, again, will help in planning for the forthcoming session. Participants must have the opportunity to inform you if they are unable to attend the following session.

**ACTIVITY**

For your chosen sport structure a coaching session which has a central theme. This should be apparent within the warm up, the main activities and the cool down. Clearly identify what you are hoping to achieve.

## CASE STUDY

The Funbury Leisure Centre volleyball team, which plays in the local league, has undergone preseason training and is now preparing for their first competitive league game of the season. There are two more coaching sessions before the first game and the focus is on improving the team's overall team strategies and tactics, with special emphasis on serving and receiving.

The coach continues to plan each session and adapts the plans for the final two sessions before the first game. The goals, agreed with the team, focus on a percentage of serves in and serves received. The emphasis of the session is on quality and repetition and as everyone has to serve the coach ensures that each individual reaches an acceptable level. Some players need their serve breaking down into parts to improve, others need practice.

The session ends, before the cool down, with a game where each 'focus and objective' is put into a realistic situation.

1   Why is it important to keep clear records of coaching and player profiles from preseason work and how can they be used in the future?

2   What information should the coach give to the players, and what arrangements should the coach make, at the end of the second training session?

## PROGRESS CHECK

1   What are the two main types of coaching style?

2   Why is it important to establish a theme for your coaching sessions?

3   Explain the coaching process of whole–part–whole and provide an example of where it may be used.

4   What considerations should be taken into account before using demonstrations?

5   What are the key points to inform participants about when ending coaching sessions?

# Looking after your athletes

The health and fitness of an athlete will greatly affect their performance. As a coach you have control of what performers do during your training sessions. It is important that you are able to instruct them on how to look after their bodies, and achieve their optimum performance through safe and legal practices, especially when they are on their own. At the centre of these issues are physical fitness, nutrition and drugs.

## Physical fitness

Before looking to improve fitness, you need to ask what you want your performers to be fit for. Each sport requires different components of fitness, and the more competitive you are the fitter you have to be. The individual's physique (height, weight and body type) can also affect fitness levels. Fitness is not being healthy, but certainly can improve your general well being, and should be part of a health programme. As a coach you need to know these components of fitness, and how they can be assessed and improved.

### Aerobic capacity

This is often referred to as stamina or cardiovascular endurance. It is the ability to take in and use oxygen, over continuous periods of exercise such as running and cycling. Aerobic capacity is required in most sports, even those associated with large components of sprinting such as tennis. This is because having a good aerobic capacity will enable you to recover more quickly during training and practice sessions. A person's aerobic capacity is also known as the $VO_{2(max)}$, which is the maximum volume of oxygen that can be taken in and used by the body.

There are several ways a coach can measure a person's aerobic capacity. The National Coaching Foundation has developed the Multistage Fitness Test. In this an athlete performs 20 m shuttle runs to an audio tape, which clicks at ever-decreasing intervals. The athlete must cover each leg of the run between clicks, and so has to go faster as the test progresses until they can no longer keep up with the sound track. This test is unsuitable for young children and often is not performed to the maximum by adults who know they are to be retested. It is a good idea to use this at the start of training, occasionally during the season and at the end of the season. If performed correctly this test is a useful measure of aerobic capacity.

GOOD PRACTICE ▷ *When assessing performers it is useful to compare their outcomes over a period of time. For this to be meaningful you should assess the same way each time.*

The 12-minute Cooper test is a simpler test, which requires an athlete to run as far as possible in 12 minutes. This has an element of technique and judgement to it, but again can be used as a good comparative means of assessing aerobic fitness.

To improve your performers' aerobic capacity you need to work at a prolonged level of intensity. This will allow you to train aerobic capacity without fatiguing too early. Fatigue is caused by lactic acid build up in muscles, which prevents maximum performance. The athlete's pulse rate (either from the neck (carotid) or the wrist (radial) – Figure 10.8) will indicate the level of intensity.

Training intensity can be measured roughly by taking the resting heart rate and adding 60% of maximum heart rate minus the resting heart rate. Maximum heart rate is roughly 220 less the person's age.

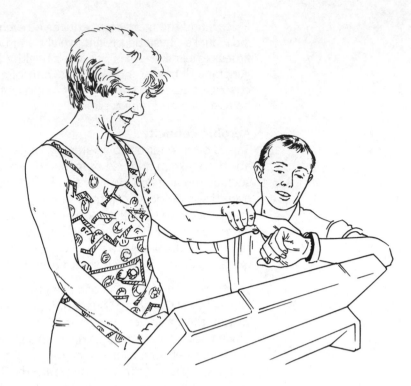

**Figure** 10.8    *Taking the pulse*

For example, for an athlete of 30 with a resting pulse of 63 training intensity

=    62 + 60% of (190–62)

=    62 + 60% of 128

=    62 + 76.8

=    139 beats per minute.

Aerobic capacity can be improved by continual running at your optional pulse rate or by using specific running methods. The Fartlek method involves moving continuously at different speeds and over different terrain. A typical Fartlek run would include a series of sprints, interspersed with periods of jogging and walking, up and down hills as well as on the flat.

Interval training includes runs over a certain distance. The number of runs, the distance and rest in-between can all be changed depending on what you want to work on. For example:

4 × 200 m at 32 seconds      2 minutes recovery

6 × 100 m at 15 seconds      1 minute 30 seconds recovery

10 × 40 m at 6 seconds      50 seconds recovery

**Flexibility**
An athlete's flexibility is the range of movement around a joint, and is often referred to as suppleness. Being flexible can help to prevent muscle soreness and injury. There are several ways to improve flexibility, which include static and ballistic stretching and proprioceptive neuromuscular facilitation (PNF).

Flexibility training can be used before and after your training sessions and should be incorporated in your warm ups and cool downs. At least three times a week stretching should be performed to a point at which you feel the muscle tighten but it is not painful. In static stretching (Figure 10.9), the stretch is held in a position for 10–20 seconds and should be repeated on each side of the body.

**Figure 10.9**   *Static stretching*

An individual's flexibility can be measured by using specialist equipment, depending on what flexibility measurement you require. The most-used test is the sit and reach test. In this test, the person removes their shoes and sits with their feet pressed against the sit and reach box. He or she then leans forward along the box as far as they can. The further they can reach, the greater their flexibility.

GOOD PRACTICE ▷

*When stretching, start with static stretches, and move to ballistic and PNF stretching when you have warmed up. Start from the head and work down through the body to the feet, thus ensuring that you cover all the parts of the body that are going to be required for exercise.*

**Muscular strength**

Strength in sports can be used to describe an individual's ability to lift objects, or hold off an opponent. Generally, strength is the ability to hold or move resistance. There are three types of strength.

- *Maximum strength*, which is the greatest weight you can hold or move. The simplest method of measuring maximum strength is to assess how much a person can lift using free weights or multigym equipment. An example of equipment to develop maximum strength is the bench press.

211

- *Power* is the ability to move resistance at speed. Power might be used in throwing, hitting or sprinting exercises. It can be measured by assessing a vertical jump or standing long jump. More sophisticated measurements can be done with the Wingate test, which uses specialist bikes

- *Endurance strength* is where the muscles can work for extended periods without fatigue. This can often be a major factor when sports games are near completion. It can be measured by sit ups, press ups and dips.

## ACTIVITY

In pairs research your chosen sport and list the most important fitness attributes of that sport. You may also wish to contact successful players in your sport and ask for their opinions. Compare your findings with those of other groups.

To train to improve your strength, you need to use the principles of training such as progression and overload. Weight-training programmes include repetitions ('reps') and sets. The number of reps is how many times you perform the exercise and makes up one set. Strength routines usually have high weight, low reps and sets. Power programmes have submaximal weight, slightly higher reps and sets. Endurance uses lower weight and higher reps and sets.

An example programme for improving strength in the chest area, using a bench press, is shown in Table 10.1. The maximum weight the person can lift on the bench press is 90 kg.

*Table* 10.1

| Aim | Weight (kg) | Reps | Sets |
|-----|-------------|------|------|
| Maximal strength | 86 | 3–5 | 2 |
| Power | 72 | 6–8 | 3 |
| Endurance | 45 | 9–18 | 3 |

### Speed

Speed, basically, is how fast a person can move part or all of their body. Foot speed is measured by multiplying stride length by stride frequency and is represented in metres per second. However, some players are able to react quicker to situations and signals than others and hence reaction time in the brain is also a factor in a person's overall time in sprint racing. Foot speed is often measured, especially in American sports, by a 40 m sprint. This is a running start and the time is taken between two parts 40 m apart.

> **REMEMBER**
>
> *Coaching to improve speed should be done with control. Going quickly does not necessarily mean doing better.*

To improve speed the interval and Fartlek techniques discussed earlier are good methods to use. Circuit training also allows specific skills to be tested and timed. Bounding – hops, over obstacles, depth jumping (known as plyometrics) – can also help to improve speed and leg strength.

## Drugs and sports

This subject continues to be topical as the rewards for winning are increasing and as athletes look for methods to improve performance. It is important as a coach to inform performers about the nature of drugs and what constitute legal and illegal substances. Many organisations, such as the Sports Council, fight against drugs in sport and protect the ethics of their game. There is also a lot of social influences, especially on young people, to drink alcohol and smoke. Drugs testing is becoming more common at higher levels of sport.

### Defining drugs

Any substance that may affect a person's emotions, behaviour or physical actions can be classified as a drug. This includes a variety of medicines, but not all are banned by the governing bodies in sport. For example, athletes suffering from a common cold are allowed to take paracetamol but not products that contain ephedrine.

The following drugs have different effects but are all considered to improve performance and are banned. They form the major part of antidoping regulations.

- *Stimulants*, such as amphetamines, increase the heart rate and are taken to give a person more energy. This can lead to increased blood pressure
- *Narcotic analgesics* raise the pain threshold, allowing an athlete to continue to perform even if injured. This can often cause further and more permanent injury
- *Anabolic steroids* are synthetic hormones that (unnaturally) help athletes increase their strength and power. They often have a range of adverse side-effects, such as aggressive behaviour
- *Beta blockers* are tranquillisers which help to calm down athletes, by reducing the heart rate and blood pressure. They can be addictive and taken in excess lead to depression
- *Diuretics* are used to help remove fluid from the body and thus reduce body weight. Boxers and jockeys have been known to use diuretics. However, essential salts are lost in the urine, which can lead to muscle damage.

### Supplements

Ergogenic aids are taken to improve the physiological performance of an athlete in an attempt to optimise the production of energy and improve the recovery time so as to enable an athlete to perform again. However, a balanced diet will most often provide athletes with all they require. It is important to inform your performers, who are exposed to advertisements for supplements, what each contains and what natural products they can be found in.

- *Vitamin* supplements are available in all health stores. However, these vitamins are mostly excreted from the body without providing any advantageous effect
- *Bicarbonates* are used mostly by athletes for high-intensity exercise. The evidence for performance improvement is inconclusive and certainly not in sports lasting long periods
- *Caffeine* can be found in coffee, tea and chocolate and is a stimulant. There is some evidence to show it can improve endurance, but it is a prohibited substance if the concentration in urine is too high. Caffeine is also a diuretic
- *Ginseng* taken in its natural form, the root, is a permitted substance. It is meant to act as a 'pick up' or restorative agent and is often found in tablet form. However, these forms often also contain other, banned, substances
- *Creatine* plays a major role in the production of energy and can be found in meat and fish. It is not conclusive as to how much creatine is required and what improvements can be made

**Figure** 10.10  *Leaflets are there to inform you – don't just ignore them!*

GOOD PRACTICE ▷  *Get a list of banned products and substances from the governing body of your sport and give them to each player. A list of medications allowed for athletes who are ill should also be available.*

The benefits of supplements are often not conclusively shown, as scientists continue to discuss their effects. What is known is that they are expensive and a balanced diet can provide the body's requirements.

214

### Social drugs

Tobacco, alcohol and other social drugs are taken by people in social situations such as pubs and night clubs as a means to relax and make us feel good. However, these drugs are harmful and have negative effects on the body. The pleasant effects are only short-term effects and the negative effect on the fitness and long-term health of sports people can be life threatening.

- *Alcohol* is perhaps one of the oldest known drugs. Taken in moderation, alcohol causes little harm but excessive intake has serious effects on health, such as damage to the liver. Alcohol is a diuretic and can therefore cause dehydration. Players often like to socialise and relax with a couple of drinks after training or a game. You must make sure that people under the age of 18 do not drink alcohol and that any drivers are discouraged from doing so.

- *Tobacco smoking* has an adverse effect on fitness. It decreases lung capacity and increases the risk of heart disease. Areas where smoking is allowed should be avoided by performers as passive smoking can cause harmful effects.

- *Soft drugs* such as cannabis are also becoming more easily available and are taken by more people. It is a criminal offence to supply or to possess these substances, and their use reduces performance in sport.

If you suspect anyone is using or supplying drugs you should inform the police. If you discover any drugs, remove them from where you found them (have a witness present) and inform the police. Record the time, place and any particulars of the incident. Place the items in a container and wait for the police to arrive.

> ### REMEMBER
>
> *Always wear protective gloves if you discover a needle and handle it with care.*

## Diet and exercise

It is likely that your performers will be leading busy lives involving work, training and playing matches. A balanced diet will provide the energy and nutrients they need for training and recovery and maximising their performance. Your players should understand the components of diet, what and when to eat when preparing for sport and the importance of fluids.

### Components of diet

The body needs the following nutrients to survive.

- *Proteins* help to build and repair muscles. They can be found in meat, fish and cereals

- *Carbohydrates* are essential nutrients as they provide energy for our muscles. The best forms of carbohydrate are the complex carbohydrates (such as starch), which are found in whole-grain breads, rice, wheat and vegetables

- *Fats* are also an essential part of the diet, and are also used as a source of energy, although too much fat can cause obesity and heart disease. Many animal products such as red meat, milk and butter have high levels of fat

- *Vitamins and minerals* have a variety of roles to help the body function correctly. The different minerals and vitamins can be found in many foods such as dairy products, nuts, fruit and green vegetables
- *Fibre* provides the roughage for our digestive system. Fruit, nuts and vegetables are all good providers of fibre.

**Nutrition for sport**

The amount of energy (food intake) you require depends upon the amount and type of sport you are doing. Weight can be gained or lost by altering the amount of energy taken in and the amount expended. The dietary requirements of a typical athlete are shown in Table 10.2.

*Table 10.2*

| Dietary component | Percentage of diet |
| --- | --- |
| Carbohydrate | 55 |
| Fat | 25 |
| Protein | 15 |
| Vitamins and minerals | 5 |

Inform your athletes to keep their salt and sugar intakes to a minimum and ensure that they are eating plenty of fibre.

Before training/competition, athletes should eat at least 2 hours before exercise. Complex carbohydrates, such as pasta, are the best source of energy ('carbo loading'). After exercise, the stores in the body need to be replenished. Breakfast bars, sandwiches with low-fat filling and scones are good food sources and easy to eat.

GOOD PRACTICE ▷

*When playing games away from home, and where travel makes it difficult to obtain food, take a supply of the following foods:*

- *plain biscuits*
- *sports drinks*
- *apples, bananas*
- *pitta bread with low-fat fillings*
- *dried fruit*
- *crackers.*

**The importance of fluid intake**

Fluids are an essential component of the diet. Dehydration occurs when we lose too much fluid and this can affect our heart rate, strength and endurance.

**Figure** 10.11    *Always eat a balanced diet, even if you're travelling*

Athletes sweat when performing to regulate their body temperature. It is essential to take in water to replace that lost during exercise. Even a sedentary person requires about 1.5 litres of water a day, so anyone performing exercise should drink plenty of fluid before, during and after exercise (anyone exercising will need about 1 litre per hour). It is important not to wait until you are thirsty before drinking when exercising – by that point you are already dehydrated.

Drinks that are or contain diuretics, such as coffee, cola drinks and alcohol, should be avoided. Fizzy drinks can cause bloating and gastric upset and are best avoided during exercise. Sports nutrition drinks are designed for rapid replacement of carbohydrate, salts and water lost during exercise. Their use will delay the onset of fatigue and will help the rate of recovery.

KEY TERMS

*You need to know the meaning of the following words and phrases. Go back through the chapter to make sure that you understand.*

| | |
|---|---|
| Analysing and problem solving | Autocratic and democratic styles |
| Being a role model | Coaching theme |
| Code of conduct | Developing self learning |
| Ethics | Identifying coaching needs |
| Planning and preparation | Preparing athletes |
| Solving problems | Whole–part–whole |

# Glossary of terms

**Activity register** – A list of the names of participants that are under the supervision of a leader or coach

**Analysing and problem solving** – Examining issues and trying to find the best solutions

**Autocratic and democratic styles** – Styles of leadership. Autocratic leaders tend to make all the decisions; a democratic leader often includes other people in the decision-making process

**Being a role model** – Being in a position to influence others, setting a good example of behaviour and practice

**Booking sheet** – A method of recording who has booked what facilities. Also acts as a method for monitoring sales

**Booking systems** – Manual (e.g. booking sheets) or computerised systems to record the facilities that have been booked and by whom

**Business systems** – A general term used to describe an organisation's methods of controlling and organising their business. An example is a management information system

**Child development** – The mental and physical aspects of a child's growth

**Child protection** – Children who are in need of independent support and safety are often protected by child support agencies

**Civil law** – Law that has been created by previous civil (as opposed to criminal) cases. Individuals bring action against another party to claim for damages or costs incurred

**Cleaning rotas** – Identify people's duties for cleaning and the dates and times they should carry these duties out

**Coaching theme** – Where a coach has a specific focus for a training session to help ensure the participants concentrate on particular aspects of their game

**Code of conduct** – A list, drawn up by a sports governing body, a club or its representatives, stating their policy on individual and team behaviour

**Communication process** – The exchange of information between two or more people

**Conditioning the activity** – A coach or leader places restrictions on a game or activity. For example, allowing an individual only two touches when playing football

**Conflict** – Disagreement between two or more people

**Criminal law** – An act of parliament, designed to regulate behaviour. These are enforced by representatives of the government – such as the police – who can prosecute if the acts of parliament are broken

**Customer comment system** – The process by which an organisation provides an opportunity for customers to give their opinions on the organisation's products and services

**Customer survey** – A market research method to ascertain customers' opinions on the quality of the products and services an organisation offers

**Database** – A collection of files, information and records, stored on a computer or manually in cards and folders. Customer details can be kept on a database for easy and quick retrieval of information

**Decision making** – A process resulting in action, such as making up one's mind on designing a programme after assessing all the information available

**Delivery note** – A form detailing the items sent by a supplier to a customer

**Developing self-learning** – Encouraging individuals to continue to learn skills and techniques on their own once they have been taught sound practices

**Discounts** – Reductions in the published/standard prices of a product or service for specific target groups such as pensioners or for buying in bulk

**Duty of care** – A term in civil law, expressing our obligations to our neighbours (i.e. those affected by our actions). If we cause damage to others by our actions we have broken our duty of care

**Equal opportunities** – An expression highlighting the rights of different people in society to be equal, regardless of age, sex, race or religion

**Equity** – Often used in financial terms, but in the context of this book refers to providing equality in sports provision

**Ethics** – Moral codes and values of behaviour that should be endorsed by coaches and sports leaders

**Ethnic groups** – Specific groups of people with the same cultural background

**Evaluation** – A method used by coaches, managers and sports leaders to reflect and analyse a course of events in order to make future improvements

**Feasibility** – An analysis of the advantages and disadvantages of proposed projects

**Feedback** – Providing or receiving information from individuals to assist and influence future courses of action

**Finance and budgetary control** – Comparing proposed costs with actual expenditure and the subsequent course of action chosen

**Fund raising** – Attempting to raise money to support an organisation's activities by various methods (e.g. holding a summer fayre). Often associated with voluntary organisations

**Gross and net profit** – Financial terms. The gross profit is the profit calculated by subtracting the cost of sales from sales. Net profit is the amount left after subtracting interest and taxes paid from the gross

**Groups** – A number of people with a common link join together to achieve specific tasks

**Guarantee** – Written assurance from a provider of a product or service that it will meet certain standards or specifications

**Hazards** – A hazard is something that could cause injury to a person or damage to property

**Identifying coaching needs** – A process of decision making aimed at identifying what a coach needs to be able to increase his or her performance in terms of achieving set objectives

**Improvisation** – Sports leaders and coaches have to react to situations that do not follow the proposed course of action (perhaps required equipment is not available) by changing their plans to fit what is available (improvising)

**Inventory** – A detailed list of goods, such as equipment in a store room

**Legislation** – Act of parliament (such as The Children's' Act) or process of making laws, and the laws that are made.

**Maintenance schedule** – A timetable for servicing and keeping in working order equipment and facilities

**Market segmentation** – The way organisations divide the total market for their product or service into smaller groups with common elements (e.g. by age group or by sex)

**Marketing mix** – Once known as the 'four Ps', but now the 'seven Ps' (product, price, promotion, people, physical evidence, place and process). Marketers place emphasis on the different elements of the mix to ensure success

**Negotiation** – A discussion between people aimed at producing an agreement

**Networking** – Conscious effort to meet and develop contacts in industry who may be able to help achieve objectives

**Operating procedures** – Instructions on performing tasks and following systems at work designed by the organisation

**Organisation and methods** – A way of analysing the most efficient methods of performing tasks, usually within the service sector

**Organisational chart** A diagram showing the division of responsibilities within an organisation, the lines of authority and the channels of communication

**Overuse injuries** – Injuries in certain parts of the body caused by over-exercising those parts

**Peak/off-peak** – The times of greatest (peak) and least (off-peak) demand on facilities. Peak times for health clubs are at weekends and evenings, and off-peak periods are usually during the day on weekdays

**Personal protective equipment –** Equipment that employees are required by 1992 EU Directives to wear to protect themselves from harm when handling hazardous substances – goggles, gloves, etc.

**Personal selling –** Encouraging buyers to use your products or services by talking to them yourself

**Planning and preparation –** Used by coaches and sports leaders before an activity to help them ensure that they meet the needs of the participants, as well as their own objectives

**Policies –** An organisation's statements as to how it will achieve its mission statement and objectives

**Preparing athletes –** Coaches try to ensure that their athletes are in the best mental and physical shape for the forthcoming competition

**Primary and secondary research –** Methods of collecting information. Primary information comes straight from the source, for example by direct observation. Secondary research gathers information second-hand, for example by collating information from several books or newspapers

**Product knowledge –** An employee's understanding of the products and services the organisation he or she works for has to offer

**Programme balance –** The range of activities a facility has to offer is very often dictated by demand. However, most organisations (especially those in the public sector) provide a variety of activities to a range of different user groups. Balance includes flexibility, equity and reliability

**Programme patterns –** The elements of a programme and the factors that affect them, such as time, space and the seasons

**Programming for specific groups –** Arranging activities aimed at specific groups of people – for example, women-only swimming sessions

**Prospective customers –** Individuals who might become customers – such as families of existing customers

**Quality standards and procedures –** Quality is about providing a service well, but can also be measured by national and international standards, such as ISO 9000

**Risk assessment –** Thorough inspection of potential risks and identification of hazards in the workplace

**Safety programme –** A series of structured measures that comply with legal requirements to ensure the safety of staff and visitors to a facility

**Solving problems –** Finding solutions to difficult tasks

**Special needs –** A general term given to people with disability – for example, partially sighted people, people in wheelchairs

**Sponsorship –** An organisation will provide money, goods or services to another in return for promotion of their name. For example, a sports manufacturer will supply a local football team with shirts for free, but with their logo or name on them. Both sides benefit – the team from the shirts and the manufacturer from the advertising

**Spreadsheet –** A computer application using numbers in tabular form to help calculations, forecasting and displaying information

**Staff appraisals –** A system for reviewing an employee's performance and goals

**Stock check –** The process of counting the amounts of goods an organisation has in a certain area at a certain time

**Stress –** The non-specific response of the body to the demands made upon it

**SWOT analysis –** Examination of an organisation's strengths and weaknesses, the opportunities and threats in the market place

**Teams –** Similar to groups, but team members are more dependent on each other than group members to achieve shared goals and objectives

**The Children's' Act –** Devised in 1989, this came into force in 1991. It comprises legislation aimed at improving the care and upbringing of children

**Unique selling point –** An organisation's product or service that makes it different from the competition

**Whole–part–whole –** A coaching method in which all skills are taught together, broken down into individual points and then taught simultaneously again

**Word processing –** Creation, amendment, storage and printing of documents (letters, memorandums, etc.) on a computer

# Useful addresses

Allied Leisure PLC
Commercial Centre
Poole
Dorset
BH12 4NY
Tel: 01202 716 010
Fax: 01202 716 122

Bass PLC
20 North Street
London
W1Y 1WE
Tel: 0171 409 1919
Fax: 0171 409 8503
Website: www.Bass.com

Brent Walker PLC
53-55 Brooks Mews
London
W1Y 2NY
Tel: 0171 465 0111
Fax: 0171 629 6955

British Institute of Sports Administration (BISA)
24 Southfields
East Molesey
Surrey
KT8 0BP
Tel: 0181 224 0712
Fax: 0181 224 0712

British Nutrition Foundation
High Holborn House
52–54 High Holborn
London
WC1V 6RQ
Tel: 0171 404 6504
Fax: 0171 450 6747
Website: www.nutrition.org.uk

British Olympic Association
1 Wandsworth Plain
London
SW18 1EH

Tel: 0181 871 2677
Fax: 0181 871 9104
Website: www.olympics.org.uk

CCPR
Francis House
Francis Street
London
SW1P 1DE
Tel: 0171 828 3163
Fax: 0171 630 8820

David Lloyd Leisure PLC
The Arena
Parkway West
Cranford Lane
Hounslow
Middlesex
TW5 9QA
Tel: 0181 564 8877
Fax: 0181 564 8777

Department of Culture, Media and Sport
Sport and Recreation Division
2–4 Cockspur Street
London
SW1Y 5DH
Tel: 0171 211 6000

First Leisure Corporation PLC
7 Soho Street
Soho Square
London
W1V 5FA
Tel: 0171 437 9727
Fax: 0171 439 0088

Fitness Industry Association (FIA)
5–11 Lavington Street
London
SE1 0NZ
Tel: 0171 620 0700
Fax: 0171 620 0300

Foundation for Sport and the Arts
PO Box 20
Liverpool
L13 1HB
Tel: 0151 259 5505
Fax: 0151 230 0664

Granada Group PLC
Stonaway House
13 Cleveland Row
London
SW1A 1GG
Tel: 0171 451 3000

Health Education Authority
Hamilton House
Mabledon Place
London
WC1A 9BD

Information Centre English Sports Council
16 Upper Woburn Place
London
WC1H 0QP
Tel: 0171 273 1500
Fax: 0171 383 5740
Website: www.english.sports.gov.uk

Institute of Leisure and Amenity Management
ILAM House
Lower Basildon
Reading
Berkshire
RG8 9NE

Institute of Sports and Recreation Management
Giffard House
36/38 Sherrard Street
Melton Mowbray
Leicestershire
LE13 1XJ
Tel: 01664 565531
Fax: 01664 501155
Website: www.isrm.co.uk

Littlewoods Organisation PLC
100 Old Hall Street
Liverpool
L70 1AB
Tel: 0151 235 2222

London Central YMCA
12 Bedford Square

London
WC1B 3NQ
Tel: 0171 580 2989
Fax: 0171 436 1278

National Coaching Foundation
114 Cardigan Road
Leeds
LS6 3BJ
Tel: 0113 231 1310
Fax: 0113 231 9606

National Council for Vocational Qualifications
(NCVQ)
22 Euston Road
London
NW1 2BZ
Tel: 0171 509 5555
Fax: 0171 509 6666
Website: www.open.gov.qca/uk

National Sports Medicine Institute
St Bartholomew's Medical College
Charterhouse Square
London
EC1M 6BQ
Tel: 0171 251 0583
Fax: 0171 251 0774
Website: www.nsmi.org.uk

Rank Leisure Ltd
6 Connaught Place
London
W2 2EZ
Tel: 0171 706 1111
Fax: 0171 262 9886
Website: www.rank.com

Royal Life Saving Society (RLSS)
Riverhouse
High Street
Broom
Warwickshire
B50 4HN
Tel: 01789 773 994
Fax: 01789 773 995

Scottish and Newcastle PLC
Abbey Brewery
111 Holyrood Road
Edinburgh
EH8 8YS
Tel: 0131 556 2591

Fax: 0131 558 1165
Website: www.scottish-newcastle.com

Scottish Sports Council
Caledonia House
South Gyle
Edinburgh
EH12 9DQ
Tel: 0131 317 7200
Fax: 0131 317 7202
Website: www.ssc.org.uk

SPRITO
24 Stephenson Way
London
NW1 2HD
Tel: 0171 388 7755
Fax: 0171 388 9733
Website: the.nto.@sprito.org.uk

Sports Council for Northern Ireland
House of Sport
Upper Malone Road
Belfast
BT9 5LA
Tel: 01232 381 222
Fax: 01232 682 757
Website: www.sportscouncil-ni.org.uk

Sports Council for Wales
National Sports Centre for Wales
Sophia Gardens
Cardiff
CF1 9SW
Tel: 01222 300 500
Fax: 01222 300 600

Sports Aid Foundation
Lynton House
7–12 Tavistock Square
London
WC1H 9TL
Tel: 0171 233 7747
Fax: 0171 380 0283
Website: www.sportsaid.org

Sportsmatch in England
4th Floor
Warwick House
25–27 Buckingham Palace Road
London
SW1 OPP

St John's Ambulance
1 Grosvenor Crescent
London
SW1X 7EF
Tel: 0171 235 5231
Fax: 0171 235 0796

The Camelot Group PLC
Camelot Tolpits Lane
Watford
Hertfordshire
WD1 8RN
Tel: 01923 425 000
Fax: 01923 425 450
Website: www.national-lottery.co.uk

UK Institute for Careers and Qualifications in the
Outdoor Industry
c/o Ian Lewis
Tracey College (Exeter) Ltd
East Gate House
Princeshay
Exeter
Devon
EX1 1LY
Tel: 01392 272 372

Whitbread PLC
The Brewery
Chiswell Street
London
EC1Y 4SD
Tel: 0171 606 4455
Fax: 0171 615 1000

Women's Sport Foundation
305–315 Hither Green Lane
Lewisham
Surrey
SG13 6TJ
Tel: 0181 697 5370

Youth Sport Trust
Rutland Building
Loughborough University
Loughborough
Leicestershire
LE11 3TU
Tel: 01509 228 293
Fax: 01509 210 851
Website:
www.educate.co.uk/youthsport/youthsport.htm

# Index